Re
 na

ONE WEEK LOAN

CT 2004

Inside Popular Film

General editors Mark Jancovich and Eric Schaefer

Inside Popular Film is a forum for writers who are working to develop new ways of analysing popular film. Each book offers a critical introduction to existing debates while also exploring new approaches. In general, the books give historically informed accounts of popular film which present this area as altogether more complex than is commonly suggested by established film theories.

Developments over the past decade have led to a broader understanding of film which moves beyond the traditional oppositions between high and low culture, popular and avant-garde. The analysis of film has also moved beyond a concentration on the textual forms of films, to include an analysis of both the social situations within which films are consumed by audiences, and the relationship between film and other popular forms. The series therefore addresses issues such as the complex intertextual systems which link film, literature, art and music, as well as the production and consumption of film through a variety of hybrid media, including video, cable and satellite.

The authors take interdisciplinary approaches which bring together a variety of theoretical and critical debates that have developed in film, media and cultural studies. They neither embrace nor condemn popular film, but explore specific forms and genres within the contexts of their production and consumption.

Already published:

Harry M. Benshoff *Monsters in the closet: homosexuality and the horror film*
Joanne Hollows and Mark Jancovich (eds) *Approaches to popular film*
Jacinda Read *The new avengers: feminism, femininity and the rape-revenge cycle*

Forthcoming titles include:

Joanne Hollows *The state of the heart: re-mapping the field of women's genres*
Bennet Schaber *Everyday life and popular film*
Esther Sonnet *Sexuality and popular film*
Ben Taylor *Film comedy*

Realism and popular cinema

Julia Hallam with
Margaret Marshment

Manchester University Press
Manchester and New York
distributed exclusively in the USA by St. Martin's Press

Published by Manchester University Press
Oxford Road, Manchester M13 9NR, UK
and Room 400, 175 Fifth Avenue, New York, NY10010, USA
http://www.man.ac.uk/mup

Distributed exclusively in the USA by
St. Martin's Press, Inc., 175 Fifth Avenue, New York,
NY 10010, USA

Distributed exclusively in Canada by
UBC Press, University of British Columbia, 2029 West Mall,
Vancouver, BC, Canada V6T 1Z2

British Library Cataloguing-in-Publication Data
A catalogue record for this book is available from the British Library

Library of Congress Cataloging-in-Publication Data applied for

ISBN 0 7190 5250 5 *hardback*
     0 7190 5251 3 *paperback*

First published 2000

06 05 04 03 02 01 00   10 9 8 7 6 5 4 3 2 1

Typeset in Sabon with Frutiger
by Northern Phototypesetting Co Ltd, Bolton

Printed in Great Britain
by Bell & Bain Ltd, Glasgow

Contents

List of illustrations   *page* vi

Acknowledgements   vii

Introduction   ix

Part I

1 Realism and film: discursive formations   3

2 Realist moments: representation and reality   24

3 Realism and genre: realising fantasy   62

4 The epic of the everyday: notes towards a continuum   97

5 Discerning viewers: cognitive theory and identification   122

Part II

6 Re-visioning history: realism and politics   145

7 Space, place and identity: re-viewing social realism   184

8 Violent appropriations: realising death   220

Bibliography   257

Index   270

Illustrations

1 *Saturday Night and Sunday Morning*
(Reisz, GB 1960).   *page* 48

2 *Saturday Night and Sunday Morning* (Reisz, GB 1960).   50

3 *Straight Out of Brooklyn* (Rich, US 1991) reproduced
by kind permission of Artificial Eye.   59

4 *Once Were Warriors* (Tamahori, NZ 1994) reproduced
by kind permission of the New Zealand Film Commission,
the producers Communicado and Entertainment Film
Distributors Ltd.   204

5 *La Haine* (Kassovitz, France 1995) reproduced by kind
permission of Metro Tartan.   209

6 *Ladybird, Ladybird* (Loach, GB 1994) reproduced
by kind permission of Film Four International.   212

7 *Henry, Portrait of a Serial Killer* (McNaughton, US 1986)
reproduced by kind permission of MPI Media Group and
Cavis Marketing DBA Omni International as agent for
Amerina Corporation.   235

All stills courtesy of BFI stills archive.

Acknowledgements

This book is dedicated to our students past and present whose enthusiasm for popular films continues unabated in spite of our attempts to deconstruct their pleasures. It aims to provide a contemporary framework for the critical articulation of ideas about realist aesthetics which, like films themselves, are often difficult to express although easy to understand.

Margaret Marshment and I began work on the project as a collaborative venture early in 1996 and shared the construction of its conceptual framework. Margaret wrote sections of the chapters on genre and cognitive theory and contributed to two of the case studies; the book has benefited throughout from her critical commentary and editing skills. In the event, the task of completion fell to me and although I am responsible for the final text, the use of 'we' reflects the process of constructing the text and our consensus on many of the issues discussed. John Corner provided unfailing support throughout the project, useful references and inspirational commentary during the preparation and writing of the manuscript. He is, properly, the book's third collaborator, his input extending far beyond the call of collegiality and we thank him for his energy and enthusiasm.

I am grateful to Katherine Reeve at Manchester University Press for encouraging us to co-author the text, Mark Jancovich for his helpful comments on the proposal and Matthew Frost and Lauren McAllister for steering the project to completion. Thanks to my immediate colleagues in Communication Studies at Liverpool University, Kay Richardson, Margaret Scammell and Peter Goddard, who enabled the study leave that allowed me to complete the writing; and to Nickianne Moody at Liverpool John Moores University who good-humouredly tolerated the dereliction of my duties as joint co-ordinator of the Association for Research in Popular Fictions. We are grateful to Karen Boyle, Ian Conrich, Sean Cubbitt, Martine Hollins and Robin Nelson for providing additional source materials and commentary on the text. Thanks to the library staff at the British Film Institute for offering valuable help and advice with the research. An immeasurable debt is due to all the friends and colleagues who encouraged the project and gave unfailing encouragement and personal support, in particular Nuria Triana-Toribio, Elizabeth Harvey and Steve Brie.

Finally, we would like to thank the BFI stills archive and the film production companies and distributors who have granted us permission to use stills from their films: the New Zealand Film Commission, Communicado and Entertainment Film Distributors for *Once Were Warriors*; Metro-Tartan for *La Haine*; Artificial Eye for *Straight Out of Brooklyn*; Film Four International for *Ladybird, Ladybird*; MPI Media Group and Cavis Marketing DBA Omni International as agent for Amerina Corporation for *Henry, Portrait of a Serial Killer*; and Linda Baird for her efforts to secure permissions for *Schindler's List* from Universal, who finally refused to grant us a licence 'under any circumstances'. Thanks also to the copyright holders of stills for *Saturday Night and Sunday Morning* whom we have been unable to trace; these copyright holders are invited to contact the publisher.

                                                              Julia Hallam

Introduction

During the 1980s in Britain, oppositional cultural producers were increasingly encouraged and supported in their attempts to enter the mainstream by a chorus of academic voices from within cultural studies who believed that the avant-garde no longer provided a useful or serious position from which to mount an effective critique of the dominant culture and its ideologies. Only by infiltrating the mainstream and using its common language could oppositional voices hope to make themselves heard. Not all cultural producers and critics, of course, were convinced that such a strategy could be successful, many agreeing with bell hooks that 'you cannot dismantle the master's house by using the master's tools', but others decided to take on the task of 'dismantling from within' by infiltrating dominant institutions and offering a critique of the *status quo* from a position of insider knowledge, if not authority.

This book is an attempt to re-evaluate some of these strategies by mapping the spaces culturally occupied by realist film texts produced to challenge, in various ways, the dominant *status quo*. Within this process, variously defined as infiltration or incorporation depending on your viewpoint, we acknowledge the director of the text as a primary agent of the production process, not because of naïve assumptions about the authorship of moving image texts but because directors, rightly or wrongly, continue to wield considerable cultural power both as individuals within and without the institutions of film production, and as a discursive construct within Western culture generally. A Spielberg film is recognised as a kind of movie experience very different from that of an Oliver Stone or a Ken Loach film. If we are to understand how challenges to the dominant *status quo* can be achieved within mainstream filmmaking practice, the politics and practices of film production need to be more securely anchored to successful interventions at a number of levels. Although it would be possible to examine a number of textual strategies from a postmodern perspective that foregrounds the play of difference, intertextuality, parody and pastiche, these tools of analysis are often only able to offer a critique of many mainstream texts in terms of 'lack' or the 'insufficient density' of their signifying systems. The texts examined here could all be accused of 'failure' in this sense – a failure to critically engage the viewer, a failure to address an imagined audience critically, a failure to play with their own terms of signification. Most demonstrate a lack of textual awareness of the means of their construction, creating forms of transparency between text and viewer that constitute one of the cornerstones of critique of the realist text – that it cannot deal with the real in contradiction.

As the dominant form of representation in our culture, however, realism is arguably also the most powerful. To dismiss realist texts – and those who advocate realist strategies – without further examination is to dismiss a huge proportion of the mainstream cultural products that most people consume and enjoy. Academic analyses of generic fiction have established how popular texts function on patterns of recognition and difference; it is these patternings that constitute the basis of formal generic categorisation. But little attention has been paid in recent years to realist aspects of popular moving image texts, and how changing patterns of narrative organisation and structure create opportunities for a wider range of engagements as the audience for films becomes both more globalised (in terms of standard Hollywood production and distribution) and more localised (as national and regional production continues to cohabit – albeit often unwillingly – with the Hollywood film). Realism, in this context, is less a metaphysical problem than a contextual one.

While nineteenth-century proponents of realism felt able to claim a correspondence between the employment of a specific artistic form and the reality it purported to represent, this confidence is no longer possible. Realism is now considered to be a matter of form, with a very debatable relationship to the real. The formal qualities of realist texts that distinguish them from, say, fantasy or the avant-garde, can be identified – secularism, material plausibility, verisimilitude of mise-en-scène, for example; but there are too many differing forms and uses of realism to be able to define realism as such. Rather, we need to see it as locally and historically specific. The Hollywood film

industry, with its assumption of 'universal' criteria of what constitutes reality – powerfully reinforced by the worldwide appeal of its
products (no doubt facilitated by widespread familiarity with American culture) – tends to obscure this relational view of realism. But it
is important to recognise the degree to which all definitions of realism are locally (regionally, nationally) specific; exactly what the Hollywood film, with its 'universal appeal', is not. In this sense all
definitions of realism are necessarily locally contingent, hinging on
their fidelity to perceived notions of the familiar and the 'other' that
constitutes audiences' experiences of one mainstream movie as
'more realistic' than another. As Noel Carroll puts it, 'realism is not
a simple relation between films and the world but a relation of contrast between films that is interpreted in virtue of analogies to
aspects of reality' (1996: 244). A film or film style may be deemed
realistic because it differs from current films or film styles, where the
difference is construed as revealing a reality that was formerly
hidden or absent. Carroll maintains that because realism is a term
whose application rests upon a historical comparison with other
films and film styles, it cannot be used unprefixed; hence the use of
terms such as Soviet realism, neorealism and 'kitchen sink' realism
are all descriptions of attempts to depict a reality that was absent
from other styles at the time of the conception of the category.

It is our contention that realism continues to be used as a yardstick
in this way, as some of the studies in this book will demonstrate. In
terms of fiction films, the assessment is often based on an assumption
of a dominant form, most usually in the case of American and British
critiques, the Hollywood text. Hence our attention to Bordwell,
Staiger and Thompson's model of the classical Hollywood film as a
paradigmatic textual style. This form of assessment tends to be based
on empirical judgements of characters and events, such as: how
familiar are these characters? do they act in ways which we would
deem realistic? do they represent a believable set of circumstances
and actions in recognisable settings and time frames?

How often, when we hear one film described as 'more realistic'
than another, do we assume it is a positive assessment? What are the
underlying assumptions that such a judgement is based on? Scant
attention has been paid to these issues in recent years; yet in popular
journalism and discussion of film and television, notions of 'realisticness' are bandied about freely. It is easy to think that these judgements are subjective responses, the result of individual interactions

with texts, and as such not worthy of further investigation. One person's 'realism' is just another person's fantasy. This, of course, is true, as far as it goes; but it is not a very useful way to think about the most dominant form of representation in Western culture, its wide range of aesthetic strategies and its appeal to millions of people. Nor does it address the ways in which realism, as the dominant form, is part of a discursive struggle to make sense of our realities, albeit primarily through forms of address that support dominant beliefs and values, but also in ways that can refract those beliefs and values through a critical prism by revealing the very conventionality of their own systems of signification.

Critics and theorists have paid surprisingly little attention to these issues in the past twenty years. Since the debate in *Screen* in the mid-1970s, when realism was accused of being an inherently conservative mode of representation, incapable of embodying a progressive politics, realism has been largely ignored in academic analysis of film. It remains, however, the most pervasive aesthetic form in Western culture and the dominant mode of all popular mediated forms of representation. As such, it is an important barometer for measuring shifts in regimes of representation over the past two decades concerning, for example, race, gender and sexuality, as well as constituting the site of fictions engaging with, for example, the politics of class, international relations and war. Film criticism, both academic and journalistic, has implicitly acknowledged this in debates on particular films, genres and issues: on whether, for instance, certain texts can be read as feminist or anti-racist, in studies of popular television genres such as soap opera, or in audience studies. 'Realism' is taken for granted in these debates; it may be alluded to (as when a text is criticised for being 'unrealistic') but it is not analysed in its specific manifestations as the source of a text's meanings and pleasures. Form seems only to be the focus of critical interest when the text is non-realist, and can perhaps be seen as 'modernist' or 'postmodern'.

We are not seeking to define realism as a mode of representation in terms of its relation to philosophical concepts of realism and the real. Instead, we begin with a basic definition of realism as a mode of representation that, at the formal level, aims at verisimilitude (or mimesis). The dominance of realism in this sense, in painting and prose fiction, is historically related to a shift from a religious to a secular world view, although degrees of mimesis are to be found in most

forms of representational art in most periods. Allied to the more
formal concept of realism as verisimilitude is the notion of truth
telling. Here realism is seen as being appropriate for, and being
obliged to, represent social reality in the interests of knowledge and
social justice. This has been the rationale behind many 'realist
moments', both creatively and critically, from the 'manifestos' of
Courbet and Zola in the nineteenth century, through the
Brecht/Lukacs debate in the 1930s to debates about 'progressive
realism' in 1970s *Screen* theory. We will examine some of these
debates with particular reference to film. Where realism has been the
subject of critical discussion it has taken one of two major forms: (a)
as praise for a text or movement's 'greater realism' (as with British
'New Wave' in the early 1960s); (b) as a critique of realism's decep-
tiveness and consequent power to reproduce dominant ideology (as
in the 1970s critiques by Barthes, MacCabe). Both of these conceptions depend on a model of realism predicated on the Hollywood
paradigm outlined above. We will examine what has been at stake in
these processes of critical differentiation which, on the one hand,
claim that certain forms of realism can present 'a more realistic' or
accurate fictional representation, and, on the other, claim realism as
a deceptive aesthetics which constantly reinforces dominant ideas
and values. Somewhat buried beneath these debates are the actual
uses of realism by filmmakers marginalised from the mainstream,
whether that mainstream is national or international. Realism has
often been used to critique both local traditions of filmmaking practice and the Hollywood model. Our analysis of pivotal historical
moments of realist debate points out what was at stake culturally
and politically in the processes of aesthetic differentiation. We will
also consider certain moments in the history of film when forms of
realism emerged in opposition both to the dominant Hollywood
model and to more local, conservative, traditions. These will include
early Soviet cinema, Italian neorealism, British war-time cinema and
the 'New Wave', and the more recent example of African-American
urban films.

An understanding of the relationship between realist aesthetics
and contemporary popular cinema can only be developed if the
historical conditions that have given rise to popular forms of representation are sufficiently acknowledged. In film terms, the most
thorough and useful account of the development of what is
commonly understood today as the classical or 'realist' style is

Bordwell, Staiger and Thompson's analysis of the Hollywood film industry between 1917 and 1960. Their work provides the foundation on which our own analysis and arguments are built. Identifying the 'invisible' formal structure that underlies popular films reveals the taken-for-granted assumptions that underlie many contemporary discussions and debates, such as, for instance, whether a popular film can be feminist or challenge racist ideologies. Our discussion of realism and genre suggests that contemporary Hollywood is moving away from a filmmaking style based on a compositional model of narration favoured in classical filmmaking towards aggregate formats of entertainment, where the plot serves as a weak connecting mechanism for dispersed actions and events that are highly real-ised through the use of special effects cinematography. Bordwell *et al.*'s model proposes four sources of narrative motivation in classical films, with compositional motivation generally overriding the other three elements of realism, genre and artistic motivation. In Bordwell's paradigm, generic motivations work hand in hand with compositional motivations to create the 'invisible' style of the classical film text. But genre films are often sharply delineated from everyday conceptions of reality by their fantastic elements. In the third chapter we explore the relationship between realism and genre, paying specific attention to the motivational role played by realism. We discuss genres such as science fiction and the musical which seem to transgress the primary compositional motivation of plausibility, and genres that are more dependent on compositional logic, such as the gangster film. (In the former, for example, realist motivations may serve to anchor implausible events in order to give them conceptual credibility. In the latter, the conventions of the genre not only render the narrative credible, but also serve to elicit appropriate emotive responses from the audience – such as the lack of emotion felt over certain types of death.)

A crucial aspect of the critical definition of realism has been an underlying assumption that formal innovation could shift the parameters of textual interpretation from an emotional to an intellectual engagement with contemporary issues and concerns. The implication behind this assumption was that form is a container of meaning in a one-way communicative process. While we have no wish to reify a film or TV text's formal properties as the source of its many and varied interpretations, form is, as Corner recently put

it, instrumental in cueing various acts of both knowing *and* feeling
– of finding sense and significance and having emotions – which is
what happens when we view a film or watch a television programme. Since the 1970s, work with audiences in television studies in particular has emphasised the interpretative aspect of the
communication process. Although some attention has been paid to
the role played by realist texts in this context (Ang 1985, Corner
1992), little of this work has addressed questions about realism
more generally. In addition, there are more popular discourses concerning the power of realism over audiences in relation especially
to violence and sex. Many of the texts that we will consider in Part
II have been remarkably successful in awakening public knowledge
and creating public debate on particular issues. The source of our
interest is how popular realism *manages* contentious content, and
by doing so, removes the text from its status as 'only' fiction or
drama and brings it into the public realm, where its status as fiction, although recognised, is altogether more ambiguous. Our
interest is not in the 'truthfulness' or not of the sounds and images
on the screen but in the aspects of the text that have cued a range
of responses in the public realm that effectively constitute intervention.

Our aim then is to investigate realism for its range of aesthetic
strategies. In Part II of the book, the analysis extends to the specific
uses of realism in contemporary films drawing on the theoretical
conceptions developed in Part I. Having established the wider parameters of definitions and debates about realism, the second section
of the book consists of a series of case studies which demonstrate
the range of realist strategies in common use in recent years. All the
films selected for analysis here use realism to present a potentially
oppositional point of view to the dominant *status quo*, but as the
popular critical response to these texts demonstrates, there is no
guarantee that a text will be read in this way. On the other hand,
many of these texts have been remarkably successful in awakening
public awareness and stimulating public debate. Our categorisation
of these texts is suggested as a starting point from which further
work in this area can develop and is in no way definitive, but it does
suggest that the strategic use of realism can raise issues in the public
sphere that otherwise would have remained obscured or hidden
from popular scrutiny. It is our contention that within the (huge)
body of films that could be seen as not only realist in terms of their

dominant representational mode but also as socially 'progressive' or 'oppositional' to dominant ideas and values, a wide range of aesthetic and ideological strategies are available and employed. Realism is *not* a single, homogeneous mode that always works in the same way; on the contrary, it is important to identify the particular strategies at work in any particular text. For example, audience identification may be invited, subverted or denied. A plot may follow the 'classic' trajectory of disruption, complication, resolution or may appear simply episodic, lack resolution or subvert the resolution. It may be based more or less on historical reality or on the historical reality of an individual's situation or be a fictional recreation of a known contemporary social issue. The text's dominant realism may incorporate non-realist features such as fantasy, the surreal, direct address, voice over, and non-diegetic music. And it may be constructed through the familiar conventions of dominant cinema, or through what are arguably equally familiar alternative practices, such as *cinéma vérité* techniques, using black and white instead of colour, shaky rather than smoothly controlled camerawork. What we want to stress is that this variety is present within a body of films which would not usually be thought of as non-realist or as genre films, and that, perhaps because of this, the specific realist strategies employed usually receive little detailed critical attention. Realism is the taken-for-granted mode; it is non-realism that gives cause for comment. Here, that situation is reversed: this book is devoted to an analysis of that which is commonly taken for granted, the discursive contexts in which realism is mobilised both as a film style and a mode of critical practice.

Part I

Chapter 1

Realism and film: discursive formations

To be realist a cultural form must be compatible with an ontology rooted in secular and scientific cosmology. And more specifically in a scientific cosmology (based on Galilean and Newtonian concepts) that is primarily mechanistic. (Abercrombie, Lash and Longhurst 1992: 118)

Introduction

Realism is a contentious arena of debate across a broad field of scholarship embracing philosophy, aesthetics and the social sciences in an on-going dialogue about the role of all forms of representation – from fine art to photojournalism, autobiography to scientific reports – in the construction and understanding of the social world. Debates about realism and representation in European culture can be traced back to Plato and Aristotle, but take on a particular intensity in the nineteenth century with the development of what Winston (1995) terms 'lens culture'. The development of an empirically grounded analysis of the material world, aided by scientific ways of seeing, created a shift in nineteenth-century culture that has parallels with the shift in our own times from analogue to digital modes of representation. In this introductory chapter, we will concentrate on the principal strands of thought that have informed debates about realism in film studies. A brief outline of the historical context in which realism develops as a mode of representation in the nineteenth century is followed by a discussion of the critical contexts in which realism is mobilised as a film style. The critical approach to realism in film studies is informed by two strands of thought, both of which have their roots in formalist conceptions about how film texts are structured and the effects of that structuring on our abilities to comprehend artistic products. One strand embraces debates which situate realist films as breaking with or departing from the codes and conventions of mainstream, commercial film practice; the other is inflected by ideological approaches, which treat all mainstream film texts as versions of the classic realist text developed in the nineteenth-century novel. In working through these approaches, what emerges is that realism cannot be confined to a particular style of representation; it is always contingent, always in flux. This notion, that 'the real' is 'a site of contest, of change and redefinition' (Gledhill 1992: 132) is now a common assumption. Here, we draw on recent historical work in film studies which traces the formations of critical debate about realism through shifts in nineteenth-century literary and dramatic forms and their influence on the development of narrative cinema.

Realism and narrative in the nineteenth century

Whilst narrative is not an inevitable destiny of the cinema, it was 'an inevitable destiny of any cinema created in a Western culture addicted to narrative – i.e. the only cinema there is'. (Winston 1995: 26)

Realism and narrative are inseparably linked in nineteenth-century Western art and culture, their development spread across a wide spectrum of leisure and entertainment practices. Winston, somewhat pejoratively, links the development of cinema to an increasing fascination in late nineteenth-century popular culture, art and literature to ways of showing and telling that cast the representation of the material world in mimetic rather than symbolic terms. In fine art, the term 'realism' is applied to the style of a group of nineteenth-century painters who between 1840 and 1870–80 made their mark by seeking 'to give a truthful, objective and impartial representation of the real world based on meticulous observation of contemporary life' (Nochlin 1971: 13). At the same time, the development of photography led to predictions that painting would soon become obsolete, its impressionistic mimesis replaced by the empirical objectivity of the photographic image. In literature, the early realists cast themselves as careful painters of human life, asserting that 'Art always aims at the representation of Reality, i.e. of Truth', but by the latter half of the century writers became aware of the

inherent deficiencies of the formulation and the compositional difficulties that such a project entailed. George Eliot, foremost
amongst the realist writers, demonstrates her awareness of the central difficulty of realism in chapter 17 of *Adam Bede*: namely, how
does a writer translate a true (but necessarily subjective) vision into
words? By the end of the century, writers are less sanguine about
their ability to create truthful representations of material life; the
writer Guy Maupassant (1888) suggests that realists should call
themselves illusionists, while Henry James in *The Art of Fiction*
(1884) favours a verisimilitude defined by an 'air of reality' and an
'impression of life' (Furst 1992: 27–8).

Meanwhile, Emile Zola formulated a theory of fictional representation which he called 'naturalism'. According to Zola, the writer
should study men and women as the naturalist studies animals,
observing and reporting, while eschewing judgement or any subjective perspective. The aim was to be as objective as the scientist: the
facts would speak for themselves, but only, of course, if they were
accurately and fully presented. 'Naturalism', therefore, demanded
comprehensive and meticulous description of the material world
inhabited by its characters, as well as of the characters and events
themselves.

Naturalism has taken its place in the critical vocabulary as an
extreme form of realism, in which observation and the reproduction
of detail are often seen, rather derogatorily, as ends in themselves. It
is very arguable whether Zola's own practice conformed to his
theory, but Lukacs, in taking up Engels's comment that Marx preferred the conservative novelist Balzac to the more left-wing Zola,
drew a distinction between the former's 'critical realism' and the
latter's 'naturalism' as the basis for judging Balzac to be the better,
and more radical, novelist. This is, however, essentially a value
judgement rather than a formal differentiation, while the more current version of the distinction, which claims that naturalism aims at
verisimilitude as an end in itself, is grounded in assumptions about
authorial intention, which again is not a formal distinction.

We have, therefore, chosen not to use this distinction in our
examination of realism in film. Gerhardie's definition of naturalism
as the desire 'to resurrect the complete illusion of real life, using the
things characteristic of real life' (Gerhardie 1979: xvi) can equally
apply to realism – in the novel, in theatre and in film. Similarly, the
naturalists' preference for dealing with the unpleasant and taboo

aspects of life and society in order to 'tell the whole truth', their often reforming impulse, and their aim to make their representations a 'slice of life' are all characteristic of early realists in the novel and drama, and continue to be the self-consciously avowed aims of critical filmmakers such as, amongst others, Costa-Gavras, Oliver Stone and Ken Loach.

In contrast with realism's concern with observation and depiction of character psychology, situations and events, melodrama is characterised as primarily concerned with situation and plot. It employs a more or less fixed complement of stock characters or emblematic types, the most important of whom are a suffering hero or heroine, a persecuting villain and a benevolent comic. Acting is typically gestural, relying on particular movements to illustrate emotional states. The action takes place against elaborate scenic backgrounds accompanied by music to underscore dramatic effect. Recurring themes – the triumph of virtue and the punishment of vice – are given added substance by drawing from a range of sources that represent and mediate views of contemporary life, such as popular novels, newspaper reports and social documents. Melodramatic protagonists pit themselves against an unpredictable world, untroubled by self-doubt or personal reflection on events. Their adversaries are evil men (sometimes women), a different social group, a hostile ideology, an accident or chance event, or a malign evil force. It is this dependence on external foes that finally separates melodrama from all other dramatic forms. As we will explain in more detail below, melodrama formed the basis of early film narratives until the use of techniques taken from the realist stage became more common.

The philosophical and intellectual impetus for the realist and naturalist movements came from social conditions and intellectual currents felt throughout post-Enlightenment Europe. For heuristic purposes, these can be divided into three strands: religious influences, the impact of scientific thought and the socio-political critique of Marxism. Throughout the eighteenth and nineteenth centuries, new theological ideas challenged the traditionally accepted meaning of existence, opening the door to greater freedom of personal decision-making, but also to a greater sense of personal alienation. In the literary theatre of the late nineteenth century, spiritual doubt and religious degeneration were in part responsible for a growing critique of melodrama which postulated its world view on traditional religious foundations and comforts. The realist writers typically pictured a world without a god and without the consoling illusions of religion, often a world of accident and chaos. Scientific method implied that the truth was out there, waiting to be discovered, a product of experiment, not of spiritual revelation. Careful observation and reportage, it was believed, would lead to scientific truth, and this empirical truth would answer all the needs of mankind. These ideals were assimilated by realist writers and playwrights along with the overwhelming spirit of optimism that surrounded scientific activity in this period.

The new scientific outlook is perhaps encapsulated by Darwin's evolutionary theory, which emphasises the descent of man from a primitive mammal and the adaptation and survival of the fittest: 'Man' (sic) is a character inseparable from his environment – and from his natural characteristics as well. Within this context, discoveries in the emerging field of psychology started to question easy assumptions about the underlying causes of behaviour; psychologists began to speak of aberrant, anti-social or 'unnatural' human behaviour in terms of subconscious drives, not conscious choices. The stereotypical 'types' and contrived plots of melodrama produced a naïve form of dramatic motivation that looked increasingly contrived to realist playwrights. Realist drama, predicated on the desires and motivations of individual characters, gave semblance to the increasing emphasis on individual responsibility favoured by realist writers.

The sordid materiality of the industrial revolution coupled with the spreading claims of communism and socialism led to a questioning of the exploitative basis of capitalism and strengthened class antagonism throughout Europe. There are numerous depictions of this changing socio-political context in realist novels and in realist theatre, from Gorky's experiments with the 'mass hero', where a number of suffering alienated workers provide the focus of interest rather than a single, individual character, to the breakdown of class barriers depicted seriously in Strindberg's *Miss Julie* and humorously in Shaw's *Pygmalion*. Ibsen investigated the corruption of capitalist enterprise in plays such as *The Wild Duck* and *An Enemy of the People*, portraying the chaos of a fragmented citizenry. Social concerns found their theatrical expression in the development of the social problem play. In Shaw's commentary on *Widowers' Houses* (1892), an attack on slums and absentee landlords, he informs the reader that the play 'deals with a burning social question and is

deliberately intended to induce people to vote on the Progressive
(liberal) side in the next city council election in London' (Bentley
1947: 103). The use of realist strategies to persuade audiences to
support social and politically inflected projects continues to this day,
as we discuss in more detail below.

What seemed new at the time was the conviction that a play need
not be just entertainment, manipulating an easy response to familiar
tricks and situations, but that it could be a penetrating enquiry into
the way we live. This conviction drew its strength from the prestige
of scientific method, backed by the achievement of the novelists in
recording and analysing complex social changes. The conception of
realism in fiction and drama towards the end of the century is very
similar. Both are positivist, both are sceptical of metaphysics. Reality is to be found in the world of science where everything, in principle, can be verified by observation. Ethically, the picture is a good
deal less simple. Not only do the writers diverge from each other,
but the majority of them are fiercely critical of the bourgeoisie from
which they came and in which their own values had been formed.
For drama, as well as for the novel, the essential point is that scientific positivism, theoretically a dispassionate account of reality, was
in practice usually appropriated by the values of a single social class.
Although aimed at reforming the popular commercial theatre, realist drama paradoxically cultivated a small audience amongst the
literati – the sophisticated upper middle class – an audience in tem-
perament and education very like the playwrights and critics themselves.

The drive towards realist narratives and stage scenarios was
accompanied by a similar quest to visualise the world through what
Brian Winston has described as the development of 'lens culture'
(Winston,1996: 10–38). Visual 'real-isations' in the form of Panora-
mas, Dioramas and magic lantern shows were part of a developing
entertainment industry in the rapidly growing cities. These 'real-isations' contained elements of narrative sequencing, often in the form
of journeys or transformations, and a panoply of techniques for
melding the sequences together. Winston argues that 'the propensity
to arrange images in a logical order and then to display them at a
fixed pace before an audience is, at the very least, a mark or trace of
addiction to narrative' (1996: 26). This 'addiction' reaches its
apotheosis on the melodramatic stage; realism becomes spectacu-
larised, its dramatic potential harnessed to the demands of a plot

driven by the Manichean forces of chance and coincidence. The commercial stage was increasingly dominated by productions where the special effects aimed to create a believable setting in which the unbelievable, the fantastic and the spectacular could take place. In melodrama, the plot is often a vehicle for a series of dramatic tableaux, fixed points in the action, where great attention is paid to the realistic detail of setting. Melodrama shared with the Diorama and other visual entertainments increasingly sophisticated technologies of realistic representation, often combined with the use of living and 'real' props such as animals, trees and water.

Nicolas Vardac (1949) has argued that the spectacle of 'the real' dominated the melodramatic stage for half a century before the moving image slowly displaced theatrical illusions of pictorial reality. Cinema develops in the context of these fascinations, its pre-conditions of existence firmly rooted in the dispositions of nineteenth century audiences for forms of storytelling accompanied by various techniques of visualisation. Throughout the century, mass migration from the countryside into the cities created an increasingly lucrative market for all forms of popular spectacle (Hobsbawn, in Winston 1996: 27). By the middle of the century, metropolitan audiences had grown accustomed to sitting in rows of seats in darkened auditoria to watch entertainments designed to appeal to a wide range of different social groups. Between the 1860s and the 1890s, theatre owners and producers became increasingly organised: chains of theatres were built, and touring shows block-booked to fill them. Shows were marketed through mass circulation newspapers and magazines on the reputations of their leading performers, actor stars who attracted large audiences. Winston makes the point that by 1895, the year of cinema's invention, the broad mass of the audience, addicted to naturalistic illusion and narrative, were sitting watching

> highly professional entertainments created by a logistically complex, capital-intensive industry. Theatrical products became highly differentiated, often along class lines, although theatres remained places where 'commoners' could mix with the 'well-to-do'. By the end of the century, theatre had come of age: developed into an industrially organised 'show' business, it now served a mass public ready and eager to be entertained. Both producers and consumers were by this time ready and 'waiting for cinema'. (Winston 1996: 31)

Critical contexts: literary realism and bourgeois ideology

Dominant Anglo-American theories of the rise of the novel create an inseparable link between the establishment and development of novelistic form and a concurrently emerging mercantile class able to take advantage of the social and economic changes instigated by capitalism. In *The Rise of the Novel*, Ian Watt argues that the 'formal realism' emerging during this period in the novels of Defoe, Richardson and Fielding represents the defining characteristics of this new form, and can be generalised to the novel genre as whole (Watt 1957). More importantly for our purposes here, Watt conceives the genre as inseparable from the liberal ideology of the emergent bourgeois class. But there are two senses in which liberalism can be understood in this context. As Gasiorek has pointed out, liberalism is equated in economic terms with *laissez-faire* politics and free market endeavour associated with possessive individualism; but it is also associated with a humanist sensibility that favours open-mindedness, tolerance and breadth of vision. It is one thing to associate the eighteenth-century development of the novel to the rise of a class produced by a liberal economic system, but quite another to claim that liberalism is a structure of feeling, a literary sensibility, rather than an economic or political doctrine (Gasiorek 1995: 7). Nonetheless, it is the latter view that has tended to prevail in critical evaluations of novelistic realism; many Anglo-American critics have associated realism with liberalism, for example linking the crisis in post-war British society with a crisis in novelistic form.[1]

The association between the formal characteristics of realism and political liberalism is a tenacious one; post-structuralist critics such as MacCabe, Heath and Belsey take the argument a stage further, outlining the key characteristics of realism as 'a transparent tool that relies on a reflectionist aesthetic; relatively stable characterisation; a universalising metalanguage that establishes a hierarchy of discourse, producing the 'social' as the 'natural'; and closure' (Gasiorek 1995:9). Their position argues that realism is a rule-governed system that determines how our perceptions of the world are structured. Realist representations mirror the world, claiming that their accounts are self-evidently natural, when they are in fact socially and historically contingent. The broad perspective shared by post-structuralist critics is that language is necessary for thought, and therefore precedes independent entities, which can only be made intelligible by differentiating between concepts. Because realism is forced to create 'juxtapositions and complexities from what we already know ... it is a predominantly conservative form' (Belsey, in Gasiorek 1995: 9). Realism does not reflect reality, but the order inscribed in particular discourses. Since there is no unmediated access to the world, the correspondence theory of truth is eliminated; there is no external reality which language can be measured against or claim to transparently represent because language constructs our perceptions of that external reality. Language, as a system, is independent of a pre-existing mental reality that gives shape and structure to the world. To use an aphorism that was common in 1970s debates, language thinks us; it is a system of differences that produces what we know and what we construct as knowledge of the world.

Realism, film and ideology

In film studies, the post-structuralist position on realism is forcefully argued by Colin MacCabe in his well-known essay 'Realism and the cinema: notes on some Brechtian theses' (MacCabe 1974). Mac-Cabe argues that the so-called classic realist text of the nineteenth-century literary novel is defined by a hierarchy of discourses comprising its textual structure. Each of these discourses proposes a version of reality, but only one discourse is privileged as the bearer of the truth; this discourse functions as a 'metalanguage' against which the truth or falsity of the other discourses can be judged. The metalanguage corresponds to the narrating source of the fiction, no matter whether the narrating voice is explicit (first-person narration) or implicit (third-person narration). The reader is positioned by the narration, given a place in the story from which they are able to pass judgement on what should be the case and who should be believed.

A similar structural hierarchy applies in film: conventional documentary films, for example, often have an overt metalanguage in the form of a voice-over commentary that binds together the different versions of reality presented by numerous voices and images to perform a truth-telling function. MacCabe claims that fiction films are similarly structured, but with images taking precedence over words. The image track shows the spectator what really happens, the camera providing the metalanguage by situating the spectator within the fictional diegesis of the film. MacCabe uses as an example a sequence from *Klute*, a Hollywood film of the early 1970s that was influenced by developments in European art cinema, to illustrate his point. *Klute* has an ambiguous ending because the soundtrack and the image track provide two alternative solutions to the central character's dilemma. On the one hand, her voice-over establishes her doubts about leaving the city to live with her lover, whilst the image track shows her packing her cases, as if she has already decided on a course of action. MacCabe argues that the truth of the situation is established by the image track; we believe what we see, that she is leaving, rather than what we are told. In filmed fictions, the narrating discourse provided by the camera tells us the truth in a manner that resists questioning. Because the narrating discourse is rendered transparent, the truth is revealed to us as obviously self-evident. This coincidence of truth and vision puts 'the real' beyond argument, placing the spectator in a position of 'dominant specularity', a position of fulfilment, in possession of complete and final knowledge of events, 'locked into a paralysing fixity, with no perspective for struggle or possibility of transformation. In dissolving all contradictions, the metalanguage places the spectator outside production, outside conflict, outside history' (Lapsley and Westlake 1988: 173). The transparency of the classic realist text is therefore conservative and ultimately reactionary because it is unable to mobilise a subject in process, one who is consciously aware of the relationship between the knower and known.

MacCabe's formulation has been criticised by David Bordwell as a 'general and loose one' which applies to a great many texts in both common and specialised use – everything from newspaper reports to scientific documents. Nor does MacCabe's category of the nineteenth-century novel distinguish between sub-genres, such as the Gothic romance and novel of manners, or the varieties of point of view (omniscient, restricted) which are a feature of all written narratives. Bordwell argues that filmic narration is a process, and as such cannot be reduced to that of other media; he suggests that formal and generic conventions can make empirical realism a secondary factor. Futhermore, rather than conceptualising the nineteenth-century novel as monologic and subject to a hierarchy of discourse, Bordwell favours Bakhtin's theory of heteroglossia, or dialogue, where conflicting visions of the world struggle to articulate themselves through various discourses. Bordwell concludes his piece by claiming that MacCabe's formulation reduces the range of filmic narration. By equating the metalanguage with the camera, camerawork is privileged at the expense of other filmic techniques such as speech, gesture, written language, music, colour, optical processes, lighting, costume and even off-screen space and off-screen sound. The ambiguous ending of *Klute* is open to a range of interpretations; there is no reason to decide that the image privileges the sound track because each are given equal interpretative weight. Filmic narration 'can often be better characterised by the interplay of potentially equivalent narrational factors than by the flattening of all elements under a monolithic "metalanguage"' (Bordwell 1988: 18–20).

Bordwell, Staiger and Thompson's account of the development of American narrative films in *The Classical Hollywood Cinema* is the most comprehensive account to date of how a particular mode of film production can give rise to a certain kind of film style. Their conception is based on a neoformalist perspective that foregrounds narrative causality as the driving motor of Hollywood cinema in the studio era, subordinating other influences such as popular music and melodrama to the needs of a narrative logic based on causality, plausibility, linearity, character motivation, psychological realism and compositional unity. But they do not claim that it is a realist style *per se*; the confusion here seems to stem from the use of the term 'classical'. In tracing Bordwell and Thompson's use of this term through various editions of *Film Art* between 1979 and 1993, Christopher Williams points to an unacknowledged broadening of the concept of 'classical Hollywood cinema' to 'classical narrative cinema' which he claims effects a rhetorical move closer to MacCabe's formulation of the 'dominant narrative' of the classic realist text (Williams 1994: 275–92). Williams goes on to state that 'Realism is not a singular or univocal style. It is not a homogeneous or finished effect, nor is it a side effect of a genre ... Nor can it meaningfully be divided into two distinct, antagonistic entities – illusionist realism on one side and formal and intellectual consciousness-raising anti-realism on the other' (Williams 1994: 289). It is our contention that this binary division, between the so-called 'transparency' of popular conventions and the 'opacity' of films that use non-realist strategies with the aim of creating a different vision, a different view of reality, continues to inflect critical attitudes to the uses of realism in popular cinema.

Realism and film form

The neoformalist position on realism and film style has its roots firmly embedded in Russian Formalist theories of art dating from the 1920s. Formalists claim that what makes a work of representation a work of art is its technical deviation from existing, conventionalised forms of representation. Form, in the formalist conception, is a container of meaning: new meaning can only be achieved if the shape or pattern of the container is changed. This has particular implications for our analysis because for neoformalists such as Bordwell and Thompson realism can only be achieved if it breaks with familiar, conventional patterns. Defamiliarisation is the name given by the formalists to this process. Formalism is a consistent mode of analysis practised by early film theorists such as Munsterberg, Malraux, Arnheim, Balazs and Eisenstein, most of whom had a background in a wide variety of other art forms (Andrews 1976: 134). Formalist theories of film remained dominant until the end of the Second World War, becoming mollified in the late 1940s by the voice of André Bazin, whose theories coincided with a new interest in a form of filmmaking practice epitomised by Italian neorealism.[2] One of Bazin's recurring concerns was the dependence of cinema on reality. This has led to a rather reductive view of Bazin in contemporary accounts of his theories as an unreformed humanist, but his ideas some fifty years on remain suggestive. Bazin set out to show that cinematic signification is a continuum from the most unadorned forms of signification to the most abstract and obviously constructed. He aimed to debunk the idea that only the most abstract techniques can lead to the judgement of a film as truly cinematic, bringing to light numerous types of films and techniques neglected by the formalist approach. Today, Bazin is most remembered for his opposition to montage. Bazin conceived of two different types of montage, one of which has its roots in the associative montage of Soviet cinema, the other in the repertoire of techniques generally associated with the continuity editing style of mainstream films; montage is always a telling or an ordering of events to suit rhetorical ends. Bazin showed a consistent preference for the long take and depth within the image, claiming that such a style was inherently more realistic, that certain kinds of events demand this more realistic treatment, and that such a treatment confronts our normal psychological processing of events, therefore making us aware of a reality we often fail to recognise (Andrews 1976: 146–57).

Although challenging many of the basic tenets of formalist thinking, Bazin too favours a defamiliarisation technique that breaks with already established codes and conventions in the interests of generating realism and interpretative ambiguity. Mainstream popular cinema is governed by fidelity to narrative causality; it has an official look and uses a dictatorial language which determines the kinds of subject matter that it can deal with and rules out the possibility of a reciprocal relationship between the spectator and the objects or events represented on the screen. In contrast, Bazin advocates a realistic cinema that preserves the freedom of spectators to choose their own interpretations of an object, character or event. This concept of realism respects perceptual space and time, advocating depth-of-field shooting and the long take which remain at the level of recording events as they take place. But as Andrews points out, technique alone cannot guarantee that a 'realistic' cinema will result from its use (Andrews 1976: 162–4). It is ultimately Bazin's commitment to a correspondence theory of representation favouring the use of particular techniques in the interests of 'truth' that is so at odds with contemporary theories of representation today.

Traces of the Bazinian legacy are found in neoformalist approaches to film. In *Breaking the Glass Armour*, Kirsten Thompson argues, drawing on some of Bazin's ideas, that whole films, existing against specific historical backgrounds, create the effect of realism. In the broader sense of the term, all art has natural links to reality which engage with some aspect of an experiential relationship to the world and can therefore be judged as 'realistic' on the basis of some criterion or other. The temptation is to attempt to define a set of traits that constitute a more specific realist style. For neoformalists, the concept of types of motivation is the main tool for distinguishing realism. Motivations can be compositional (essential in the case of Hollywood films to their structural unity of character-centred causality), artistic (defined in mainstream films as shows of technical virtuosity or physical skill), transtextual (generic) or realistic. Thompson states that 'if the cues ask us to appeal to our knowledge of the real world (however mediated that knowledge may be by cultural learning), we can say that the work is using realistic motivation. And if realistic motivation becomes one of the main ways of justifying the work's overall structures, then we generalise and perceive the work as a whole as realistic' (Thompson 1988: 197–8).

It therefore follows that in any film history constructed around formalist criteria, realist films depart from the prevailing conventions of mainstream films. In an Italian neorealist film such as *Bicycle Thieves* (De Sica, 1948) realism is achieved where the film significantly departs from the mainstream studio-based practice of late 1940s Hollywood cinema. Thompson identifies five aspects of the film's text and viewing contexts which situated it as a realist film in its day. First of all, the subject matter of the film draws on an historical notion that a concentration on the lives of peasants and the working class make for more realistic action. This stems from a reaction against traditional conventions in art and literature that depict the common people as comic or allegorical figures without the full subjectivity and authority given to biblical subject matter or to those occupying positions of power. Secondly, the narrative strays from a tight causal link between character and action typical of mainstream film narrative by introducing peripheral events and coincidences. Trivial events are included that serve a variety of functions: they furnish an appearance of everyday life, adding small but significant details that will be important to later events, or they can suggest symbolic or social meanings that fill out the depiction of contemporary life. When combined with the use of coincidence, the overall effect is an appeal to the chaotic and random nature of everyday existence. In spite of these chance occurrences and events, the narrative structure of *Bicycle Thieves* is quite tightly constructed around a series of internal deadlines such as meetings and appointments that form a temporal continuum, rather than relying on a logical chain of character-driven causes and effects, characteristic of mainstream films. Thirdly, and most obviously within the context of a studio-bound mainstream film practice, the use of non-actors and location shooting make the style of mise-en-scène and cinematography seem realistic for its time. Looking at the film today, there is a notable disparity between what we might now consider 'realistic shooting' and the obvious technical artistry brought to the illumination of interior studio-shot sequences. Thompson suggests that these conventions of classical filmmaking were invisible to the audiences of the day, who based their criteria of 'realisticness' on the content of the image and the obvious authenticity suggested by the unglamorous faces, the shabby clothes worn by the characters, and the poverty of their environment. The film focuses on an incident related to unemployment, a pressing problem in post war Italy, but rather than advocating a solution to the problem or a critique of the social order, it presents an apparent position of neutral objectivity. The political dimensions of the story become submerged in the psychological realism of the relationship between father and son, creating a compassionate, humanistic viewpoint which ultimately contributes to the film's impression of realism. Finally, the mise-en-scène of the film includes numerous references to Hollywood cinema: posters of Rita Hayworth, a market stall selling movie magazines, and a comment from a man in the street who remarks that he finds movies boring. The film flags up its difference from mainstream films, calling attention to itself as a more authentic representation, one that is closer to the truth of everyday experience.

Thompson completes her analysis of *Bicycle Thieves* with the irony of its reception not as a popular film among working people in Italy (who preferred commercial mainstream products) but as an art house commodity admired by an elite audience. In the United States, where it was circulated through the network of art house cinemas and university campuses, the film was received as a realistic tale of a little man struggling against adversity, a theme with 'universal' implications. It is unlikely that a more polemical film about Italian unemployment would have received such an enthusiastic reception. *Bicycle Thieves* fitted a growing conception of realism becoming a new norm at that time; that of the psychological drama, unhappy ending and ambiguous causality. All these traits were to become central to developments in post-war European art cinema in the 1950s and 1960s (Thompson 1988: 203–17).

Thompson's case study provides an excellent account of how a film that breaks dominant conventions comes to be judged as a realist film by film aficionados, scholars and reviewers. The film was clearly at one with the values of a liberal cultural elite committed to finding and promoting artworks that corresponded with their own cultural taste and value system. But inherent within this conception of realism as defamiliarisation, as breaking conventions, lies an implicit assumption that the popular film, by definition, can never be a realist film. For a more nuanced account of the relationship between realist codes and popular cinema, we have to look elsewhere.

Realism and melodrama

A different reading of what might constitute the aesthetics of main-stream film is proposed by Gledhill, who argues that the development of Hollywood film style can be read in terms that suggest a modernisation of nineteenth-century melodrama. The Bordwell, Staiger and Thompson model of the classical Hollywood film emphasises general characteristics associated with realist forms of representation; chance, coincidence and episodic structure are elim-inated in favour of the needs of narrative logic and compositional unity. Romantic music and the expressive elements of mise-en-scène are subordinated to psychological realism and verisimilitude. By way of a contrast, Gledhill emphasises the aesthetic dimension of melo-drama rather than its formalist attributes, drawing on Peter Brooks's definition of melodrama as a 'structure of feeling' that pervades European culture from the time of the French Revolution to the pre-sent day. Brooks situates melodrama not 'as a theme or a set of themes, nor the life of the drama *per se*, but rather melodrama as a mode of conception and expression, as a certain fictional system for making sense of experience, as a semantic field of force' (Brooks 1976: xiii). Melodrama comes into being 'in a world where the tra-ditional imperatives of truth and ethics have been thrown violently into question ... [melodrama] becomes the principal mode for uncovering, demonstrating and making operative the essential moral universe in a post-sacred era' (Brooks 1976: 14–15). Melo-drama articulates 'the moral occult', the hidden sacred values of Western societies whose traditional ways of life have been trans-formed by the massive changes wrought by industrialisation, secu-larisation and mass migration. In a de-sacralised world the only remaining source of moral and ethical values resides within the human personality itself. An increased emphasis on the individual actor as the locus of dramatic force and action on the melodramatic stage towards the end of the nineteenth century corresponds to the increased social and political power vested in individuals through an extension of the voting franchise. Citizens are responsible for the moral and ethical health of society, a responsibility that many took seriously, reflected in the growth of numerous reform movements seeking to infuse the developing entertainment industries with a sense of moral and social duty.[3]

Realism and melodrama are often posed as antithetical aesthetic

terms, with realism connoting authenticity and truth and melodrama exaggeration, sensationalism and sentimentality. The discursive split occurs around the end of the nineteenth century, as
literary and dramatic critics start to give cultural value to realism at
the expense of melodrama, denigrating its expressive style in favour
of a more restrained method of performance. Gledhill points out
that the struggle to define a new kind of realism, epitomised in the
work of the realist and naturalist writers and dramatists, was a
struggle to open a new territory for representing changing social
mores and values. The values at stake were those of a different
social class of writers – 'literati rather than entertainers – on behalf
of a different audience – the intelligentsia rather than a popular
middle-class or working-class audience' (Gledhill 1992: 133).
This cultural disengagement from melodrama is found in collec-
tions of late nineteenth-century critical writing. Performances
begin to be judged in terms of their 'restraint'; suppression of emotions is linked with 'masculinist' notions of virility, intelligence and
adulthood, in opposition to the 'feminising' sensationalism and sentimental emotions of melodrama (Gledhill 1992: 135). Expressiveness comes to be seen as a feminine characteristic of drama, and in
English criticism in particular, as a lower class attribute. In North
American criticism of the same era, considerations of class are displaced by a concern with gender, no doubt because the United
States considered itself a classless society. Realism is conceived in
terms of the same masculine values which informed the pioneering
spirit: strength, virility, energy and violent expressiveness are preferred to the discourse of restraint favoured by English critics. In
American realism, it is the 'heart of Man' that is at stake; masculinity needs to be protected not from emotion but from feminine class
affectation (Gledhill 1992: 136). An aggressive, independent masculinity is seen as a necessary corrective to a society in danger of
being overwhelmed by artificial mannerisms and inauthentic attitudes. This polarisation between the pioneering attributes of 'natural' man and the softer 'civilising' influences of femininity is found
in many popular novels of the day, such as the western and the
crime novel, genres that become mainstays of popular American
cinema in the 1930s, 1940s and 1950s.

Realism and authenticity become key terms at the turn of the century as theatre seeks to reclaim literary and cultural respectability,
denigrating melodrama as an entertainment only fit for children and

women. But the two terms are not antithetical – they present different approaches to shared ideological and cultural conditions. During the nineteenth century the two develop in tandem in what Vardac has described as a 'romantic–realist' aesthetic which was most pronounced on the melodramatic stage. In its early stages of development, cinema offered a superior means of achieving the realist representation of romantic fantasy. Producers then sought a higher paying audience, which entailed the transformation and modernisation of melodramatic practices and themes in line with the prestige of the New Drama, realism and 'naturalism', changing social mores and new criteria of verisimilitude. Melodramatic narratives function around missed opportunities, repetitions and coincidences that finally explode, allowing unexplained and therefore unexpected dramatic energies to emerge that over-determine causal effect. In classical narration, everything is motivated by plausible causes; melodrama is accused of contrivance and coincidence, the most obvious example being the happy ending which often seems contrived in order to make a moral point. Realism emphasises the ordinary, not the extraordinary, rejecting unbelievable plots and implausible characters. The new dramatists wished to substitute the one-dimensional heroes and villains of melodrama, whose personalities were often signified by physical attributes, with the more complex, multi-dimensional and psychologised characters created by the literary realists. The realists paid attention to 'insignificant' redundant detail, which often meant writing dialogue that accurately reflected a character's social identity, as well as, or instead of, forwarding the plot. In production, realist effect was created through props and sets that reproduced everyday life in great detail, whether or not the action required them.

Pearson has traced the emergence of the realist psychological narrative through a change in performance style from a melodramatic or histrionic code to a more realistic, or what she terms 'verisimilar', style in the Biograph films of Griffith between 1908 and 1913. Claiming that the widespread and indiscriminate use of the concept of the melodramatic in film studies has rendered the term all but meaningless, Pearson advocates a method of analysis which attempts to understand the aesthetic standards of another time and place through textual and intertextual analysis. A new acting style, the verisimilar code, was increasingly discussed in the critical writings of the day and in the trade press. This style depended on actors delivering delicate hints and nuances in their performances, rather than the obvious gesticular movements of the histrionic code inherited from the melodramatic stage. On stage, melodramatic actors play to the gallery, using a repertoire of stock gestures and responses to convey particular emotions and character traits, judged by their ability to create striking attitudes and poses in fixed tableaus that present performance as spectacle. The use of this histrionic code, in a somewhat attenuated form, is evident in the early Griffith Biograph films, but by 1912 the balance shifts in favour of a more extended use of the verisimilar code (Pearson 1992: 50).

Actors employing the verisimilar code, like dramatic and literary writers, use a wealth of detail to create 'realistic effect': this detail, referred to as 'byplay', emphasises personal physical mannerisms, adding small touches that suit a character's station in life. Actors are encouraged to accumulate nuances and detail by the scientific observation of real human beings, to make a connection between artistic representation and the actual experiences of everyday life. Within the box set favoured by realist dramatists, the actors play to each other, ignoring the audience, acting as if they are unseen and unheard. In this way, the realist stage aimed to create the illusion of everyday life. By 1912 there was an increasing demand for natural, sincere, unmelodramatic acting in popular film: critics and writers point to instances of verisimilar by-play and restraint as proof that the histrionic code is being displaced by verisimilar acting. Gunning (1990a) and Thompson (1985) have stressed that the use of the face and eyes constituted an important aspect of this new code, presenting a restrained performance that nevertheless conveyed the detail of a character's emotional and psychological traits. The desire to see the actor's face predates cinematic techniques such as the use of close-up which developed to highlight facial expression. By 1911, reviewers were criticising filmmakers for not bringing actors close enough to the camera: the face and eyes were thought to reflect characters' thoughts and emotions, and therefore facial expression was considered an indispensable part of the verisimilar code's construction of a psychological character (Pearson 1992: 125–7). In the trade press, there was a similar disassociation of popular film from theatrical melodrama. Filmmakers were urged to hire writers of realist narratives, and to encourage them to follow the example of the well-made play. Actors imported from the literary stage served to legitimise film acting by using the verisimilar style with the new realist narratives, providing adequate psychological motivation for character action.

Changes in the organisation of film exhibition accompanied this shift towards a newly perceived realism on the screen. Public-spirited citizens denounced the shop front nickelodeons as dens of vice, breeding grounds of physical and moral degeneracy, their lower-class immigrant audiences overly susceptible to the 'immoral' and corrupting influence of melodrama. In contrast, 'good' drama was viewed as 'educative in the best sense, developing taste, social responsibility and human sympathy' (Pearson 1992: 130). By 1908 the Motion Picture Patents Company, headed by the Edison and Biograph studios, vowed that films would become 'moral, educational and cleanly amusing' in their bid to woo the 'the better classes'. Trade papers started to reiterate these sentiments: 'The motion picture, the greatest factor in the future instruction and amusement of mankind, must range itself with the forces that make for good, that mean progress and spell advancement' (Pearson 1992: 131). Those sympathetic to the film industry argued that it could be a repository of cultural and moral values, a force for education and change. The industry, keen to avoid public censure, turned to producing more respectable entertainments, distancing itself from the cheap amusements abhorred by reform organisations, churches and educational institutions.

Pearson's analysis precludes the conception of one form of representation as natural or inevitable; she is therefore against a teleological perspective that labels realism as inherently bourgeois or middle class, as Gledhill (following Belsey, MacCabe et al.) suggests above. Pearson is in agreement with Raymond Williams's view that some of the characteristics of late eighteenth-century and nineteenth-century realism, such as contemporaneity, secularity, and social inclusiveness, although initially associated with the bourgeoisie's rise to power, could be appropriated by others in the class struggle. For Pearson, codes and conventions result from struggles for meaning articulated between groups with competing agendas. We will return to the question of contemporary struggles for meaning and the shifting grounds of signification and interpretation in our discussions in Part II of the book.

Notes

1 See, for instance, the work of W. J. Harvey, George Orwell and Lionel Trilling.
2 See, for example, Bazin's (1948) essay 'An Aesthetic of Reality: Cinematic Realism and the Italian School of the Liberation' in H. Gray (ed. and trans.) (1967), *What is Cinema?*, vol. 2.
3 For a detailed account of how this relationship affected the development of early film narratives, see Black (1994), Maltby (1994) and Pearson (1992).

Chapter 2

Realist moments: representation and reality

Our own realist moment, in Western culture at the end of the twentieth century, is one in which the evidential claims of our visual and auditory recording instruments are increasingly called into question. The development of digital recording technologies and computer generated imagery has created a crisis in the representation of the real that half a century of critical and theoretical work dedicated to revealing the constructed nature of the realist image has been unable to achieve. Somewhat paradoxically, in the light of opportunities for image and auditory construction and manipulation unimagined a century ago, recordings of actuality are losing their status as guarantors of 'truth' and veracity, while the popularity of various forms of simulated reality in movies and diverse types of television 'infotainment' has never been stronger. In Britain and North America, it is various forms of realist drama that attract the largest audiences to the cinema and the TV screen, just as in popular fiction it is contemporary forms of the realist novel that consistently top the lists of best-selling fiction.

A detailed historical account of realism and the fiction film has yet to be written, although there are several books which cover in some detail aspects of its principal features, notably David Bordwell's *Narration in the Fiction Film* (1988). The key theoretical debates can be found in Christopher Williams's *Realism in the Cinema* (1980), a collection of writings and commentary compiled in the late 1970s, when debates about the political potential of realism as a mode of film style were at their height. Instead of retreading the ground covered by Bordwell or Williams here, we have selected a number of key theoretical moments when realism was the subject of intense critical attention and reflection to illustrate the different codes and conventions that are claimed as 'realist' by diverse communities of critical intellectuals in particular socio-historical contexts.

The first moment, Soviet cinema of the 1920s, a period well-known for its avant-garde and modernist filmmaking practices, may seem an odd choice; but for Soviet filmmakers issues of realism were a central concern in their attempts to forge a new aesthetic that would reflect the changed consciousness of post-revolutionary Russia. As part of this enterprise, they sought to dismantle all forms of bourgeois expression, particularly the psychological depiction of character common in popular films. Within this context, we examine the debate between Eisenstein and Vertov on how to represent historical characters and events on film, an issue that resounds with contemporary resonance in the wake of the critical controversies raised by films such as *JFK* (1991), *Forrest Gump* (1996), and *Michael Collins* (1998). The second 'moment' examines how realist films were developed to support national interests in British cinema during the Second World War through a form of propaganda that married documentary and fiction formats in an attempt to sweeten the pill of information with the sugar of adventure and romance. In contrast, the third moment investigates the neorealism of Italian liberation in the immediate post-war period, a short-lived but highly influential aesthetic movement that stimulated a new interest in cinematic realism not only in the West but in countries as far apart as Mexico, Japan and India. The fourth moment examines the legacy of European neorealism in British 'kitchen sink' cinema of the early 1960s through the critical lens of debates about gender and sexuality. Finally, African-American urban films of the early 1990s bring us up to date with contemporary critical analyses that emphasise issues of race, place and cinematic space.

Constructing the real: Soviet filmmakers in the 1920s

It is far from simple
to show the truth,
yet truth is simple. (Dziga Vertov, in Petric 1993: 1)

A consideration of the cinema of post-revolutionary Soviet Russia as a 'realist moment' appears a contradiction in terms. Artistically, the mid- to late 1920s constitutes the 'golden age' of Soviet cinema, the peak of a modernist and avant-garde moment of artistic experimentation that sought to articulate a new film aesthetics expressive of the vision and ideology of the emergent socialist society. In philosophical terms, however, the impetus behind much of this experimentation was a realist one, driven by a political desire to peel back the artifice of popular cinema and rid it of bourgeois sensibilities. Practically this involved transforming the institution of cinema politically, economically and socially, thereby taking over the means of production, distribution and exhibition and using film not only as a propaganda tool to educate and inform the working class, but as a means of expressing an evolving working-class subjectivity.

The Russian film industry was virtually destroyed by the Revolution of 1917 and the years of civil war that followed. Many filmmakers fled the country, taking with them any equipment they could transport. Those who stayed found it increasingly difficult to obtain film stock, which had to be imported. The new Soviet government struggled to gain control of the industry, but in the immediate aftermath of civil war many of the studios were in ruins, and much of the distribution infrastructure in a state of collapse. In spite of these problems, a few films were made, primarily newsreels and propaganda films. Cinema was considered a powerful means of communication and expression, one that could carry the revolutionary message and signify revolutionary consciousness to a largely illiterate and massively scattered populace. In 1919 Lenin nationalised the film industry and set up the State Film School to train a new generation of young filmmakers. Here Lev Kuleshov developed a workshop that explored film technique in a climate of harsh economic deprivation, using old films and limited film stock. Kuleshov is credited with exploring an editing technique that became central to the development of montage theory and film style in the mid 1920s: the basic premise is that spectators construct spatial and temporal connections between separate shots even without an establishing shot to aid their interpretation. The most famous experiment described by Kuleshov involved the selection of a close-up shot of an actor with a neutral expression on his face; when the same footage of the actor's face was edited with shots of a bowl of soup, or a dead body, or a baby, Kuleshov claimed that ordinary filmgoers praised the actor's performance, believing that his face had registered an appropriate response to what they had just seen. This, and other experiments, led Kuleshov to conclude that viewer response was less a product of the individual shot than of the meaning generated from juxtaposing shots in the editing – the montage process.

Although many Soviet filmmakers remained committed to traditional forms and methods of filmmaking practice, those most familiar in the West are renowned for creating new forms of cinematic expression using montage in an attempt to represent the revolutionary visions and aspirations of the newly liberated working class. Politically motivated filmmakers formed loose collectives with visual artists, theatre practitioners and other artistic experimentalists seeking to develop new means of expression. Although they often held conflicting ideological positions, these collectives promoted artistic freedom and experimentalism in an attempt to find ways of re-visioning the nascent socialist society.

There was little general agreement amongst filmmakers and intellectuals about what forms of filmmaking practice could achieve these aims. A focus on one key area of debate, the representation of historical events, and the contrasting views on this issue by two of the most well-known montage experimentalists of the era, Eisenstein and Vertov, reveals a schism that continues to reverberate today in debates about how films can mediate the 'facts' of history and the 'truth' of historical events. While both filmmakers were united in their rejection of popular forms of bourgeois melodrama – the 'photoplay' as it was more commonly known – they could not agree on either a method of collective filmmaking practice or a suitable form of representation for informing and educating the audience.

Between 1923 and 1928 the Russian Left Front of the Arts, a loose association of artists and critics from the Futurist, Constructivist and Formalist movements, published two successive avant-garde journals, *LEF* and *Novy Lef*. In his assessment of the form/ideology debates in these journals, Christopher Williams claims that, broadly speaking, writers took up positions against realism and the imitation or copying of life (which meant that they were against most known forms of literature and art) in favour of developing art forms which emphasise the nature of the artistic material and the process of artistic production. It was hoped that the overt construction of new artistic forms would parallel the construction of new forms of social and economic life lived under socialism. The journals devote several articles to film questions, but the debates are often confused, leaving their participants in the difficult position of rejecting both realism and the use of art as an instrument of knowledge, yet simultaneously calling for a cinema of fact which could be socially and politically useful (Williams 1980: 111–52).

The film debates were led by the Constructivists, who view the artist as a species of engineer whose job it is to build the foundations of a new society. Constructivist theories are more concerned with the structure, utility and function of artworks than their expressive and decorative aspects. The Realist Manifesto of 1922 claimed that 'art is the realisation of our spatial perception of the world' and that the artist 'constructs his work as the engineer builds his bridges and the mathematician establishes his formulas of the orbits' (Gabo and Pevsner 1922: 3, quoted in Petric 1993: 5). Dziga Vertov, a committed Constructivist and documentary filmmaker and one of the first people to record on newsreel the Soviet revolutionary struggles, believed film could be a universal language of expression intelligible to all people regardless of class and national boundaries. It was not religion that was the opium of the people in Vertov's estimation, but the photoplay and the bourgeois novel. For Vertov, the camera is an instrument for penetrating external reality, enabling people to see 'through and beyond' the mundane realities of everyday life. At the same time he wanted to demonstrate cinema's exceptional power and how it could be used educationally to build a new society. To achieve these aims, he demanded that filmmakers abandon the narrative and theatrical conventions of popular cinema in order to create new forms that would captivate a moviegoer's 'dormant' consciousness and foster an active engagement with the film. For Vertov, this entailed a commitment to revealing the expressive mechanisms at work in the process of making a film within the filmic product itself. The aim was to direct the attention of the viewer to the non-narrative formal structures of the work rather than to the content. Vertov used a gamut of special techniques to achieve these aims – lighting, montage, distorted camera angles, fast or slow motion, freeze frame and flicker effects among them – in an attempt to force the viewer to acknowledge and recognise films as reconstructed realities rather than a mirror or reflection of pre-existent events. By shooting 'life-unawares' and subsequently restructuring the footage through montage, Vertov believed that the camera operator could use the camera as an omnipotent eye that would, through the process of montage, reveal processes and structures invisible to the human naked eye. Vertov and his collaborators, the *kinoks*, sought both to preserve the sense in which actuality filmmaking captures 'life as it is' and to express a different vision of that reality, a vision constructed by the use of montage. The 'Film-Truth' principle respects the authenticity of individual shots; while the 'Film-Eye' method recreates events cinematically through the editing process. An objective recording of events (Film Truth) is merged with the subjective interpretation of the filmmaker (the Film Eye) through the use of montage.[1]

A significant influence on Vertov's ideas was the Constructivist critic Aleksei Gan who founded the first Soviet film journal *Kinofot* in 1922, using it as a platform from which to expound his views of cinema as a 'factual' art. Gan claimed that cinema had been exploited in bourgeois society for recording theatrical events – the photoplay. In the new socialist society it should be used as 'a creative vehicle for witnessing everyday life, a conscious extension of the proletarian state' (Gan, in Petric 1987: 15). In post-revolutionary Russia, to achieve the type of cinema that contributed to the ideological struggle, it was necessary to develop new theoretical concepts based on an aesthetic attitude totally different from that governing the narratively bound bourgeois film. Gan denounced fiction, narrative, illusion and all forms of 'fabricated art', because they sought to evade reality rather than confront it. Traditional art was tainted with escapism which 'through film mesmerism' paralysed the conscious mental activity of its consumers (Petric 1987: 18). Although the relationship between Vertov and Gan was later fraught with disagreements regarding the function of ideology in art, they were united in their resistance to the 'threat' of narrative cinema, which they perceived as masquerading in the form of newsreels, particularly in the work of Sergei Eisenstein.[2]

Eisenstein began his filmmaking career after a period working with Vsevolod Meyerhold, the acknowledged supremo of Soviet Left theatre. By 1923 he accepted, along with his other avant-garde associates, that experimental art had to be justified in forms that had recognisable content and would serve revolutionary aims. In the winter of 1922–23 he briefly attended Lev Kuleshov's State Film School workshop, assisted Esfir Shub in editing a German film for Soviet distribution and began work on his first feature-length film *Strike*. *Strike* bears the hallmark of Eisenstein's background in the Proletkult theatre, combining exaggerated performances of comically grotesque capitalist villains with a more realistic portrayal of the effects of a strike on the daily lives of factory workers. Shot

between June and December 1924, *Strike* established Eisenstein as a
young director of some significance. He accompanied the release of
the film with a polemical article 'The Problem of a Materialist
Approach to Form'.

Eisenstein's most elaborate theoretical disagreement with Vertov
appears in this essay. It stems from the divergent definitions of 'ontological authenticity' held by the two filmmakers; that is, the extent
to which a viewer accepts an event presented on the screen as actually taking place in the real world. Eisenstein did not believe that the
camera – a mere tool or instrument – was capable of penetrating
reality or revealing a hidden reality behind everyday events as other
Constructivists claimed. Such revelations, in Eisenstein's estimation,
depended upon the filmmaker finding the best expressive means and
stylised devices both before and after shooting that would jar the
viewer's consciousness. Vertov, in contrast, opposed any stylistic
interventions, trusting the camera to reveal those aspects of the
filmed event that under normal circumstances cannot be perceived.
The candid recording of 'life-facts' – everyday reality caught
unaware – was the basis of the Film-Truth principle. Eisenstein considered this an artistically useless, purely mechanical device that created a static shooting method lacking in metaphorical implication:
he claimed that Vertov 'selected only those facts from the outside
world which impressed the filmmaker', and not those that could
'plough up the viewer's psyche' ('Toward the Question of a Materialist Approach to Form' in Petric 1987: 52). Eisenstein sought to
'infect' the spectator with feeling, aiming to create spectacles that
generate emotional or psychological influence through the manipulation of physical response: hence his insistence on the need to shock
the audience. Spectacle can stimulate the viewer even if it does not
resemble the real world. Images achieve perceptual and emotional
power through juxtaposition, as the Kuleshov experiments had
demonstrated. Eisenstein responded to Vertov by proclaiming the
principle of relativity: that a filmmaker is free to choose any signs or
symbols he pleases in order to make his message work. 'Whereas
today the strongest audience response is provoked by symbols and
comparisons with the machine – we shoot the 'heartbeats' in the battleship's engine room – tomorrow we might exchange them for false
noses and theatrical make-up' (Eisenstein 1925). For Eisenstein and
others drawing on Marxist ideas, displacement of the real world is
carried out in the name of an idealist conception of realism based on

essences rather than appearances. The principal point of controversy between Eisenstein and the more dedicated Constructivists,
especially Vertov, was that for a Constructivist, form determines the
message. Vertov, a purist in his choice of formal vocabulary,
reproached Eisenstein for betraying the cause of revolutionary art by
using actors, traditional narrative components and symbols to depict
real events.

David Bordwell claims that Eisenstein's silent films can be usefully
understood as part of a broader tendency toward 'heroic realism' in
1920s Soviet art (Bordwell 1993: 40–3). Before socialist realism
became the official Soviet style, Eisenstein explored a range of aesthetic options taken from a diverse range of traditions. These innovations are exemplified in 'plotless' cinema, a new form of narrative
film which abandons the notion of events caused by the individual
motivations of characters in favour of a narrative where events are
driven by collective action, by the 'mass protagonist' exemplified in
the use of typage. The concept of 'typage', which casts non-professional actors according to their physiognomy, facial expression and
physical stature, is a central aspect of Eisenstein's theory in the
1920s. Typage is the representation of character through external
traits of class or role. Although not specific to Eisenstein, he
exploited typage as a non-psychological means of depicting character and is often credited with inventing the technique. In *Battleship
Potemkin* (1925) and *October* (1928), both films that reconstruct
heroic revolutionary moments, Eisenstein uses typage to distinguish
the oppressors from the proletariat. Vertov disagreed with the inclusion of any artificial elements in documentary films and, conversely,
any quasi-authentic elements in fictional films. The use of non-professional actors in staged films was incompatible with the notion of
'life-fact' because such a practice 'impedes the evolution of the documentary film ... newsreels have their own path of development, the
staged films should not follow the same path, the inclusion of newsreel technique into the organism of staged cinema is simply unnatural' (Vertov 'In Defence of Newsreels', quoted in Petric 1987: 53).
When Eisenstein chose an ordinary worker to play the part of Lenin
in *October* the *LEF* critics supported Vertov's position, claiming that
Eisenstein was being 'totally insensitive to the historical truth' and
using a 'most shameful method' to depict historical fact (Brik, in
Petric 1987: 54). The poet Mayakovosky attacked Eisenstein for
dramatising the revolution 'in a disgusting manner', pointing out

that the workers' revolutionary newsreels produced by the *kinoks* were a correct approach to the representation of history (Mayakovsky, in Petric 1987: 54). Eisenstein was judged to be encroaching upon inappropriate territory; the point at issue was not that he had created a fictional account of historical events but that he had used documentary filmmaking techniques to authenticate his interpretation. The blurring of boundaries that incensed Eisenstein's compatriots is illustrated by the film's reception in the West, where it was interpreted as a documentary of the 1917 Revolution.

The mid-1920s were a fervent period of growth in Soviet film theory, led by montage filmmakers interested in developing a scientific understanding of cinema. Although riven by internal debate and disagreement, the montage directors (notably Eisenstein, Vertov, Kuleshov and Pudovkin) developed an international reputation. Their films, distributed on the international market, aided the recovery of the ailing film industry. Ironically, their success was increasingly criticised at home; official policy accused filmmakers of making films for the sophisticated tastes of foreigners rather than the uneducated indigenous population. In 1928, with the instigation of the first five-year plan, the cinema was fully centralised in order to tailor the production process to meet the needs of addressing workers and peasants. Experimentation was interpreted as a form of elitism, with the result that attacks on montage filmmakers intensified. In 1929 Eisenstein left the Soviet Union for Mexico, only to return in 1932 to a climate of increasing hostility. Vertov retreated to a provincial outpost to make his most experimental montage film, *Man with a Movie Camera* (1929). In 1934, the doctrine of socialist realism was imposed on all artists and writers, requiring them to follow Communist Party dictates. The model of artistic practice advocated by the party was based on the European realist novel of the nineteenth century: artworks were required to be free from all formal experimentation and stylistic elements that would make them difficult to understand. This resurrection of traditionalist methods forced montage filmmakers, along with modernist artists in every medium, to adopt more accessible styles. The official line promoted socialist realism: an idealised, optimistic image of Soviet society. Positive images of heroes based on worker/peasant stereotypes became the order of the day (Thompson and Bordwell 1994: 294–5).

In their preface to *Eisenstein Rediscovered*, Christie and Taylor

state that the debates that raged in the early 1920s about the relative
merits of documentary as opposed to fiction film, or of the proper
role of cinema in the forging of post-revolutionary Soviet culture
and the shaping of new Soviet man, have their echoes in contemporary discussions about the role of cinema in society. Films continue
to have a role to play in effecting the cultural and psychological revolution in human consciousness necessitated by the economic and
political transformation of the former Soviet Union into modern
democratic societies and states governed by the rule of law. In Western democratic societies, debates about the representation of historical events continue to be fuelled by similar concerns *vis-à-vis* the
relative merit of documentary or fiction films to represent historical
events, while debates about how to represent marginalised subjec-
tivities and unpopular identities have oscillated between the respective merits of foregrounding form or prioritising content. The legacy
of the Soviet modernist filmmakers and their theoretical agendas
continues to haunt contemporary film theory and practice today,
albeit often hidden in the transmuted voices of cine-psychoanalysis
and postmodernism.

'Realism and tinsel': British cinema

One way of interpreting the history of British cinema is to examine
how both filmmakers and the critical machine have aimed to differentiate the British product from its Hollywood counterpart. At certain historical moments, realist aesthetics have been heavily
implicated in this process of differentiation. Realism in this context is
used to project an aesthetics of 'Britishness' through the use of strategies which present the experiences and sensibilities of British characters in settings and situations which are recognisably familiar to both
the native and international audience. Two historical moments stand
out as significant in this respect: war-time cinema and the 'New
Wave' films of the late 1950s/early 1960s. The prominence of a
comparatively small number of films that form the corpus of both
moments is due to the influence that they have had on the subsequent
development of British film culture, undoubtedly the result of the
intense intellectual engagement they engendered at the time and
subsequently. Although there are significant differences between the
two moments, the overall realist impetus shares some broad general
characteristics. Both periods are distinguished by critical intellectual

disdain for the vast bulk of popular film production, whether British or American, which was either disregarded as a mass cultural form not worthy of serious critical attention or denigrated and accused of undermining traditional cultural values. Within this context, the realist critics aimed to promote a national film culture which would receive international recognition and acclaim for its distinctively British aesthetics. This can be understood as an attempt to encapsulate British sensibilities, British values and the British way of life. In social and political terms, realism was constructed as an aesthetics of responsibility with a mission to incorporate its citizen subjects within the public sphere by addressing the social issues of the time. Morally, such a cinema had to demonstrate the sincerity of its objectives through forms of signification that would be seen as an authentic and truthful account of how things actually were. This entailed creating representations that audiences would recognise as truthful accounts of their experiences, which included, in war time, recognition of family separation and death, and, in the late 1950s and early 1960s, the everyday lives of the working class.

The first moment, war-time realism, forms a transitional point between the documentary movement of the 1930s, valorised at the time as Britain's unique contribution to the art of the film, and the subsequent development of a popular form of cinematic depiction that integrates aspects of documentary filmmaking practice with the narrative conventions of mainstream film in the interests of forging a 'national community'. The second moment – the British 'New Wave' – lays claim to a similar fusion of documentary and narrative film conventions, but to rather different ends. Whereas the war-time films use this fusion of strategies to emphasise a sense of national community and belonging, the New Wave films depict the aspirations of the (mainly northern) working class through aggressive individuals who feel alienated from the (relative) abundance and affluence of post-war society. New Wave films were influenced by Italian neorealism and the French New Wave and are discussed after the section on neorealism.

Projecting the real: British war-time cinema

Undoubtedly, it is the influence of realism on the British film in war-time which has given it its new and individual character and which has weaned it away from being an amateur and clumsy pastiche of its Hollywood counterpart. (Michael Balcon (1946), quoted in Higson 1995: 213)

The realist moment of British war-time cinema is characterised by the conjunction of two modes of filmmaking practice: the documentary film of the 1930s and the popular fiction film. The birth of a national popular cinema in Britain is attributed by many contemporary commentators and film historians to a relatively small number of war-time films that typically combine documentary strategies with the psychological realism of conventional narrative fiction. The integration of these two elements forged a new kind of film, one that inter-mixes what Higson has termed 'the public gaze of the documentary with the private gaze of individual narrative protagonists' (1995: 179). Amongst the wealth of critical commentary and re-assessment of the role of the numerous films produced by this method of filmmaking in British film culture, one film stands out as epitomising the form and the moment of which it is a product: *Millions Like Us* (F. Launder/S. Gilliat 1943). Although only moderately successful in box-office terms,[3] the extensive body of commentary accrued around this one text provides a useful background to the necessarily brief commentary given here.

The exigencies of war time created an awareness of the importance of film as a propaganda medium: films could combine the informational role of documentary in creating an informed citizenship with the engaging values of narrative fiction in providing light-hearted entertainment. These elements were viewed by government and socially-committed critics alike as an ideal vehicle for addressing the nation and projecting a sense of the British people as a national community united against the threat of Fascism. The Second World War saw an unprecedented level of state involvement in all aspects of film production through the aegis of the Ministry of Information Films Division (hereafter the MOI). In addition to sponsoring newsreels and documentaries, scripts for feature film development had to meet with government approval. The Films Division also sponsored a number of feature films. Although there was no absolute blueprint of what a film had to be about, the MOI encouraged scripts which emphasised a democratic way of life, depicting the British as a free people united by a common cause. Various combinations of information and fictionalisation were favoured by the Ministry, who believed in 'sugaring the pill' of propaganda to retain audience interest.

Millions Like Us, initially conceived as an MOI documentary project, was produced by a commercial production company,

Gainsborough Pictures, renowned for its popular historical films and 'escapist' melodramas, with the support and encouragement of the MOI. The film tells the story of a young woman from a lower middle-class background called up to support the war effort. She finds herself posted to an aircraft factory, becoming part of a female community undertaking traditionally masculine production work. She meets a young airman, falls in love and marries him, but he is killed on a mission. The film was described in a *Kine Weekly* review of the day as 'at one and the same time a rough sketch of working-class family life in war time, a gigantic newsreel summarising salient events on the home front since war began and a tender if ingenuous love story with an aero-engine factory employing women from all walks of life for its background' (September 1943, in Higson 1995: 220).

The film combines documentary techniques with a melodrama of war-time romance and loss, creating what Andrew Higson suggests is a key text in the formation of a relatively distinct British genre: the melodrama of everyday life (Higson 1995: 176–271). The form has its roots in 1930s story documentaries such as *Night Mail*. Corner points out that story documentaries are discernible from fiction films in a number of ways, the most obvious of which is the relation between the 'core' of the story and the wider project of documentation. The story documentary has an economy of depiction which continuously registers the nature of the circumstances surrounding the narrative through an excess of contextual details or a focus on particular procedures (Corner 1996: 35). In *Target for Tonight*, (Watt 1941) a popular war-time story, documentary, drama and documentary techniques are combined to produce a realistic account of an RAF attack on an enemy target. The film merges fidelity to the actual processes of planning and enactment of the mission with a fictional account of the crew who carry it out. The first section of the film depicts in considerable detail the process of planning the mission; narrative pace is sacrificed in favour of technical detail, foregrounding the use of photography, maps and radio. The second section shows a fighter plane 'F for Freddie' hit by anti-aircraft gunfire while bombing a German fuel depot, injuring a crew member and disabling the aircraft. The strategies used here depend heavily on expressionistic techniques and associative montage sequences: the film cuts between long shots of planes in the sky, close-ups of the crew members in the aircraft cockpit and silhouettes of shadowy figures on the ground briefly illuminated by bursts of gunfire. The scenario is performed by RAF personnel playing 'themselves'. Characterisation is sacrificed in favour of depicting official procedures, but none the less the film conveys one of the primary themes of wartime cinema, a group of people from diverse class backgrounds and geographical regions who overcome individual differences in the interests of working together for a common cause.

By way of contrast, *Millions Like Us* foregrounds Celia's story against a contextual background of mobilising and defending the home front communicated through a series of documentary montage sequences. The opening of the film, with its authoritative voice-over and pre-war seaside montage sequence, resembles a contemporary newsreel. Later, actuality footage focuses on war-time events and incidents, including the blackout, evacuating children from the cities to the country, soldiers on the move, air raids and the removal of signposts and the mining of the beaches. All these details emphasise measures that need to be taken to defend the home front. A later documentary sequence depicts daily work at an aircraft factory, from the arrival of the (primarily female) workforce at the factory gates through an account of the production process – including smelting the raw iron ore and the casting and assemblage of parts – to the final take-off of the finished fighter plane. The montage sequences are clearly separate from the diegetic fictional flow of the film, remaining outside its motivationally driven systems of narrative logic. Unattached to the film's narrational schemata, unsutured into its system of looking relations, these sequences project a neutral, observational gaze at events, characteristic of public information films of the period. In this context, the sequences function as reportage rather than representation, mediating events in a form familiar to the war-time cinema audience from their experiences of watching cinema newsreels and documentaries.

Having set the stage for the public significance of the private drama enfolding within the narrative space of the film, the montage sequences become less frequent, replaced by an intermittent focus on particular procedures and processes that again appear excessive within the film's internal economy of narrative motivations. When Celia (Patricia Roc) is called up for war duty and attends for interview at the Ministry of Labour office, as she gazes at a recruitment poster for women in the armed forces she imagines herself in a number of heroic female roles. These daydreams are represented by

romantic conceptions of femininity that were popular in the Hollywood styled fictions of the day. A slow track in to Celia's face
accompanied by swelling romantic music dissolves into a montage
of images. Celia is seen in an RAF uniform helping a pilot into his
cockpit, as an ATS soldier driving a car and lighting a cigarette for
her superior officer, as a land army worker who attracts the attention of a country gentleman and as a nurse engaged to marry her
patient. These romantic fantasies are sharply interrupted by the
stark reality of war-time work for women as the voice of the ministry recruiting officer orders her to report for duty in a munitions
factory. In the ensuing interview, essential government information
is included in the dialogue: 'Mr Bevan needs another million
women ... You can help your country just as much in an overall as
you can in a uniform these days.' Communicating information that
is excessive to the economy of narrative causality is often regarded
as a hallmark of the realist film (Higson 1995: 227); the overall
effect can be didactic. In *Millions Like Us* this excess is apparent at
various times in the film, particularly in its depictions of routine factory work and the detailed exposition of the response to certain procedural events such as air raids.

Higson points out that the narrative structure of the film differs
significantly from the standard Hollywood film of the day; it has a
number of mini-dramas constructed around other characters which
never fully develop into parallel narrative trajectories, but constantly
intersperse Celia's story with small details about other characters'
lives (1995: 226). Celia's sister Phyllis, her friend and co-worker
Gwen and the upper class Jennifer appear in episodic interludes,
their presence unmotivated by the causal logic of narration. These
intermittent snapshots create a sense of Celia living as part of a wider
community, extending the diegetic space of the fiction and adding to
the effect of the real. Working against the generic conventions of the
romantic melodrama, the film ends not in the happy-ever-after of the
heterosexual couple, but in the supportive community of women
workers. The final sequence shows the newly widowed Celia reinte-
grated into the group, singing along with the others. The family,
destabilised by war-time conditions, is replaced by a young female
community wherein lies hope and promise for the future. Caroline
Lejeune, the astute but somewhat acerbic *Observer* film critic commented, 'You should applaud this honest, quietly-observant British
film ... It's real' (3 October 1943, in Higson 1995: 221).

Numerous war-time films similarly combine attention to realistic details of mise-en-scène, character motivation and dialogue with stories of everyday life lived within the confines of the war-time environment. *Went the Day Well?* (Cavalcanti 1942), the only war-time film to depict an imaginary German invasion of Britain, combines a standard narrative of detection with an ensemble cast who achieve heroic status by virtue of their spirited defence of their village in the face of enemy attack. Directed by documentary film-maker Alberto Cavalcanti, *Went the Day Well?* uses a combination of continuity shooting and editing, documentary observation and modernist montage to depict a contrast between a romanticised pastoral image of English country life and the sudden violence and death that disrupt it. A cast of eccentric English character types, many of whom bear more than a passing resemblance to the characters found in Agatha Christie's country house detective novels and the later Ealing comedies, discover that their village is occupied by German paratroopers posing as a British squadron. Once detected, the Germans become aggressive and violent. Returning by bicycle from a tour of duty, the Home Guard are mown down by enemy gunfire in a single medium long-shot. No point-of-view shots are proffered; no emotion or response depicted on behalf of any of the characters. This detached mode of filming stands in sharp contrast to the depiction of violent acts by the villagers. The village post-mistress, an elderly woman, kills an unsuspecting German soldier billeted in her house with an axe, an act that seems all the more extreme because of the manner of its depiction within the overall context of the film's visual style. A rapidly-edited montage sequence of angled, distorted shots disturbs the rhythm and tenor of the film, emphasising the unexpected passion lurking beneath the surface image of romanticised bovine complacency.

In a pamphlet brought out in 1945, 'Film and International Relations', Sidney Bernstein, cinema owner and MOI films advisor (later founder of Granada Television), pointed out that audiences were attracted to violence and passion, to the exceptional rather than the everyday, and that the realist path might be difficult to follow once the war was over (Murphy 1989: 96). His view was prophetic; in spite of the passion of the critics for films that aimed, in their view, to realistically depict changes in post-war society through a combination of melodramatic and documentary strategies, the audience longed for Hollywood styled escapist fantasies, stories of passion and adventure, to relieve the gloom of war time and immediate post-war life.[4] Only Michael Balcon at Ealing studios remained dedicated to producing films that represented the 'tenor and texture of national life' in the comedies and social problem films that formed the bulk of Ealing's output until its final demise in the early 1950s.

The neorealist moment

Like most realist movements in the arts, neorealism was an attempt to get closer to reality by refusing old and outmoded conventions which inevitably falsify our picture of it. (Armes 1986: 22)

Neorealism is regarded by film historians and scholars as one of the most significant filmmaking legacies to emerge from the debris of the Second World War, at the core of developments in cinematic modernism, influencing practitioners as far apart as Spain, Japan, France, Poland, India, Greece, Latin America, Britain and the USA (Liehm 1984: 130). The *Encyclopaedia of European Cinema* defines neorealism as a generic term used to describe a body of films made in Italy in the years immediately following the liberation (1943–45). The central characteristics consist of a method of filmmaking practice (location shooting and the use of non-professional actors), the attitude of the filmmakers (who aim to get close to their subject), their choice of subject matter (the lives of ordinary people), and the ideological/political slant of the films (broadly left wing/liberal humanist). Inevitably, like all attempts to define and categorise a body of films, the above summary reveals the features that are now perceived to constitute the corpus, but conceals the historical matrix that gave birth to its conception.

Sorlin traces the use of the term 'neorealism' to a group of philosophers in the 1900s who maintained that objective facts exist independent of human thoughts. The term resurfaces again in the late 1920s, where it was used in literary criticism. By the mid-1940s, neorealism was a vacant signifier available for adoption; foreign critics start using it as a way of defining the blend of traditional Italian melodrama and new style acting and filming that was first perceived in *Open City* (*Roma, città aperta*, Rossellini 1945). There was no general agreement about what the term defined; some claimed it as a description of the moral and physical destruction of people and environment brought about by war; others that it provided a metaphysical image of human despair. Like other stylistic definitions (*film noir* is the most obvious case in point), neorealism is a flexible container for a range of non-classical variations found in many Italian films of the day; domestic dramas, adventure films, even comedies, portray a range of neorealist qualities. Thompson and Bordwell (1994) link neorealism to a realist impulse developing in Italian literature and film during the waning years of the Fascist regime, but arguably a similar impulse can be found in many pre-war European countries (Britain and France, for example). Nor can the filmmakers be identified as constituting an artistic or political movement in the conventional sense; there was no manifesto of agreed aims and principles, no agreed method of filmmaking practice. Rather, there was what Sorlin describes as an array of negative convictions opposed to the formulaic depictions of commercial cinema and the belief that films should be a source of knowledge and reality – ideas nursed by Italian filmmakers since the silent days. Unity, such as it was, came from a moral commitment to the creation of a new Italy, rather than an explicit programme of aesthetic or political aims. Once the initial optimism of the post-war period started to wane, this fragile alignment fractured into the factional interests that characterise Italian society in the late 1940s (Sorlin 1996: 86–91).

Nonetheless, by the early 1950s, neorealism came to occupy a central place in discussions about the position of the cinema in Italian social and economic life. The word had accrued political connotations. Championed by the Left and numerous critics writing in influential film magazines and journals, it was despised by the Catholic church and the ruling Christian Democrat party. But it was not only artists, intellectuals and the political Left who supported neorealism. In popular weekly magazines, the term became synonymous with Italy's international prestige and artistic reputation. Sorlin's examination of three best-selling weekly magazines of the period reveals the influence of neorealism on the popular press. The films' themes were used to stimulate debate on contemporary social, economic and moral issues, such as unemployment, corrupt business practices and sexual behaviour. Even the illustrations emulated neorealist style: black and white photographs copied the compositions, character arrangements, framing and lighting design (Sorlin 1996: 106). Although many of the films fared poorly at the home box office, their success on the international festival circuit was a source of popular nationalist pride. The French critic André Bazin played a

major role in bringing neorealist films to the attention of an international public, ensuring their presence at festivals and circulating
numerous articles and reviews. Bazin sought to liberate French
cinema from the dictates of commercial producers in the interests of
establishing a film culture in harmony with the political aspirations
of the post-war generation. In neorealism he perceived a cinema
totally in sympathy with these aims; it became a cornerstone in the
theories of cinematic realism for which he is so well known today.

Accounts vary as to the number of films that actually constitute
the neorealist canon, but most critics agree that the core films were
produced during the 'Italian Spring' of 1945–48.[5] Today, a handful
of films are taken as representative: *Open City* (Rossellini 1945);
Paisan (Rossellini 1946); *Shoeshine* (Vittorio De Sica 1946); *La terra
trema* (Visconti 1948); *Bicycle Thieves* (De Sica 1948); *Bitter Rice*
(Guiseppe De Santis 1948); *Umberto D* (De Sica 1951). In 1948 the
short-lived period of political optimism, the 'Italian Spring', ended.
Liberal and left wing parties were defeated at the polls; the new right
wing government instituted a law to protect the national industry
from American competition, at the same time reintroducing strict
censorship through state control of all aspects of the film industry.
Neorealism had put Italian cinema on the international map, opening up new markets for Italian films abroad: yet it was precisely these
films that the new government accused of tarnishing Italy's international reputation. The committed social and political slant of the
neorealist films revealed the poverty, unemployment and corruption
of everyday life and its effects on ordinary people. Such films were
no longer considered suitable ambassadors for a government anx-
ious to demonstrate the effectiveness of its modernisation policies
and the country's growing economic strength.

In retrospect, as with most films deemed realist in their day, it is
difficult to fully appreciate the significance and impact these films
had at the time. An examination of any of the key films now considered central to the corpus shows a continuing adherence to many
classical norms. Whether we are examining *Open City*, often considered as the first neorealist film, or *Bicycle Thieves*, now considered a paradigm of neorealist technique (see Chapter 1), smooth
camerawork privileges character as the primary point of camera
focus and there is a careful regard for balanced composition in the
frame. Editing shows slight variations from classical norms, particularly in character interaction, favouring two-shot compositions and

point-of-view shots rather than the more usual eyeline match combinations used in classical films: in *Open City*, close-ups are often cut in without regard for character viewpoint. Bazin noticed that neorealist films tend to dwell on the microactions of daily life, drawing attention to the minutae of daily detail that conventional techniques treat as redundant to the forwarding of narrative action. The films have a looser, more episodic plot structure that rejects the rigid causality of the classical film. Longer takes create more real-time equivalence, creating an observational space that is somewhat analogous to the public gaze outlined by Higson in his account of British war-time films (above) but with a greater emphasis on the relationship between character and setting.

The use of music in these films is particularly interesting, often signalling a change of plot direction as well as a change of mood. Near the beginning of *Open City*, a military march heralds the arrival of the soldiers before we see them: an operatic chase theme, reminiscent of the accompaniment to silent comedies, begins before Manfredi starts to run from his pursuers. Underscoring as a precursor of plot action is used selectively throughout the film to underline threat or danger to the indigenous community, rather than to emphasise character emotion as in mainstream films. Significance is given to the magnitude of external events and disruptions rather than to individual response to personal tragedies or moments of romantic revelation. Such details, while as self-consciously composed as the norms of pre war Italian genre films, enhance a sense of difference in the treatment of subject matter. By not conforming to either the fictional or newsreel and documentary norms of the day, a hybrid form was created that gave stature to ordinary subjects. These innovations in film form were, and continue to be, a source of interest for film historians who find in neorealism's innovative techniques not only the mediation of a particular world view and political attitude, but a unity between form and content, expression and theme, that invites ambiguity, speculation and reflection.

Sorlin claims it is the quality of these films that explains their influence. Well made, with good scripts, elaborate dialogue, excellent shooting and editing techniques, the plots develop against backgrounds which, instead of being merely evocative settings for action, play an important role in disclosing the meaning of the stories. Many were located in rural environments, evoking the problems of fishermen, farm-workers or co-op members. They have no

counterpart in other European countries, offering an exotic ethnographic view of Italian rural life, whereas the urban films deal with
comparable problems of other major cities such as unemployment,
black market racketeering and prostitution but, because of their
location shooting, offer a unique vision of Italian cities. Among the
films that now define the corpus, few conform to the rigorous definition set out above; most use professional actors (although rarely
stars), many interiors were studio rather than location shot, and the
banal events of everyday life feature in many of the standard melodramas of the day. The documentary impulse was in part inherited
from Fascism, in part enforced by post-war necessity. The Fascist
dictatorship had taken Soviet cinema as their model for a national
film industry; the works of Eisenstein and Dziga Vertov were familiar to the neorealists, who tended to follow Vertov's practice of
aiming to 'catch life unawares' (Liehm 1984: 104). Pre-war Italian
films were known throughout Europe for their magnificent studio
settings and opulent visual style, but war damage to the principal
studios drove filmmakers onto the streets in search of suitable
shooting locations. Creating realistic sound was less of a problem in
Italy, where dubbing foreign movies had created expertise in post-
synchronisation. Footage shot on location was sound dubbed
during the post-production process, often by professional actors;
naturalistic regional dialects were usually sacrificed to make the
films intelligible to a broader audience.

For Sorlin, critical acclaim is a sociological phenomenon rooted in
the cultural investments and motivations of a small group with high
levels of 'cultural capital'; without this enthusiastic approval, the relatively small number of neorealist films would have disappeared
unnoticed amidst the commercial hurly-burly that characterised
domestic production in the post-war years. Foremost amongst these
motivations are the nationalistic desires of intellectuals, politicians,
Roman Catholics and committed filmmakers to make their mark on
the world stage, to produce films that would draw attention to the
emerging identity of the newly liberated Italian state. As long as the
'popular front' remained united, it was possible to locate a new sensibility of progress and renewal in certain forms of filmic depiction.
Once it collapsed, the films became a signifier of Italy's artistic excel-
lence and intellectual regeneration.

Neorealism's abiding legacy combines unique content with re-
invigoration of form defined by aesthetic difference from the generic

traditions of Italian commercial production, but driven by nationalist desires for a cinema independent of American control and domination. A similar rejection of both national tradition and American
infiltration of domestic exhibition was common throughout post-
war Europe, in part inspired by the Italian example. Neorealism's
influence on cinematography and film style shaped what has become
known, rather reductively, as European art cinema. This artisanal
mode of production, politically and philosophically committed to
freedom of political expression and personal vision, stood in con-
tradistinction to the globalising tendencies of the Hollywood dream
factory and the nationalised propagandist cinemas of communist
and Fascist states. Inspired by the neorealist example, the art cinema
served as a model of personally committed political filmmaking
practice as well as an aesthetic inspiration to the developing national
cinemas of post-war Europe.

The British 'New Wave'

The 'New Wave' is the name given to a group of British films produced between 1959 and 1963. The roots of the social realist aesthetics of these 'kitchen sink' dramas are found in the British
documentary movement of the 1930s (particularly the poetic realism of Humphrey Jennings), the Free Cinema movement of the early
1950s and a new class consciousness in British theatre and literature
centred on the experiences of aggressive and rebellious working-
class males – the so-called 'angry young men' epitomised in successful plays such as John Osborne's *Look Back in Anger* and novels such
as Alan Sillitoe's *Saturday Night and Sunday Morning*. The Free
Cinema Movement shares some characteristics with similar cinema
movements in post-war Europe. Broadly, these can be summarised
as a commitment to a socially aware form of filmmaking practice
operating from an independent artisanal production base which
allows maximum freedom to work on self-selected film projects outside the confines of commercial constraint. Neorealism had a major
impact on the New Wave style of the films, although, as John
Caughie has commented, the late arrival of European influence in
British cinema can be read as a backwash of a wave that had already
happened elsewhere (Caughie, in Vincendeau 1995: 61).

As in other realist moments, the New Wave needs to be seen in the
context of dominant trends in mainstream cinema at the time.

British cinema was undergoing something of a transformation: the cinema audience was falling and television ownership growing rapidly.[6] The American majors, subject to falling box-office receipts on their own domestic market, were re-organising their financial agreements with British producers and distributors, intent on retaining their overall control of the British exhibition circuit. The Hollywood film, forced to compete with television for an audience it had taken for granted, became more visually spectacular. Technological change increased the use of colour and widescreen formats such as CinemaScope and experimentation with 3-D, transforming the viewing experience. Sexual depiction on the screen became far more explicit following changes in censorship, and in Britain, the introduction of the 'X' certificate.

Against this background of technological change and heightened commercial competition the feature films produced by the New Wave filmmakers were heralded as a renaissance of artistic quality and social commitment. Emanating in part from the documentary ethos of the Free Cinema movement, but relying for their commercial success on adapting successful novels and plays, it is arguable that the films were less dependent on the documentary roots of the filmmakers than cinema's ability to represent the social realist content of novels and plays. The first production, an adaptation of the best-selling novel *Room at the Top* (Clayton 1959) that tells the story of an ambitious working-class man who marries the daughter of a rich industrialist, became an international success, winning two academy awards at the 1959 Oscars. This was swiftly followed by a filmed version of *Look Back in Anger* (1959) following a successful run of the play on the West End stage. Instigating a style that is now short-handed as 'kitchen sink' realism, most of the films feature working-class characters in dramas of everyday life set against the drab industrial landscapes of post-war northern Britain. The films focus on the personal experiences of primarily young male characters and their sexual relationships with women. The realism attributed to these films at the time and subsequently is based on their (for the time) explicit depiction of sexual relationships, a vernacular use of language and breaking of conventional shooting techniques. This combination of new content for commercial cinema, and a new form of depiction based on location shooting, earned the films a radical reputation. By introducing new characters and subject matter for popular cinema, the films arguably broke the stranglehold of a conventional and repressive style that had dominated the 'social problem' films of the 1950s.

Raymond Williams suggests that realism has a political dimension that overrides technique: the bringing of hitherto neglected groups onto the screen, the speaking of previously unheard truths and unexpressed attitudes (Williams 1977b). The character of Arthur Seaton in *Saturday Night and Sunday Morning* (Reisz 1960) stands out as a major breakthrough in terms of such a depiction. Played by newcomer Albert Finney, the determined aggressiveness of Arthur is brought home in the opening sequence of the film: he is shown, in medium close-up, at work on a factory lathe, repeating the same task over and over again while his voice-over intones, 'Don't let the bastards grind you down. That's one thing you learn. What I'm out for is a good time. All the rest is propaganda.' The popular appeal of this character undoubtedly played a major role in the film's success at the box office. The producer, Harry Saltzman, claimed that young people and working people totally identified with the character (Walker 1974: 85). Arthur's rebellious tone extended to his aggressive behaviour and forthright use of language. Scenes of drunkenness and a frank depiction of his adulterous relationship with a married woman gained the film an 'X' certificate. Arguably, the social realism of the film rests upon the hitherto unexpressed subjectivity of a character situated within an authentic setting – the Raleigh bicycle factory in Nottingham. New technology adapted from television news-gathering equipment allowed greater freedom of camera movement on location, creating a more fluid shooting style. The use of black and white filmstock associated the film with the liveness and immediacy of television documentary and reportage, providing a stark contrast to the colourful spectacle of mainstream cinema (see Figure 1).

Critical re-evaluation of the New Wave films has tended to emphasise the formal aspects of mise-en-scène and shooting style rather than other elements of realism such as acting style and characterisation, thus equating New Wave films with an excess of 'surface realism' and an over-abundance of descriptive detail of place which is somewhat at odds with plot development and character motivation. Following Higson (1984), Hill analyses this 'excess' of description primarily in terms of camerawork and shooting style, emphasising the extended use of establishing shots. For example, the opening of *Saturday Night and Sunday Morning* depicts a factory floor with a

1 Arthur (Albert Finney), Bert (Norman Rossington) and Doreen (Shirley Anne Field): domestic interior in *Saturday Night and Sunday Morning* (Reisz, GB 1960).

slow track into a medium close-up of the principal protagonist, Arthur Seaton. Similarly, *A Kind of Loving* (Schlesinger 1962) begins with shots of cobbled streets, terraced houses and a church wedding which slowly becomes the focus of character depiction and narrative action. The films are punctuated with these extended establishing shots, many initially empty of both characters and events. This technique accentuates a sense of place, which, according to Hill, creates a visual spectacle of the squalor and poverty of the working-class urban environment. Landscape and setting are afforded an integrity outside the demands of narrative causality; although they provide a sense of place, the aestheticism of the image suggests that they do not adequately address the effects of environment on character as in the work of avowed nineteenth-century naturalism or provide contextual background detail for the 'core' of the story. Rather, place is presented as an exotically realistic spectacle for consumption by those who do not have to inhabit it (Hill 1986: 135–6).

Lovell argues that the viewpoint of the films is that of the aspiring working-class male, the post-war grammar school boy who has left his roots and is now looking back, not in anger, but with regret and nostalgia for a way of life he has lost. This viewpoint is encapsulated in an enduring image found in many of the films, dubbed by Lovell 'that long shot of our town from the hill' (Lovell 1990: 369). The shot has its forerunner in *Millions Like Us*: the high-class factory worker Jennifer and her factory foreman boyfriend, from their position at the top of a hill with the town in the valley below, guardedly discuss the possibilities of sharing a life together in the post-war world if promises for a more equal society are fulfilled. In *A Kind of Loving* and *Saturday Night and Sunday Morning*, similar shot sequences are used, but now reverberating with connotations of personal freedom and entrapment rather than inequality and class difference. For Vic and Ingrid in *A Kind of Loving*, the hill is a place for sexual expression, free from the restraint of a stifling domestic situation. For Arthur, the new estates creeping out into the countryside epitomise a life style he has been trying to resist, a future of domestic entrapment tied to working in the factory that he loathes, but to which he seems destined (see Figure 2).

From *Saturday Night and Sunday Morning* to *Up the Junction* (1967) it was the films that documented 'low-life' environments in the most detail – where the excess of mise-en-scène is integral to the psychological development of characters – that proved popular at the box office. Less successful commercially were the films that strayed from this, in particular the films of Tony Richardson and Lindsay Anderson which inherited the 'poetic' realism of Free Cinema. The emphasis in films made by these latter directors is on the stylistic excess of creative montage: *A Taste of Honey* (1961) and *This Sporting Life* (1963) exemplify the techniques. Based on Shelagh Delaney's play, which was stage set in a 'comfortless flat in Manchester', *A Taste of Honey* depicts the relationships of an unmarried pregnant girl with her often absent mother and a young gay man who befriends and 'mothers' her. Lovell claims that the insertions of place in *A Taste of Honey*'s filmic narration represent a male viewer's perspective on a drama that was essentially concerned with domestic space and a young woman's life. For example, when Jo accompanies her mother and her new boyfriend on a trip to the seaside, the couple dance to the sounds of a popular tune. The shots of obvious pleasure on the faces of the couple are intercut with a close-up of the laughing face of a clown (used in an earlier documentary on Southend and Margate, *Oh Dreamland*) that seems to

2 The new estate: location shooting in *Saturday Night and Sunday Morning* (Reisz, GB 1960).

mock their enjoyment, critiquing the commercial culture that is the source of their delight. These inserted montage 'comments' from the filmmakers, while a source of critical acclaim, appear to have been less popular with audiences, and perhaps contributed to the film's relative lack of success at the box office.

Interestingly, the depictions of aspirant working-class characters in these films have no place in the working-class landscape described by New Left intellectuals of the time, such as Hoggart, writing about his own childhood in the 1930s, or in the sociologial studies and ethno-gaphnies which inscribe working-class life for women in terms of 'our mam' and the community. Single mothers, pregnant schoolgirls and abortions, which feature in several of these works, are a notable absence in these more documentary accounts.[7] There is something of an incongruity in Hill's and Higson's arguments, identified by Murphy in his comprehensive analysis of 1960s British cinema. In spite of the fact that realism is an acknowledged set of conventions, Marxist critics accuse New Wave realism of fetishising the character in the landscape and creating a 'surface realism' (often referred to as 'naturalism') at the expense of depicting 'real' working-class people and the 'real conditions of working-class life' (for such critics, 'socialist realism') as if there could be an unmediated referentiality of everyday life which is in some sense more truthful or more accurate than the one depicted.[8] Discussing the relationship between form and ideology in *Realism and the Cinema*, Christopher Williams points out that Theory, under its Marxist name of Knowledge, finds it difficult to cope with some of the visual aspects of cinema, claiming functions for them that seem far from proven (Williams 1980: 186). What is interesting in these debates is the extent to which critics are prepared to argue the inauthenticity of representations based on certain formalist criteria such as mise-en-scène and narrative structure, while largely ignoring other criteria of realist depiction and referentiality, such as the iconicity of the image. In particular, aspects of characterisation, dramatic performance and dialogue are ignored, yet the success of some of these films at the box office, as the producer of *Saturday Night and Sunday Morning* Harry Saltzman astutely noted at the time, depended upon young people identifying with the characters. The Marxist tradition of ideological critique inherited from Soviet and Brechtian theories views recognition and familiarity with characterisation and location as 'ideological effects' of the text; rarely are they accorded any positive values.

In spite of the rather tarnished image of 'kitchen sink' realism today as misogynist, drab, dramatically dull and visually unremarkable, the move out of the studio and on to the northern streets inaugurated a new era of filmmaking practice in Britain. Not only did the New Wave films break up the stale clichés of studio convention, creating an exciting intervention into the depiction of working-class characters at the time by placing them at the centre of the narrative, but they encouraged the vision of an independent, de-centred, regionally-based filmmaking practice rooted in local writers, actors and filmmakers. By bringing new talent into the film industry, the stranglehold of a relatively small London-based coterie slowly began to be challenged. In their determined efforts to make films differently, the New Wave filmmakers redefined some aspects of conventional filmmaking practice in Britain, opening up a space for films on controversial social topics. This legacy, kept alive in British television drama throughout the 1960s and 1970s, re-emerges in some of the films produced by Channel 4 in the 1980s and 1990s, a point we return to in Chapter 7.

Black urban cinema: a contemporary realist moment

*If the practice of black cinema is derived from that of Hollywood, then
it will serve to reproduce the unequal relations characteristic of blacks
in society.* (Yearwood 1982: 7)

The early 1990s saw a flourish of Hollywood films commissioned
from African-American filmmakers as the major studios recognised
the commercial potential of this rich tradition of independent filmmaking practice. Amongst the most well-known films of this type
are the spate of 'ghetto, guns and violence' movies exemplified by
Do the Right Thing (Spike Lee 1989), *New Jack City* (Mario Van
Peebles 1991) and *Boyz N the Hood* (Singleton 1991).[9] Many of
these films are dubbed 'cross-over' films because they mix the techniques garnered in independent practice with mainstream generic
values. Successful 'homeboy' films such as *Boyz N the Hood* share a
number of features with traditions of African-American cultural
production that use the city as the locus of identity and experience.
Drawing both on images of the city as a mythologised utopia, a place
to escape to that promises freedom and social mobility in early
twentieth-century literature, and later, dystopic visions, place
becomes mapped differently from the conventional depictions
found in mainstream film and television. Here, that difference is
traced through the strand of African-American independent filmmaking practice that informs contemporary realist practices, using
strategies that engage with the lived realities of ghetto life to depict
the psychological and social consequences on character of racism
and marginalisation.

African-American cinema in the early 1990s is characterised by
the number of films that take as their theme the violent culture of
the ghetto that is often prevalent in news media depictions of black
urban life. These films are frequently read for their social and political implications and 'granted a relation to "real life" that is quite
unusual amongst today's media-wise audiences and film critics'
(Mermin 1996: 3). Manthia Diawara, for example, argues that the
use of linear narrative time in recent urban films such as *Boyz N the
Hood* coincides with a 'coming of age' thematic, producing 'an
effect of realism by creating an overlap between the rite of passage
into manhood and the narrative time of the story' (Diawara 1993:
20). Diawara suggests that the new realism 'imitate[s] the existent
reality of urban life in America', because for young black men the

journey to manhood is 'a dangerous enterprise which leads to death both in reality and in film' (Diawara 1993: 23–4). Other critics and commentators suggest that the films can be read as 'authenticating documents' in the tradition of the slave narrative, their realism functioning as a marketing strategy to distinguish them from more conventional Hollywood genre products.[10] While these critics all agree on the 'realism' of this group of films, most place them within a tradition of independent African-American filmmaking practice that emphasises the content of the films rather than their formal aspects. Mark Reid, for example, suggests that critics and historians

> must analyse the independent film in terms of the filmmaker's efforts to create films that explore serious social issues and present balanced images of black women and men, and of the African-American community in general. In developing such a cultural, ideological, socioeconomic analysis of black film, critics and historians must describe how, by what means, and to what extent black independent filmmakers have chosen to be responsive to the needs of the black community. (Reid 1993: 135)

Reid implies that black filmmakers and critics have a responsibility to the black community to produce 'politically correct' images and readings of black life; but, as Kobena Mercer has pointed out, the problem with this approach is that it saddles black artists with the impossible task of carrying a 'burden of representation' for a community which it is complexly heterogeneous rather than homogeneous.[11] In contrast, Elizabeth Mermin is less concerned with the social responsibility of the filmmakers or how closely the black urban films approximate political and social realities than with how the films use expectations of cinematic realism and constitute a genre. Taking issue with the exclusion and marginalisation of these films within the film studies pantheon, Mermin argues that their play with conventional narrative, urban space and specific street locations allows the films to be read within the context of a history of realism in the cinema, a context that denies claims by contemporary scholars such as Jim Collins (1993) that the 'window on reality' model of cinema 'died with the classics of the thirties and forties' (Mermin 1996: 13). Although the 'idealist' theory of representation that validated Bazin's claims has collapsed, his fundamental concerns continue to inform the blurred boundaries between representation and reality on which the marketing and success of these films has depended.

Mermin's argument hinges on readings of two films: *Killer of Sheep* (Burnett 1977), which she claims is a foundational film within this cinematic tradition, and *Straight Out of Brooklyn* (Rich 1991), which is used as an exemplar of the ways in which 1990s urban films work from and transform strategies used by earlier independent films. Burnett emerges from the 1970s Los Angeles school of black filmmakers trained at UCLA who sought to reshape conventional cinematic language in order to produce a different view of black cultural experiences. The challenge for this generation of filmmakers, according to Ntongela Masilela, was to find a film form unique to their historical situation and cultural experience, a period charged with the political and cultural momentum of the Civil Rights Movement, the Women's Movement, the anti-war movement, and activities in support of the struggles of national liberation movements in Africa, Asia and Latin America (Masilela 1993: 107–17). Seeking to contest the falsification of African-American history by the Hollywood film industry and the flooding of the market with commercially produced black exploitation films, the LA school drew on the family dramas of Oscar Micheaux as their model. Oscar Micheaux established the Book and Film Company in 1918; as well as providing 'positive' images of successful life in the city, Micheaux's films took as their subject matter controversial issues such as lynchings, miscegenation, gangsters, religious charlatans and their relationship to family and community. Many of the films were concerned with migration from the rural south to the northern industrial cities, themes that lie at the core of the Harlem Renaissance.[12] Blaxploitation films, like those of Micheaux, use contemporary themes associated with urban impoverishment and crime as primary motivations for character action, presenting narratives structured around crime, drugs and prostitution. Centred on the activities of law-enforcing macho heroes, these films articulated a discourse of empowerment primarily aimed at the urban African-American audience. But unlike Micheaux's films, which were circulated in the 1920s through independent black-owned exhibition sites, blaxploitation was a studio product shaped by the conventions of the commercial genre text. This invariably meant that their black heroes were firmly linked with the forces of law and order, creating in films such as *Shaft* (1971) 'a lone, black Superspade – a man of flair and flamboyance who has fun at the expense of the (white) establishment'.[13] None the less, their sexually and politically empowered male protagonists offered an alternative to several decades of Hollywood film production which only featured black characters as stereotypical 'toms' 'coons' and 'mammies' or in minor roles as petty thieves, pimps, rapists and prostitutes.[14]

The search for an oppositional film form rooted in African-American experiences led the independent school of LA filmmakers to draw on the Micheaux family dramas of the 1920s and 30s, but to shift their milieu from the middle-class home to working-class environments in which black labour was engaged in struggles against white capital. The city remains a central trope in many of these films, but the emphasis shifts away from a generic emphasis on issues of criminality that characterises 'blaxploitation' towards analysing the inter-connections between economic hardship and spiritual poverty within the confines of urban family life. These concerns are exemplified in two key films of the period, *Mama* (Haile Gerima 1974) and *Killer of Sheep* (Charles Burnett 1977) which focus on attempts to maintain integrity and empowerment within the family amidst the poverty, crime and racism of the neighbourhood.

Masilela suggests that the poetic realism of Burnett's early films are heavily reminiscent not only of Italian neorealism but also of the British documentary film movement of the 1930s; Basil Wright, one of the leading figures of that movement was one of Burnett's teachers at UCLA in the late 1960s. *Killer of Sheep* uses a non-linear narrative style to paint a bleak portrait of the poverty that circumscribes black urban life and the problems and frustrations of individuals who cannot escape from their background or their environment. The protagonist, Stan, works in a slaughterhouse, a constant point of disruption that is juxtaposed with customary scenes of everyday family life. The use of an episodic narrative structure, unknown actors and unconventional camerawork – a hand-held unsteady camera, long takes, odd angles and partial shots, coupled with grainy black and white film stock – suggest a distancing characteristic of documentary realist strategies, with the shifting position of the camera creating an interrogative relationship between spectator and text. The camera frequently changes point of view within the same sequence, oscillating between a 'complicit' look (following, looking with the actors, seeing things from their point of view) and a 'surveillance' look (observing, looking at the actors, seeing things from a detached, omniscient point of view). This alternation between an 'insider' and 'outsider' point of view structures the distance between spectators, characters and their situation, raising questions of spectator alignment. A brief example taken from Mermin's longer analysis serves to illustrate the point: in a sequence near the beginning of *Killer of Sheep* the camera is placed on a passing train and films a group of boys running along the tracks throwing stones. Before the reverse shot reveals the train as the object of their frustration, their oppositional behaviour appears to be aimed solely at the camera. Similarly, the opening sequence of the film ends with a boy receiving a lecture on his bad behaviour from his father Stan that culminates in a slap; but the hand that slaps originates from behind the camera, creating ambiguity about who exactly motivates the slapping. There are no secure point-of-view alignments offered with characters, only juxtapositions and contrasts between the hierarchical relationships in the family and community cut against images of the slaughterhouse, where the film's only white man is shown cleaning the meat hooks (Mermin 1996: 8–9). The metaphorical implications are obvious to those who want to read them: the daily grind of poverty and urban violence originates from white social oppression, but this is never explicitly stated.

Nineties ghetto films are far less experimental both in their narrative structures and their visual strategies; less concerned with revealing the transparency of conventional cinematic codes, they centre on young urban males with aspirations and desires that prove to be illusionary because choice is destroyed by the ghetto environment. The emphasis in these films is on the confinement of the urban surroundings and the impossibility of escape. As in *Killer of Sheep*, white America remains an invisible abstraction; white figures appear as indexical representatives of authority and power often in the guise of the police or as 'ambassadors' of official bureaucracies. Two films will serve as brief examples of the realist strategies at work in these contemporary coming-of-age stories: *Menace II Society* (Allen and Albert Hughes 1991) and *Straight Out of Brooklyn* (Matty Rich 1991).

Menace II Society is reportedly an enraged response to the commercialised sentimentality of *Boyz N the Hood* (Taubin 1993: 17), one which claims authenticity through the use of an objective, invasive camera that opens the film as if intent on documenting the neighbourhood as an ethnographic exercise (Masood 1996: 8). This footage is cut against pixillated images of the Watts Rebellion in 1965 garnered from official news and documentary sources. A voice-over explains the changes in the neighbourhood following these events, later identified with the leading protagonist, Caine, who articulates (sometimes unreliably) his desire for escape and the psychological dynamics that shape his life. His brutal behaviour problematises conventional identification with his character or moral alignment with his situation, but at the same time the violent treatment from the Los Angeles Police Department (LAPD) to which Caine and his friends are consistently subjected is both a critique of white racism and a means of eliciting understanding, if not con-donation, of Caine's attitudes and behaviour.[15] Diawara claims that the constant reminder of surveillance permeating the urban envi-ronment performs a similar function to that of Foucault's panopti-can. The community is kept in its place through internalising its perceived status as a deviant and criminalised group beyond the boundaries of the hood (Diawara 1993: 22). The mise-en-scène of *Menace II Society* is furnished with street signs and traffic lights that map the invisible boundaries beyond which characters risk assault and possibly death. When he takes this risk and ventures outside the neighbourhood, Caine is shot, his dreams of escape fatally fore-closed. Unlike in *Boyz N the Hood,* where it is suggested that indi-vidual will can triumph over adverse social conditions providing there is strong paternalistic support, Caine is unable to achieve his ambitions or find a way to triumph over the constricting realities that shape his life. Massood claims that this negative, 'more realis-tic' scenario could not be portrayed if it had not been for the narra-tive and spatial mapping of the 'hood already popularised by *Boyz N the Hood*. Because the 'hood already exists as a given signifying system, it is possible to rework its images as a dialogue engaged with issues of representation, breaking down the homogeneity of the 'hood as a fixed point of reference in the popular imagination (Masood 1996: 11).

Straight Out of Brooklyn contributes an East Coast perspective to this dialogue. Written and directed by film school graduate Matty Rich, who claims the film depicts his own experiences of growing up in a Brooklyn housing project, the film centres on a high school stu-dent called Dennis and his dysfunctional family, dominated by the alcoholism of his wife-beating father, Ray. Dennis dreams of leaving Brooklyn, taking his family and his girlfriend Shirley with him. These dreams and aspirations are discussed in the film against the only backgrounds that offer relief from the confined interiors and tight spatial framings that dominate the film. Walking by the river with Shirley, the skyscrapers of Manhattan outlined against the sky, a symbol of American wealth, power and success, Dennis comments bitterly that it is an edifice based on the theft of their birthright. Getting out of Brooklyn becomes an obsession; on the rooftops, again with the skyscrapers of the city looming in the distance, he discusses committing a robbery with two friends (see Figure 3). In contrast, the confinement of everyday life is spatially palpable: the family's apartment is so small that the male and female teenage children share a bedroom, the living space crowded with just enough furniture for people to sit down and eat. There are no ornaments, no embellishments of any kind. Little is shown of the external environment: bare apartment blocks, the interiors of small businesses such as a hairdresser's, a restaurant and a corner shop, the father's local bar and the garage where he works are the principal locations, along with the doorways and stairwells of the apartment blocks. Brooklyn is cold, gloomy and claustrophobic, an image intensified by a preponderance of greys and blues and a lack of any bright colours or use of green in the mise-en-scène.

Violence is all-pervasive, both outside and inside the home, permeating and corrupting all aspects of community and family life. There is no escape, no place of safety that is free from its corrosive effects. The sense of claustrophobia and the grim inertia of poverty is emphasised by the father's endless drunken tirades; the ignominy of being black, hatred of whites, his own father's lies to him about future opportunity regularly punctuate the narrative as Ray beats his wife Francie's face to a bruised and bloody pulp. The white man has colonised his mind, taken away his power to think, to provide for his family, to be an American. Amid these unremittingly painful drunken monologues and scenes of violent behaviour, mostly shot in an observational *vérité* style, Francie loses the cleaning job that provides money for food because of her disfigured face. The film is grim and unrelenting in its depictions of ghetto life. There is little to celebrate here: no extended family offering strength and support, no family gatherings, and few images of young people having fun and enjoying themselves. Dennis's mother and sister are suffering victims trapped in their domestic situation, unable to alter the conditions around them. Dennis's girlfriend Shirley tries to encourage him to stay out of trouble, away from the streets, and go to college; she rejects him once she knows he is intent on committing robbery.

3 Framed by unobtainable aspirations: Dennis (Laurence Gilliard Junior) and his friends Larry (Matty Rich) and Kevin (Mark Malone) in *Straight Out of Brooklyn* (Rich, US 1991).

Dennis has to choose between two alternatives, one vested in Shirley and the female realm which may potentially lead to happiness and personal fulfilment, the other in the public sphere of confrontation and criminality which may lead to money and power. His own domestic situation leads him to reject the former in favour of the latter, with inevitably tragic results.

The larger problem that is the source of disequilibrium in the urban films lies outside the ghetto and outside the filmic space of representation, offering no single character or point of identification whose actions are sufficiently motivated to justify the tragic hopelessness and ferocity with which the films conclude. The focus on character, at the expense of any comment on the broader socio-economic context, deflects wider political considerations towards an emphasis on individual psychology. Mermin proposes that the innovative realism of these films should not be mistaken for subversion; by keeping the enemy absent and avoiding the kinds of direct confrontation that might translate into political strategies, audiences can leave the cinema feeling disengaged, angry or hopeless (Mermin 1996: 13).

The 'hood films redraw imaginary maps of the city by placing on screen fragments of spaces which have previously remained obscured, constructing, in the words of African-American literary scholar Charles Scruggs, 'a dialogue that sets the city of the imagination, the city that one wants, against the empirical reality of the city that one has' (Scruggs, quoted in Massood 1996: 4). By placing at the centre of the screen episodic narratives that depict the daily lives of disenfranchised African-Americans, the power relations inherent in mainstream depictions are questioned and revealed. If the real-isation of these themes has become more violent and confrontational, it is perhaps because the brutal realities of which these films speak became intensely acute in the increasingly polarised economic and social infrastructure of American life in the early 1990s.

Notes

1 Vertov's ideas have some similarities to those of John Grierson, often heralded as the founder of the British documentary film movement. Grierson shared a similarly idealist vision of documentary as an informational form that is also an exercise in creativity. See J. Corner (1996: 11–27).

2 For a discussion of the blurred boundaries between fiction and documentary in Eisenstein's *Strike* (1924), see Bill Nichols (1994).

3 *Kine Weekly* survey, quoted in A. Higson (1995: 224).

4 The point is well illustrated by the critics' lauding of *Brief Encounter* (1945) while audiences flocked to see Margaret Lockwood in *The Wicked Lady* (1945).

5 This amounts to some twenty to forty films out of a total of 313 Italian films made between 1945 and 1950 (Liehm 1984: 91).

6 Throughout the 1950s, the number of TV licences issued to domestic households in Britain rose from 343,000 in 1950 to 10 million in 1960 (Docherty, Morrison and Tracey 1987).

7 See, for example, R. Hoggart (1958) and M. Willmott and P. Young (1957). In these texts the emphasis is on values of solidarity, community and stasis and the working-class mother as the focus of family life; there is no mention of single mothers or of female aspiration, social mobility and individualism. Carolyn Steedman (1986) provides an account of the latter situation.

8 See Stuart Laing (1986) for a more detailed account of possible approaches to depictions of British working-class life.

9 This film is discussed in more depth as an example of contemporary realist hybridity in Chapter 8.

10 See, for example, Valerie Smith (1992).

11 For a discussion of this issue in relation to black British films, see Kobena Mercer (1994).

12 In the 1920s, Harlem became a mecca for African-American artists, musicians, writers and performers and the centre of explicating a new aesthetic, but, with the onset of the Depression, the city within a city descended into poverty. The optimism that accompanied the Harlem Renaissance faded, but the image of the city remained central in the literature of later writers such as James Baldwin, Richard Wright and Ralph Ellison. More recently, novelists such as Toni Morrison and Rosa Guy have returned to the period, re-evaluating the cultural legacy of the imaginary constructs of the city in their own narratives. See Paula J. Masood (1996).

13 Reid, quoting from *Variety* on the advertising campaign for the film organised by the black-orientated advertising firm UniWorld (Reid 1993: 83–4).

14 See, for example, Donald Bogle (1973), and Thomas Cripps (1977).

15 See Chapter 5 for a more detailed account of shifting alignments with characters.

Realism and genre: realising fantasy

One of the earliest means used by the Hollywood studios to organise their production and differentiate their products within a competitive market place, genre is often considered a defining characteristic of mainstream feature film production. In contemporary cinema, genre continues to form the core of production, marketing and distribution strategies but is influenced by what Justin Wyatt has termed the 'high concept' aesthetics of post-classical cinema. Considerations of realism in classical Hollywood cinema have to take into account the influence of melodrama on narrative film form: similarly, any analysis of realism and genre in contemporary mainstream film practice has to reflect on the aesthetic changes that arise, at least in part, from the institutional reorganisation of film production in the post-classical era. In this chapter, we will argue that 'high concept' aesthetics permeate contemporary Hollywood filmmaking techniques, a system defined by a form of product differentiation which emphasises style rather than content and aesthetic integration with a film's marketing and merchandising opportunities.[1] An absence of artifice and contrivance is often read as a hallmark of realist works: in classical cinema, this has translated into an aesthetic often deemed 'transparent', a seamless form of storytelling that presents the story as a perceptual illusion. Bordwell argues that irrespective of whether we label it mainstream, dominant or classical filmmaking, one form of narration dominated the studio era: this typically presents psychologically defined characters engaged in struggle in order to achieve specific goals or solve a clear-cut problem. During the course of this struggle, they have to overcome obstacles in the form of other characters and external circumstances: resolution is achieved by decisive victory or defeat and attainment (or not) of the goals. This narrational mode conforms to the prototype of a 'canonic story' found in specific historical forms: the well-made play, the popular romance and the late nineteenth-century short story (Bordwell 1988: 157). In the classical text, the (transparent) unity of the work is achieved through a system of narrative motivations: motivation is the process through which a narrative justifies its content and the plot's presentation of that material. *Compositional* motivation tends to predominate in generic forms that seek to establish character-driven narratives of cause and effect, such as the crime film, psychological thrillers, legal dramas, domestic melodramas and romances. *Intertextual* motivation knowingly plays on established codes and conventions: the 'happy ending' of most Hollywood films is an established convention; the use of stars associated with particular kinds of performance creates expectations associated with their star persona; and, most commonly, *generic* conventions justify certain forms of expected activity, such as confrontational shoot-outs in westerns and characters breaking into song in the musical. *Artistic* motivation, in formalist terms, means 'to make palpable the conventionality of art' (Bordwell 1985: 21), to call attention to the status of the text or art work as a construct. Hollywood films frequently employ spectacle (and technical virtuosity), breaking their seamless narrational flow with sequences that can call attention to the film's artificiality: special effects, spectacular cinematography and various forms of choreographed performance are foregrounded in particular genres such as musicals, westerns, science fiction, some forms of horror, comedy and action adventure films. Finally, many narrative elements are justified on the grounds of *realism*; this encompasses both the creation of a realistic mise-en-scène (setting and characterisation) and plausibly motivated character actions. In classical films, realism is used 'as an auxiliary to significance – not as an object in itself' (Bordwell 1985: 19), to create characters who react plausibly to situations and events in diegetically coherent fictional worlds through the use of verisimilitude.[2] All genre films use these motivations in varying combinations; some favour strongly causal narratives driven by character action, some provide only a weak causal chain that serves as a vehicle for spectacular special effects and performative display. In this chapter, we will use the framework of motivations outlined by Bordwell to consider issues of character-driven causality, artistic motivation, realism and intertextuality in contemporary films, paying particular consideration to

Wyatt's claim that 'high concept' has weakened both causal narration and characterisation. Does this suggest that there is a move away from 'classic realism' as a representational practice based on the use of verisimilar codes and conventions of everyday life? Or is this an indication that 'high concept' aesthetics are the new codes and conventions of a contemporary version of 'classic realism'? Maltby and Craven argue that technological innovation in the cinema is motivated by economic and industrial determinations in the service of maintaining novelty within predictability rather than the desire to create a more perfect reproduction of reality (1995: 182). Yet, these innovations often seem to rely on the predictable real-isation of fantastic environments, on making scenarios that are visually and aurally credible. Are we witnessing a retreat from the narrative realism of classical texts as mainstream cinema pursues the audience by offering ever more 'real-ised' forms of audio-visual fantasy generated by the use of new computer technologies?

This chapter probes these issues in a little more depth through, first of all, an outline of genre and its relationship to 'high concept' film aesthetics. Rather than emphasise the character-centred unity of the classical text as it is commonly understood in film and media studies, part two of the chapter focuses on alternative paradigms that emphasise the gaps in narrative occasioned by excessive style, whether of music and performance, comedy, star attraction, special effects or cinematographic and technological virtuosity. In the third section, questions of realism centre on issues of mise-en-scène and characterisation, two pivotal elements in creating verisimilitude. Finally, section four provides a case study of three films that demonstrate the development of one genre, the gangster film, from its roots in melodrama and realism in the silent era to the intertexual stylistics of 'high concept' aesthetics that shape many of its contemporary formations.

Introduction

In *Alien Resurrection* (1998), Ripley is brought back from the dead to fight the Aliens one more time, the film playing on the expectations of horror/sci-fi as a genre and viewer familiarity with the first three *Alien* films. For viewers accustomed to the futuristic worlds inhabited by Ripley (Sigourney Weaver), the film offers the pleasure of seeing her fight yet another battle with her deadly adversary the

Alien Queen, combining the (by now) familiarly horrific images of the giant insect/reptilian's reproductive cycle within a new narrative of human genetic engineering and cloning. At the end of $Alien^3$ (1992) Ripley destroys herself because she is impregnated by an Alien; in *Alien Resurrection*, genetic elements of the Alien become part of her reconstituted self, a shared genetic inheritance which has horrific and monstrous implications. Although Ripley is dead by the end of $Alien^3$ (signalling the end of the *Alien* series), it is plausible within a science fiction narrative for her to be resurrected. The Organisation scientists regrow her physical body from DNA molecules rescued from her physical remains after her death. The secret of Ripley's rebirth is revealed to her (and us) when she enters a forbidden room full of large glass jars containing monstrous specimens of her 'self', a living museum of failed facsimiles in various states of torment and mental anguish who beg her to end their miserable lives. Themes of genetic engineering and cloning continue the *Alien* films' preoccupation with a monstrous reproductive and mothering process that nurtures rapacious, predatory creatures who not only feed on humans but use their bodies to incubate the young. The film both repeats and continues familiar narrative themes, exploring the boundaries of difference between human and alien, human and machine, male and female, begun in *Alien* (1979). It is both a genre film and a series film, containing essential generic tropes such as a futuristic setting, a preoccupation with manufacturing cyborgs and clones and repeating familiar series ingredients such as the Alien and the star presence of Signourney Weaver playing Ripley, promising a replay of their confrontations but changing locations, situations and events to maintain interest and variation. Similar themes and issues are common in many contemporary science fiction films: *Blade Runner* (1982), for example, explores issues of difference through a futuristic crime narrative of detection that uses a technological test to discover who has genuine rather than implanted emotions, who is human and who is a cyborg.[3]

Genre is a process of constructing meaning and interpretation that circulates between a film, the industry and the audience (Neale 1980 and 1990). A common understanding of the function of genre is shared by producers and audiences who recognise that shorthand descriptions of a film's salient features aid product identification and viewer choice. A quick tour around the local video shop reveals the common terms in use today – dramas, comedies, horror and science fiction – but in the classical period musicals, westerns and gangster movies had greater box-office currency. The industry responds to what it thinks the audience wants, its production categories shaped by the financial success of its most recent productions. Generic categories are flexible hybrids, subject to constant redefinition, division and subdivision. Hollywood's commercial logic continues to be based on combinations of generic categories that will appeal to a broad audience: in the classical period, women expressed a preference for stories of love and romance, whereas males tended to prefer action movies, war films and westerns. The two forms were invariably combined in a dual narrative structure which was repeatedly expressed in advertisements such as 'Tomorrow, the deadliest mission ... tonight, the greatest love!' for the Korean war movie *Toko-Ri* (1954) (Maltby and Craven 1995: 110). Contemporary films such as *Titanic* (1997) use a similar strategy, combining a story vehicle for male heroism and spectacular action with a heterosexual romance of cross-class conflict. Maltby stresses that producers use genre opportunistically, constantly revising their systems of classification to take advantage of audience expectation because viewers construct images and experiences of genre films even before they engage with them at the cinema. This expectation of satisfaction has limiting effects on the industry, creating 'an aesthetic regime of regulated difference, which in turn has a regulating effect on the act of consumption' (Maltby and Craven 1995: 112). The tendency is well illustrated in recent years by the production of sequels, such as the 'Police Academy' comedies and the *Nightmare on Elm Street* series, a practice which Maltby, quoting John Carpenter of *Halloween* fame, considers might be more accurately described as remakes: 'basically sequels means the same film ... (people) want to see the same movie again' (Maltby and Craven 1995: 113).

Audiences construct generic categories around their knowledge and experience of films accumulated through viewing and reading about films and their existing terms of reference. Some generic categories are based on events, such as disaster and action movies; some function on the social roles of their central protagonists, such as gangsters and serial killers, others on affective responses, such as horrors, thrillers and 'weepies'. Different genres tend to structure expectations of response in particular ways. This is obvious when thinking about how horrors, thrillers and 'weepies', for example, are all so-called because they promise a particular intensity of emotional response. If we decide to watch a horror movie it is because we are buying the expectation of being scared by uncanny, out-of-this-world events that are rooted in psychic, out-of-this-world phenomena. Thrillers deliver their shocks through tortuous guessing games, unexpected twists in their plots creating an atmosphere of uncertainty and suspense; weepies by overloading the triggers of empathetic response in favour of characters who suffer.

Many recent theorists reject the proposition that popular cinema necessarily induces illusionism in the viewer.[4] Contemporary film viewers quite obviously do not behave as if they are literally experiencing the effects of a sinking ship, an earthquake or tornado, or an alien force bent on destroying them, or as if they were pursued by a serial killer. Sometimes we watch to enjoy the physical thrills of movement, sound and spectacle, sometimes because we want to test our powers of deduction and predict the outcome of events, sometimes because we want to test our tolerance to violent entertainment,[5] to watch a favourite star, to see how well the filmmakers have adapted a favourite character from a classic novel or a comic series.[6] Quite simply, as viewers we may watch because we have paid to see the film and want to get our money's worth.

Alien Resurrection plays on a number of these desires: it provides spectacular sequences of visual and aural stimulation, such as the underwater chase sequence where, once again, Ripley and her crew are desperately fleeing from the Aliens; it generates suspense and tests viewer tolerance to violence within the safe confines of generic predictability; it provides a familiar star, known for her exploration and play with gender boundaries, this time investigating through her role the human/alien binary. As a serial film, it plays on viewer desires to see the same film again. *Alien Resurrection* is arguably a 'high concept' movie, one that calls certain fundamental tenets of classic realism into question. Rather than a narrative strongly unified by character desire and action, Ripley is driven by forces outside her personal control. In terms of narrative causation, she could be interpreted as subject to the controlling demands of the Organisation scientists, or, in her new identity, influenced by the Alien Queen. It is difficult to locate any of these causal forces as the omniscient narrating instance at the peak of a hierarchy of discourse; rather, narrative motivations are spread across the film's signifying system. Weaver's star persona ensures that narrative causality demands little by way of detailed characterisation: she is playing the same role

again, with only minor variations. Other characters slot into narrative positions as types rather than psychologically explored individuals; the film emphasises the core team as a group of people with a
range of different strengths, intellectual skills and physical attributes. Characters are easily identified as types and are, in this sense,
one-dimensional, developed to suit the exigencies of the plot rather
than reveal their personal desires and motivations. The fast pace of
the action, generated by a superficial narrative of escape and pursuit,
creates little time for reflection on why a character is responding in
a certain way, or whether there is any alternative to their situation.
In this sense, the film is like a roller-coaster, its narration motivated
by action and spectacle, the plot a vehicle for special effects, choreographed staging and performance sequences. The visual design of
the film favours a starkly industrial blue/dark grey/green colour
saturation characteristic of futuristic high-technology fantasy environments, with a suitably electronic soundtrack that foregrounds
computer-generated noise. The film is strongly intertextual, market-
led by its association with the success of other *Alien* films and its
association with the horror/science fiction genre. These various elements contribute to an aesthetics defined by Justin Wyatt as 'high
concept', a market-led integrated approach to production, distribution and exhibition that favours strongly stylised generic films led by
stars with generic associations to enable easy identification of the
film product across a range of advertising and promotion 'windows'.

The development of 'high concept' style corresponds to the
decline of the studio system and the development of the 'package-
unit system' of production. Janet Staiger describes the shift from one
individual company (studio) control to an emphasis on producer
organised projects; the producer raises the finance based on a script
or narrative property and secures both the necessary expertise and
labour from the industry pool, as well as the equipment and physical sites of production (Staiger 1985: 330–8). This shift takes place
against a gradual process of conglomeration throughout the industry, starting in the 1950s with Universal which became part of MCA,
a company with interests in musical talent and television. MCA set
the pattern for interlocking commercial ventures in recorded music
and music publishing, book publishing, retail and mail order sales,
recreation services, financial services and data processing which
became typical of entertainment conglomerates in the 1980s.
Changes at the level of industrial organisation were accompanied by

changes in the kind of product Hollywood sought to produce, shifting towards large-scale films and 'roadshowing' which attempted to
shift the activity of moviegoing into the status of a special occasion
or event (Wyatt 1994: 72). The emphasis was on large-scale spectacle: musicals such *The Sound of Music* (1965), *Funny Girl* (1968)
and *Hello Dolly* (1969) and spectacular epics such as *Dr Zhivago*
(1965) and *Ryan's Daughter* (1970). Large losses at the box office
from this type of product led to diversification and the development
of films designed to appeal to youth, such as *The Graduate* (1967),
M.A.S.H (1970) and *Easy Rider* (1969). Auteur filmmakers such as
Robert Altman and Paul Mazursky were given considerable latitude
during the 1970s, allowed to experiment under the safe umbrella of
studio funding. By the end of the decade, the poor returns at the box
office on many experimental films led to an equation of experimentation with formal and stylistic overindulgence, of which Michael
Cimino's *Heaven's Gate* now stands as the archetypical example.[7]
Budgeted at $7.5 million, United Artists seized control of the unfin-
ished film whilst still in production because costs had spiralled to
$21 million. When it finally opened eighteen months later, it was
critically slated; re-cutting failed to make any difference to its performance at the box office with financial returns of only $1.5 against
total costs in excess of $43 million.[8] This financial loss effectively
ended the period of risk and experimentation.

While the doors were open to more experimental projects in the
1970s, it was also the period in which the 'blockbuster' developed,
retaining the event status of moviegoing with all-star vehicles based
on strongly generic best-selling novels or plays with named directors. *Love Story* (1970) started the trend, followed by *The Godfather*
(1972) and *Jaws* (1975). Throughout the decade, the numbers of
films in production declined in order to divert more money into
films that were easily packaged and marketed. Wyatt notes that
adventure films and blockbusters were more easily sold abroad than
more experimental personal films, placing increasing emphasis on
producing the big budget, packaged film (1994: 80). The aesthetics
of the blockbuster and the economic forces that produced it laid the
ground for the development of 'high concept' in the 1980s. High
concept films are designed to play across the release 'windows' provided by the new television technologies – cable, home video, pay-
per-view and satellite, as well as theatrical release. Extending and
modifying significant aspects of the classical mode, high concept

style is based on two components: a simplification of character and narrative and a strong match between image and soundtrack throughout the film (1994: 18). Wyatt suggests that the narrative of high concept films is composed of stock situations set firmly within generic frameworks of viewer expectation that can be captured in a single phrase or sentence. The single sentence marketing hook that underlines high concept filmmaking communicates both what the film is about (its content) and its style and genre. The poster for the sci-fi adventure *Men in Black* (1997) proclaims 'protecting the earth from the scum of the universe', that for *Event Horizon* (1997) 'infinite space, infinite terror'. High concept films are not only intertextually generic, but are often composed of extended montage sequences set to music which are, in effect, music video sequences that fragment the forward trajectory of the narrative. *The Bodyguard* (1992) is an extended music video featuring the singer Whitney Huston, *Natural Born Killers* (1994) is in part an assemblage of montage sequences cut to music within a loose narrative structure. Wyatt argues that high concept aesthetics retain important ties to classical cinema, but are shaped by the reconfigured media market place, particularly the development of cable and home video, in the context of increasing competition and a need for product differentiation and niche marketing. Differentiation through marketing and merchandising begins at the level of the pitch: the product can be summed up and sold in a single sentence; a key image from the film is abstracted and used to market the film in advertising materials, product tie-ins and television commercials. Wyatt sums up high concept, in appropriately high concept fashion, as 'the look, the hook, the book' – the look of the images, marketing hooks and tie-ins.

Critics of the classical model of mainstream cinema are numerous; in Chapter 1 we discussed Gledhill's critique, which foregrounds melodrama as a disruptive force that creates gaps in the narrative to 'realise' the emotional state of characters through visualisation and music, rather than causal logic (Gledhill 1992). This use of the concept of 'real-isation' in the sense of reality simulation, of 'making realistic' the fantastic, spectacular elements of storytelling through visualisation and auditory effects, is a useful way of thinking about the relationship between melodrama and contemporary action cinema. Gaps are created in the chain of character-centred causality, foregrounding artistic motivation; this can take the form of spectacular action sequences that characterise films like *True Lies* (1994)

and *Cliffhanger* (1994); or of simulating visions of other worlds
through the use of computer generated special effects, as well as creating spectacular events within, for example, disaster narratives
motivated by verisimilitude in the form of cyclones, volcanic erup-
tions or sinking ships.

Real-ising spectacle

From the action cinema of *Die Hard* (1988) and *Total Recall* (1990)
to the fantasy genres of science fiction and horror, the display of situation and event can take precedence over character desire and
motivation, becoming a major part of a film's narrational structures.
The tendency towards big budget spectaculars, seen as an intrinsic
element of the contemporary Hollywood industry, favours a style of
entertainment based on aggregate forms with their roots in show
business, rather than narrative forms with their roots in novels, plays
or short stories. Aggregate forms of entertainment are essentially
non-narrative, based on a loose structure of acts which typically present the spectacle of performing. Their roots lie in nineteenth-
century entertainment forms such as the revue, the minstrel show,
variety, burlesque, circus, music hall (in Britain) and the Ziegfield
Follies, where each unit of performance, each act, each number is a
self-contained highlight. Aggregate forms are sometimes held
together by a theme   hence Buffalo Bill Cody's Wild West Show
consisted of acts of skills and daring typically associated with frontier life, such as rodeo, shoot-outs and Amerindian dance performances. Two Hollywood genres, comedy and the musical, exemplify
the integration of aggregate elements within the classical narrative
paradigm after the coming of sound in the late 1920s added a realist imperative to Hollywood's commercial aesthetics. In histories of
the cinema, this drive towards integration is often pre-figured as ideological appropriation – the structural models provided by (bourgeois forms of) literature and drama gradually supersede the
(working-class or folk modes of) performative display found in
aggregate forms.[9] Gag-based slapstick comedy films began to employ
comic performers from vaudeville, pantomime and music hall in the
Keystone comedy shorts of the 1912–16 period. By the early 1920s,
comic performers such as Chaplin had become star attractions, their
performances differentiated from those of other actors. The shift
towards feature-length films was a difficult step for established

comedians, creating an unstable combination of slapstick and narrative elements. Two directions were followed: the Keystone films starring Ben Turpin parodied contemporary (melo)dramatic or adventure films, exploiting their established framework, whilst the feature films of Howard Lloyd combined slapstick elements with 'genteel' comedy in the form of gags and incidents, which tend to be generated from the narrative by character action and desire, rather than competing with it (Krutnik 1995: 18–19). This move towards narrative integration can be seen as a precursor to the 'drawing room' comedies of the 1930s and 1940s featuring stars such as Katherine Hepburn and Cary Grant, where the plausibility of characters in recognisable situations and events becomes the ground on which comedy plays out its disruptions. In stark contrast to these smooth, bourgeois comedies (played out amongst wealthy white Americans in their luxurious domestic environments) are the anarchic (chaotic and notably haphazard) comedies of the Marx Brothers, which develop in a disordered, impromptu manner with scant regard for consistent characterisation or for a causally motivated plot. By the end of the 1930s, however, a balance had been struck between narrative and gag/spectacle, with comedians such as Bob Hope and Danny Kaye providing a predictable diet of narrative fiction and entertainment spectacle motivated by a central comic performer (Krutnik 1995: 17–38).

The musical works with a similar play-off between the integrating functions of narrative, mise-en-scène and characterisation and the disruptive carnivalesque elements of spectacle and performance. Its self-contained 'show stopping' elements emphasise exhibition rather than narrative progression, bodily display rather than character psychology. Musicals are an aggregate form that is *a priori* unrealistic because no-one ever breaks into a sudden outburst of spontaneously composed, choreographed and orchestrated song and dance. With the coming of sound in the late 1920s, musicals rapidly established themselves as box-office winners; the most popular format was the backstage musical where the song-and-dance routines were motivated by the needs of a plot with its foundations firmly laid in a plausible, everyday reality governed by character-centred desire and motivation. In the show musical, particularly those of the early 1930s such as *Footlight Parade* (Balcon and Berkeley 1933) and *Gold Diggers of 1933* (Le Roy and Berkeley 1933), the narrative theme of 'putting on a show' enables any break with the 'real' events of the diegetic world to be contained within a causal framework. The performances that we see are initially filmed from the viewpoint of diegetic spectators in the form of the theatre audience, the action located on the stage before it breaks out of the confines of theatrical space into the spectacular song-and-dance routines and cinematographic virtuosity characteristic of filmic space. No matter where the fantasy takes us in this seemingly infinite expanse, at the end of the performance sequence the camera is always (re)positioned with the diegetic audience watching the stage, aligning our view of events with theirs, back in the 'everyday' world of the fiction. The spectacular staging and camerawork of the song-and-dance sequences in these Busby Berkeley films violates realist consistency in the interests of cinematic artistic effect, but the sequences remain motivated by narrative plausibility. Similarly, the popular operatic musicals of Jeanette Macdonald and Nelson Eddy are often pre-figured around a causal mechanism for launching into song. Unsurprisingly, many of these latter films were set in historically distant places, their exact time and place hard to determine, their characters the rogues and aristocrats of popular historical romantic fiction. But even in the most unlikely of locations, musicals can still justify their excursions into song on the grounds of character-centred motivation: in *New Moon* (1940) the aristocratic character played by Jeanette MacDonald is an entertainer who sings and plays the harpsichord, a recognised sign of her upper-class status. When a stowaway below deck (Nelson Eddy) hears her performance and responds in similar vein, his singing reveals to her that he is a character in disguise, an aristocrat fleeing the French Revolution.

Plausibility of character motivation performs an essential role in establishing the grounds on which the play of sexual innuendo and mutual attraction that characterise the musical genre can be realised. Real-isation plays a similar role to that outlined earlier in relation to stage melodrama; such spectacle, (whether of song-and-dance or action sequences) uses narrative realism to establish the terms of a plausible fictional reality before fantasy can play out its utopian function through the performance of song and dance. Altman claims that the fairy-tale musical, in particular, sets up an oppositional structure that relies upon a real/ideal antithesis, out of which the sexual tension between man and woman grows. She is frustrated by her everyday reality; he is identified with exoticism, danger and the unknown. For this opposition to work, the surroundings must

appear just as exotic to the viewer as they do to the character, by presenting an image of a world we know little of. In *New Moon* this
exoticism is provided by a lack of attention to authentic historical
detail and the narrative event of a shipwreck on a desert island; this
unknown location allows freedom from conventional social (and
sexual) restraints. Altman argues that by setting its characters in a
time and space known to the 1930s audience only through travel
publicity, popular romantic fiction or society column chatter, an
opposition is set up between the spectator's reality and the ideal fantasy image of the film. In the age of the mass media and the jet aero-
plane, this fantasy image of 'exotic otherness' is harder to sustain;
places that once appeared romantic, mysterious and far away now
appear to be misrepresented, their unreality foregrounded as construction. This presents a problem for contemporary appreciation of
the musical since it is only those films that recognise the premise of
their own unreality structures, such as *Singin' in the Rain* (1952),
which escape censure by modern viewers for the perceived unreality
of their narrative supposition (Altman 1987: 182–5). Because of this
realist imperative, most musicals appear ridiculous today, their
imaginative worlds implausible and naïve.

Important to our current purpose is the extent to which artistic
motivation in the form of spectacular special effects often dominates
compositional plausibility in contemporary films. The eleven Oscars
awarded to the epic historical drama *Titanic* in 1998, the most
expensive film produced to date and a record money-maker at the
box office, are testament to the commercial aesthetics of spectacular
real-isation which currently pervades the film industry. The story of
the ocean liner Titanic's demise on its maiden voyage has survived
in popular memory as one of the great stories of human folly; the
ship, claimed its makers, was unsinkable. Yet it collided with an iceberg and did sink, drowning two thirds of its more than two thousand passengers and crew. The story of this epic disaster is retold
using the ostensibly 'true' story of a (fictionalised) survivor to moti-
vate the flashback structure of the narrative, which follows a conventional scenario of disruption, heroic action and resolution.
Structurally, the film is a traditional melodrama dressed in contemporary special effects that simulates a disaster of epic proportions.
Its huge production budget was primarily spent on attempting to
create, in action terms, the experience of being a passenger on that
particular ship at that time – and surviving. Great attention is paid

to recreating an 'authentic' mise-en-scène based on contemporary and historical verisimilitude. The opening sequence of the film, in which a group of salvage experts probe the wreck with video imaging equipment, ostensibly searching for lost treasures, has the appearance of a glossy documentary until the introduction of the fictionalised elderly survivor situates the film historically through her memory motivated flashback sequences.

In setting the scene for cross-class romance on the doomed ocean liner, the luxurious surroundings and costumes of the first class passengers create a stark contrast to the spartan accommodation and poverty of the steerage passengers below deck. The binary structure of romantic conflict has parallels with the real/ideal antithesis in the musical: sexual frisson is generated by the contrast between poverty and an exotic display of material wealth. A fairy-tale narrative of cross-class conflict and romantic love is played out amidst a spectacularly real-ised mise-en-scène of disaster as the ship slowly breaks up and sinks. In generic terms, it combines the romantic melodrama of a women's picture like *Now Voyager* (1942) with the spectacular special effects of a disaster movie like *Towering Inferno* (1974). Rose (Kate Winslet), like Charlotte (Bette Davies), undertakes a voyage of literal and metaphorical transformation, during the course of which she realises that happiness is to be found in acting on intuition and feeling, not the rigidity of social protocol and obedience demanded by her husband-to-be and mother. Her fiancé Cal is somewhat reminiscent of a villain from silent screen melodrama; dark-haired, handsome and rich but with a violent streak in his character. Rose finds the prospect of marriage to the sadistic Cal increasingly oppressive. In contrast, her young lover, played by the boyish Leonardo DiCaprio, is an unlikely hero, his naïveté and innocence strangely out of place in the world of brutal masculinity that characterises the lower class steerage passengers. The different worlds of these starkly oppositional groups are musically signified by the constrained sounds of a chamber quartet that accompanies life on the upper decks set against the lyrical strains of Irish folk melodies that transform into the unrestrained playing of an impromptu Irish band in the steerage bar. *Titanic* is structured, like most genre films, around an oppositional structure of nature/civilisation, poverty/wealth, emotion/objectivity, which places Rose's conflict of gendered social identity on the side of the earthy (natural) qualities of working-class folk, victims in this modern fairy story of greedy capitalists who satisfy their desires at the expense of any sense of duty or responsibility towards the passengers and crew. Many viewers know that this Manichean conflict between opposing forces of good and evil will end not only in disaster but also in a moral didacticism that places Rose on the side of right, a survivor changed for the better. Her emotional trial and commitment buys her freedom from the subjugation of upper-class femininity, although, as in many narratives of this sort, there is a credibility gap that fails to explain how she overcomes the potential poverty of her situation once she is rescued from the sea. In this sense the film differs from earlier women's pictures, such as *Now Voyager*, where the focus of the narrative is on how the woman achieves or maintains her social status whilst exploring and maintaining her newly discovered identity. In *Titanic*, Rose's future is revealed through the photographs she carries as memories of her past, but it is not a story we are party to.

The disastrous collision with the iceberg is real-ised through spectacular visual and sound effects using computer-simulated sequences rather than three-dimensional models, the event of the ship's disintegration narrationally motivating the last hour and a half of this long film. *Titanic* is both classic in structure and realist in intention; it is an excellent example of a film that aims to entertain through spectacular real-isation using special effects to create a believable illusion that digitally replicates perceptual realism.[10] Rather like the realistic staged spectacles of late nineteenth-century melodrama, the depiction of the ship's disintegration is structured around a romantic sentimental story. This is classical Hollywood filmmaking of a very traditional kind, taking events from history, stripping them of their socio-historical and political contexts and recycling them as entertainment. But from its inception, as Black (1994) and Maltby (1983) have demonstrated, the film industry has been driven by commercial incentives rather than a sense of social, political or moral responsibility. Louis B. Mayer, one of the founders of MGM, a studio known for its glossy, spectacular films, is said to have famously declared, 'If I want to send a message, I'll send it by Western Union.' The story may be apocryphal but no doubt James Cameron, the writer and director of *Titanic,* would share the sentiment. We return to questions raised by the mythologisation of history and the real-isation of historical events in more detail in Chapter 6.

Motivating realism

Many critics of contemporary Hollywood continue to analyse popular films in terms of the narrative coherence and unity typical of the classical narrative paradigm.[11] The critical rhetoric of realism traditionally associates lack of artifice (contrived artistic effect) with a higher claim to truth and authenticity in representation, as we have shown in Chapter 2. Films deemed 'realist' have often been held in high esteem as examples of 'quality' filmmaking practice in stark opposition to the crass commercial products of Hollywood and the mainstream.[12] The unlikely situations and unnatural events of blockbuster films are often the source of this critical disdain. *Independence Day*, one of the top box-office films of 1997, was deemed by critics a poor film, symptomatic of Hollywood's decline into the high concept formula of big budget spectacle, because the tenets of its plot were considered thin and incredible. It was scathingly termed an expensive B movie, a film crammed with spectacular special effects that none the less fails to be sufficiently entertaining because it is insufficiently convincing.[13] *Independence Day* was timed to be released on 4 July; saturation marketing ensured that the film tapped into national sentiment, slotting into celebrations of the American public holiday by becoming a 'must see' event. Read intertextually and generically, perhaps the film provided pleasures which have little to do with conventional assessments of filmic quality associated with the classical narrative text. Its parodic recreation of outsider invasion narratives, typified by the works of an earlier generation of science fiction writers such as Ray Bradbury and Richard Matheson, extends the appeal of the film beyond any single market niche into the profitable terrain of the family film. Jancovich claims that these 1950s narratives now have the status of 'trash classics': they were part of a 'cultural repertoire' of films, books and comics circulating at the time, consumed primarily by teenagers. Many contemporary filmmakers, including Stephen King, John Carpenter, Stephen Spielberg and Tim Burton, spent their teenage years watching such films and now refer to them as 'formative moments' in their subsequent careers (Jancovich 1996: 83).

Jancovich locates a major shift in 1950s horror films away from a reliance on the gothic and the use of exotic mise-en-scène towards the use of location shooting and a preoccupation with contemporary American society: 'Again and again, the threats which distinguish 1950s horror do not come from the past or even from the actions of a lone individual, but are associated with the processes of social development and modernisation' (Jancovich 1996:2). He reads the films in relation to an increased awareness of regulation permeating all aspects of American life, as bureaucracies became more centralised and the state took a more active role in controlling fiscal policy. The distinction between science fiction and horror collapsed in the group of films dubbed at the time 'monster movies', narratives of invasion where the alien or 'thing' that is perceived as a threat is as much a response to fears of mass conformity within contemporary American life as a response to the external threat of Soviet aggression, although these general features are treated very differently within individual texts. In films such as *Invasion of the Bodysnatchers* (1956) and *It Came From Outer Space* (1953) the use of location shooting grounds the credibility of alien invasion in smalltown America, a recognisable everyday space in which the metaphorical significance found in the film's themes of loss of community and mass conformity can also be linked to antecedent, pre-filmic factors. Claims of flying saucer sitings and paranormal activity, particularly around known nuclear testing areas such as Nevada, were given extensive coverage in the popular media, creating something of a national fear of the possibility of immanent invasion from outer space. Read in relation to these sensational 'factual' accounts, the visualisation of these fears in narrative form through the use of realist motivational strategies, such as location shooting and the development of characters familiar from everyday life, situates the fantasy in knowing play with rationality at the everyday level of plausible real-isation. These things could be true, they could happen because antecedent reality factors (albeit in the form of media hype of rumours and unsubstantiated evidence) suggest such events could be credible. This frisson between the real and the unknown sets in play a similar set of responses to those outlined by Altman in the real/ideal antithesis of the musical: to participate in the fiction the alien threat, like the ideal exotic location of the musical, has to be sufficiently credible to be possible in terms of what constitutes a rational possibility of the unknown. The point is well illustrated by Barker and Brooks's audience research into the film *Judge Dredd* (1995), where the scepticism of middle-class viewers towards the futuristic vision of the film was based on a 'knowing and weighting' (weighing up) attitude to images of the future because futures are about making predictions based on knowledge (Barker and Brooks 1998). This seems to indicate that the plausibility of realist intention plays an important role for some viewers in creating viable science fictions: if there is no social context in which the fiction can be plausible for the viewer, it can be judged as unfounded supposition.

Jancovich situates the science fiction horror of the 1950s in the context of rational fears because fears of invasion and bureaucratic and commercial standardisation circulated in numerous discourses in 1950s American society. He places these films very precisely within their social context, but the industrial context of film production at this time also played an important role in shifting the mise-en-scène of horror and science fiction films away from studio fantasy to location reality. The studio system of production was beginning to break down by the early 1950s due to a combination of forces, not least of which was the collapse of the audience, which fell by 50 per cent between 1946 and 1957. This dramatic fall corresponds with the development of television: by the mid-1950s, Hollywood was producing 20 per cent of prime-time network television shows in its studios, compensating for the collapse of film production which was paralleled by a corresponding rise in TV ownership. In 1949 there were 1 million TV sets in American homes, the following year there were 4 million and by 1955 more than half of all American homes had a television set in their living rooms (Hillier 1992: 13). Television brought a new sense of liveness and immediacy to moving image culture, creating a demand for filmed drama with its finger on the pulse of contemporary life. The switch to location shooting was in part made possible by new developments in camera technology developed for shooting television news that enabled economical live shooting on location to become widely available for the first time, leading to the growth of realist genres such as the police procedural and the crime series. The gradual decline of the studio system's investment in feature films opened up opportunities for independent production, small companies employing young filmmakers who were keen to try new filmmaking techniques. AIP (American International Pictures), for example, specialised in cheap exploitation and horror films favoured by the youth market.[14] In contrast, studio production sought to distance itself from the black and white immediacy of the television image, developing widescreen shooting techniques such as CinemaScope and new colour film processing methods in the interests of an increasing emphasis on both realism and spectacle.[15]

The drive towards big budget spectacle in the 1980s and 90s is similarly driven by commercial incentives; differentiation of the Hollywood product is dependent on large budgets to create the special effects that can maintain a real/ideal, known/unknown oppositional structure between viewer experience and screen fantasy. Mise-en-scène is, perhaps, the most indispensable ingredient in grounding a text in realism. The representation of a materially recognisable world is the one that the photographic media are most obviously qualified to achieve. Any departure from this recognisability is perceived as a significant departure from verisimilitude, inviting an immediate questioning of its cause or effect. Such questioning is now a common response to the classic Hollywood musical, as we noted above. On the other hand, to represent a simulacrum of the material world is to assert the fictional reality of narrative events.

The most genuine form of realist mise-en-scène is location shooting; here the real, physical world is actually, iconically represented. The camera has been physically present and recorded this mountain or this street. Whether the landscape depicted is natural wilderness or a built urban landscape, outdoors or inside public buildings such as law courts or railway stations, here is a part of the real world normally inhabited by real people outside the text. This gives credibility to the fictional characters inhabiting that landscape within the text's diegesis. A good example is provided by the opening of *North by North West* (Hitchcock 1959). The rectangular graphic lines of the titles dissolve into the façade of a modern office block, the camera pans down the building, taking in the noise and bustle of a busy metropolitan street scene (including Hitchcock catching a bus), moves into the foyer of an office block and comes to rest on a lift. The doors open, a crowd of office workers pour out of the lift, through the building and back onto the street; as this occurs, both sound and image narrow the audio-visual field, focusing on two people, a boss and his secretary, discussing his diary of events. Cary Grant, a popular 1950s star, is from here on the focus of attention, situated in the contemporary space of 1950s America.

In a realist text private interiors, such as homes or workplaces, are characterised by a redundancy of detail that convinces us that these could be the real environments of real people. The setting and props are redundant in the sense of being in excess of the demands of the narrative, though they may also serve those needs. Their purpose is to persuade us that this is the kind of environment which these people would inhabit were they real people, that these kinds of people would inhabit this environment in real life. These are the clothes they would and do wear; these are the things they would and do possess. Or 'did' in the case of historical fictions or, for contemporary audiences, in old films. In contrast, a symbolic mise-en-scène needs only those props which feature in the narrative, and may suggest the location through iconic signifiers or not at all. Few films are as minimalist as this, unless they are very short. Cartoons, however, even full-length features, tend to sketch in a physical environment just fully enough to signify the general type of location – a village, a forest, a castle for example, and to limit props to those needed for the narrative or to signify a location. Thus, for instance, in a scene from Disney's *Beauty and the Beast* where Gaston arrives at Belle's home to propose to her, all the furniture shown features in the narrative of the scene: one chair is sat on by both Belle and Gaston, the table is where she puts her book and he puts his feet, the chest of drawers has a mirror which Gaston uses to admire himself, the bookshelf is where Belle puts her book after rescuing it from Gaston's feet, and the rocking chair is thrown over by him as he pursues her. The only 'redundant' details are an umbrella stand by the door, a shelf holding a platter and a kettle to signify that this is the cottage's sole living space. Other settings are even less detailed: Belle's bedroom at the castle has only a large four-poster bed on which she throws herself; the dining room has only a table and the one chair on which she sits besides the crockery which constitute the actors in the scene; the forest consists only of bare trees and is inhabited only by the wolves that attack first her father and then Belle. Such cartoon films are, of course, not aiming at realism. Often based on fairy-tale narratives or comic book characters, they are ostensible fantasy, with magical narratives: characters are reduced to 'types', commonly of moral binary opposites; reference to the real world is mostly limited to a moral message.

Many avant-garde and art house films and some mainstream entertainment films make use of scenes that are more symbolic than realist in their mise-en-scène, but within a material context that is overall more realist than symbolic. Since the paradigmatic realist text may also use elements of mise-en-scène for narrative or symbolic purposes, it is usually a matter of degree and balance. Thus, a paperweight on an office desk may serve a narrative purpose as a murder weapon, but may only, or also, more importantly and simultaneously, contribute to the creation of a realistic office scene. Photographs on a mantelpiece may explain relationships within the diegesis, but may simply indicate the kind of thing this type of people have in their living rooms. Once a realist mise-en-scène is established, there is an impulse to read the characters and events within it according to realist expectations. On the other hand, significant departures from this realist ambience, which encourage us to read the mise-en-scène primarily in terms of its symbolic qualities, simultaneously encourage us to read the narrative action in a non-realist way – as metaphor, allegory or satire, for example. This is not to say that realist mise-en-scènes cannot also serve such functions; clearly they frequently do. Nor that what qualifies as a realist mise-en-scène does not vary historically, culturally or generically. The studio 'location' shots of 1930s and 40s films, for instance, with their use of back projection, may have been accepted by audiences as realist at that time, but now appear clearly as constructions. Yet we still perceive them as realist in intention.

The importance of mise-en-scène may be appreciated if we compare how realistic mise-en-scènes function in films and genres of films which, by many other criteria, depart substantially from the paradigmatic realist text with films and genres where the mise-en-scène is not realistic. Mainstream popular cinema has many examples of genres which, in differing respects and to differing degrees, would not qualify as realist texts in the paradigmatic sense. It can, indeed, be argued that the bulk of popular cinema, whilst realist in form, is unrealistic in content. The clearest case concerns fantasy films, particularly those within the science fiction/horror genres. There are, of course, several subdivisions within these genres and considerable overlap between them. We are not concerned to define these, but to identify structural similarities in their uses of realism. The mise-en-scène itself is often fantastic, imaging futuristic scenarios such as intergalactic travel, non-human life forms from other planetary systems and as yet non-existent weaponry and forms of space travel. Films such as *Event Horizon* (1997), *Starship Troopers* (1997), *Stargate* (1996) and the *Aliens* quartet emphasise this aspect of futuristic fantasy. In contemporary science fiction, the relationship between character and setting often parodies the exotic fantasies of early studio films in a knowing play between filmmaker and viewer, foregrounding the constructed nature of the fiction, playing the game by the rules of generic convention. *The Fifth Element* (1996) exemplifies this technique. The opening of the film features an elderly white male in an exotic desert location trying to decipher an ancient text inscribed on stone tablets; a servile 'native other' fans the 'great white sage' as he attempts to reveal the secrets of the text. The exact location of events and the time of their setting are unspecified, but the desert location and the archaeological quest narrative indicate an earlier period of generic fantasy, perhaps triggering recognition of *Raiders of the Lost Ark* (1981) or *Indiana Jones and the Temple of Doom* (1984), which are often perceived as parodies of the action adventure movie of the 1930s. Intertextuality is a recognised feature of contemporary genre production, playing on viewer complicity to establish plausible context through recognisable fictional formulas such as comic books and science fiction narratives rather than recourse to any antecedent context or reference in everyday reality. The codes and conventions in play are strictly those of fiction, hermetically sealed from any direct reference to external events, yet operating within a classical paradigm that constructs plausible, self-contained fictional worlds through character-centred action and events.

Alternatively, as in the horror films of the 1950s, the fantasy may be grounded in contemporary diegetic reality. *Jurassic Park* (1994) enacts a known/unknown oppositional structure by associating contemporary fears of genetic engineering with a fantasy of entrepreneurial excess through the plot device of a dinosaur theme park. The real-isation of the dinosaurs, which is based on scientific evidence about size, behavioural characteristics and the feeding and reproductive capacity of dinosaurs, is achieved by digital imaging. As Stephen Prince points out, this real-isation creates an obvious paradox since no-one has seen a dinosaur and paleontologists can only guess how such creatures might have moved and acted. Their 'reality' is created through 'detailed texture-mapping, motion animation and integration with live action carried out via digital imaging' (Prince 1996: 34) grounded in the plausible diegesis of creating an innovative theme park to capitalise on leisure time. Although there is an obvious ontological problem in claiming that the dinosaurs are 'real', perceptually they correspond with conventional photographic and moving image realism. What all these films share is a plot grounded in events and phenomena that are literally, according to secular standpoints, highly unlikely, but nonetheless imaginable and in some cases potentially conceivable. They are in this sense fantasies, often nightmarish fantasies which feature supernatural and/or extra-terrestrial beings that threaten human protagonists (all the films listed above), or alternatively create dystopic visions of the future, such as *Blade Runner* (1982) or *Twelve Monkeys* (1995). Their central narratives are often classical in form, ending in apocalyptic destruction or, more usually, in human victory over the alien threat.

Acting style and characterisation, in combination with location shooting, are important compositional elements of realist mise-en-scène. The shift from gesticular to versimilar acting codes noted in Chapter 1 has a significant equivalent in the early 1950s, when what is now known as the Method heralded a new era of realism in Hollywood acting style that complemented the development of widescreen spectacle. The idea underlying the Method's system of actor training was to emphasise an actor's psychology as the driving force of character depiction; such an emphasis would, it was argued, create more realistic characters who are not only effects of textual determinations, driven by narrative action and events, but respond to situations and events in ways that demonstrate underlying psychological motivations for behaviour in line with popular discourses informed by a dissemination of ideas based on Freudian psychology. The move was away from a genre-orientated typicality of character where stars use their recognisable public personas to 'play themselves' (the symbiosis between the western and John Wayne is a good example) towards a recognition of acting skills associated with theatrical techniques of 'playing a character'. The Method emphasised techniques such as improvisation, ensemble playing and emotional expressiveness, relying on the actor's own psychology as the raw material of characterisation. It aimed to fuse actor and character into a seamless, indivisible whole, creating a more 'authentic' performance that sought emotional truth drawn from an actor's own experiences and responses, rather than relying on action and plot. Difficulties of expression were understood as 'emotional blocks' that actors had to overcome through a process not dissimilar to therapy, using psycho-therapeutic theatrical techniques that helped them to 'manipulate their pyschological histories to identify with the character in performance'.[16] Based on the Stanislavski system developed in the Moscow Art theatre in pre-revolutionary Russia, the Method was, from its inception, a style developed to perform the works of realist writers such as Chekov and Ibsen. In America, the theory underlying the technique was interpreted and developed by Lee Strasberg in New York's Group Theatre during the 1930s, becoming an important force in American theatre after World War II. Actors trained by Strasberg at the Actor's Studio slowly infiltrated Hollywood, the technique gaining popularity from 1955 when *On the Waterfront* (1955) won seven Academy awards, including an Oscar for Method actor Marlon Brando as best actor. Contemporary actors such as Al Pacino and Robert De Niro have carried the torch for Method acting through the 1970s and into the 1980s, but its gradual absorption into the mainstream of American screen acting now makes it difficult to distinguish Method devotees from other actors purely on the grounds of technique.

In examining the technique of a well-known 1950s Method actor such as James Dean, what becomes evident, to couch it in Pearson's terms, is the amount of 'by-play' devoted to expressing inner psychological states. In *Rebel Without a Cause* (1955), James Dean plays Jim, a teenager who keeps getting into trouble: car theft, knife fights and gang warfare have driven his parents to move from town to town, each time in the hope that a new start will help him to stay out of trouble. Jim claims he is misunderstood, his problems being due to his father's inability to stand up for himself at home: the film is typical in this respect of many early 1950s narratives informed by popular psychoanalysis where the mother is ultimately blamed for male insecurity and anxieties.[17] Dean's performance is marked by excessive physical gestures: he tends to protect his chest with his arms, close in on himself, curl up like a baby and adopt foetal positions. At other times, he flings himself about, pounds a desk with his fists, kicks a hole in a large portrait of his grandmother, staggers to the fridge for a drink of milk, rubbing the bottle on his face. These emotional outbursts are accompanied by either a hesitancy in speaking, or the release of a tirade of accusations: emotional instability, expressed in physical actions and gestures, supports a narrative of masculine teenage anxiety about growing up. With his peer group and the gang, Dean adopts a more casual, nonchalant stance; he tries to appear confident and unconcerned, but reveals inner tension and emotion in his jumpy, inconsistent actions. Today, the acting looks somewhat exaggerated and contrived, but at the time journalistic and critical rhetoric heralded such performances as examples of the 'realism' of Method style (Maltby and Craven 1995: 262).

Wyatt claims that acting in high concept films resembles lifestyle modelling rather than characterisation, selling the film and the lifestyle on offer. He gives the example of *Baby Boom* (1987), where Diane Keaton plays an investment banker who is constructed as the New York social type 'working woman', warned by her boss that she 'can't have it all'. A relocation to the country moves the plot forward, situating the sophisticated urban businesswoman in the context of a rural small town where she meets the rustic Doc Cooper. A similar opposition is set in play to that we noted in *Titanic*, one that makes characters easily identifiable as representations of particular social groups and lifestyles. Star persona serves to underscore character typing and generic iconography as a means of economically transmitting narrative information. The lack of investment in character leads to a greater emphasis on physical types; the characters function more like fashion models constituted in the way they look and move before the camera and their taste in clothes and music; characters are sketched in referential terms through intertextuality, not through diegetic motivational forces that direct their actions (Wyatt 1994: 59–69).

Contemporary Hollywood does continue to acknowledge the star persona of actors known for their ability to reveal character psychology and motivation in performance in contrast to those who perform to type. Female stars such as Meryl Streep, Glenn Close and Susan Sarandon have secured their positions as older stars through their acting abilities rather than their physical image. Sharon Stone is a good example of a star who, having achieved a degree of success in numerous films where she played 'sexy' roles, sought recognition for her acting ability after the success of *Basic Instinct* (1991) by playing opposite Robert De Niro in *Casino* (1995). A similar tendency seems to be increasingly prevalent amongst male stars. Arnold Schwarzenegger has turned away from action adventure films such as *The Terminator* (1984) that earned him the reputation of a 'muscle man' to play roles in family orientated entertainments such as *Junior* (1994). British actors such as Tim Roth and Gary Oldman are known for their acting abilities rather than their looks; American stars Brad Pitt and Matt Dillon are known for their looks but also their ability to create convincing characters. Good acting, in the sense of a performance that engages viewers and encourages their alignment and empathy, motivates realism even in fantasy scenarios. We return to questions of acting and viewer engagement in Chapter 5.

Theme, form and intertextuality

Realism in genre films is invariably motivated by texts situated in contemporary or historical contexts that are often social or domestic in orientation, based on the articulation of anxieties, social issues and political problems within the formal structure of the classical film. The western, in its heyday, was realist in intention, aiming to recreate a credible historical image of frontier life from the point of view of the white settlers. Revisionist westerns, such as Peckinpah's *Pat Garrett and Billy the Kid* (1973) and the more recent *Dances With Wolves* (1991), aim to regenerate the cultural status of the genre by drawing on historical accounts of known antecedent events that, in the case of the former, draws heavily on realist techniques associated at the time with European art cinema, in the case of the latter by referring to a historical period that pre-dates most filmic representations. Such films, although not realist in content, are arguably realist in intention. Similarly, social problem genres, such as the domestic melodrama, the crime film and the gangster film, constantly seek to renovate tired story formulas by altering the context in which recurring scenarios are played out.

A brief historical account of the gangster film serves as an instance of a generic form that consistently effects generic renewal by weaving intertextual references and antecedent reality factors into its generic frame. Now recognised as an enduring and popular genre product, the gangster film started life as a way of articulating a contemporary social problem, the development of organised crime in the emergent modern urban society of the American 'teens and 1920s. The silent screen was filled with stories that revealed political corruption, exploitative labour practices, prostitution, white slave racketeering and illegal drug trafficking. Many of these films were melodramatic rather than realist in structure; for example the films of Louise Weber often featured stories of prostitutes and other 'fallen' women saved from their fate worse than death by religion. A fervent religious reformer, Weber favoured the use of melodrama rather than realism because of its appeal to a wide audience.[18] Geoffrey Black links these early social issue films, many of which aimed to dignify the struggles of the urban poor, to the progressive reform movement in America, which was at its height before the First World War. The movement was responsible for widespread changes in American civic life, sponsoring legislation to fight corruption, educate the poor, regulate consumer goods and make cities generally more liveable in. The reformists, primarily white middle-class Anglo/European Catholics and Protestants, sought to maintain 'traditional' American values by reinforcing nineteenth-century attitudes on morality through the introduction of protective legislation, seeking to outlaw what they considered to be corrupting influences on the poor such as drinking houses, bordellos, dance halls and other immoral entertainments, such as pulp fictions, newspapers, melodramas and, of course, movies (Black 1994: 8). The reform movement aimed to convince filmmakers that their films should educate the public as well as entertain them, promoting the use of realism which was identified with morality and truth. The development of verisimilar acting codes based on a notion of restraint takes place within this context; Brownlow points to the variable aesthetics of social problem films at this time, caught in the shift between demands for greater realism and a continuing audience demand for melodrama that characterised the development of popular film style (Brownlow 1990: 203).

The gangster film developed throughout the 1920s, creating a new kind of anti-hero, a 'dead end kid', often the son of immigrant parents brought up on 'the wrong side of the tracks' who achieves the American dream of personal wealth, power and social status by leading a successful life of crime until a tragic flaw, usually his overweening pride, cuts him down in his prime. Gangster films were popular with the public throughout the 1920s, peaking with *Underworld* (1927), which won an Academy award and established the genre as top box-office material (Brownlow 1990: 206). The coming of sound in the late 1920s brought a renewed perception of verisimilitude to the genre. During the early 1930s, the screens were flooded with gangster films, some 78 films between 1930 and 1933 (Baxter, in Black 1994: 110). Stories of young ambitious lower-class men with no respect for authority shooting their way to the top had a certain cachet in an era of depression, poverty and unemployment. Flouting the law and traditional values of hard work and self-sacrifice, these gangster gun-toting heroes lived hard and died young, enjoying money, fast cars and fancy clothes. Admired by male and female characters within the diegesis for their power and ability to make money, gangsters such as Rico Bandello (Edward G. Robinson) in *Little Caesar* (1931), Tom Powers (James Cagney) in *Public Enemy* (1931) and Tony Camonte (Paul Muni) in *Scarface* (1932) captured the public imagination, making movie stars of the actors and money for the filmmakers.

Traumatised childhoods, male bonding and adult rites-of-passage are common themes in gangster movies since the 1930s. The early films hover between rhetorical commentary on social corruption and injustice, sentimental treatment of the theme and sensational depictions of violence considered at the time highly realistic. *Scarface* is a typical example and has achieved classic status as the most violent and most realistic of the 1930s cycle of gangster films. Based on the exploits of the notorious Al Capone and his control of organised crime in the city of Chicago during Prohibition, the film was considered outrageous in its day. The Hays Office demanded that the tag line *The Shame of the Nation* was added to the title to indicate that the film industry was not glorifying yet another gangster. Ghetto life is shown as tough and corrupt, its pervasive influence on the young used to explain adult criminality, while the struggle for money and power provides a vehicle for sensational action sequences and the violent shoot-outs that are now a familiar feature of the genre. Poverty (the real conditions of existence for many in the audience) is depicted as material deprivation through a sparse domestic mise-en-scène which is contrasted with the exotic and (ideal) abundantly rich interiors of the apartments and night clubs inhabited by the gangster heroes. Public concern with the gangster problem is foregrounded in montage sequences of sensational newspaper headlines that are seen on the one hand as 'accurate reportage' of organised crime, but on the other as tabloid sensationalism, exacerbating hero worship of the criminals rather than presenting an objective, critical analysis of events. This public debate is given diegetic space in *Scarface*; a group of concerned citizens visit one of the city's leading newspaper proprietors to complain about the newspaper's sensational treatment of the gang wars and the creation of gangsters as local celebrities who capture the news headlines, firing the public imagination with dreams of illicit success. The film integrates a public critique of sensationalism with images that serve, at least within the narrative flow of information, not only to depict the problem but to present it as an entertaining spectacle, thereby actively participating in the process of sensationalism that reform organisations were critical of, but containing that critique within the fictional world of the film. This is a typical early example of the film industry having it both ways; on the one hand seeking to provide violent and sensational entertainment, but on the other claiming its products are morally responsible vehicles for public debate.

These early 1930s films exemplify the blend of realism and spectacle that characterises classical style before the enforcement of the Production Code coerced filmmakers into creating a new breed of hero, typified by James Cagney switching his gangster roles to play a lawman in *G Man* (1935), and wiping out organised crime on the screen. By 1934, pressure groups in American society associated with the Catholic Legion of Decency had gathered sufficient momentum behind their campaigns to persuade millions of churchgoers to stay away from films that were considered morally salacious or excessively violent. This threat to box office dividends finally persuaded the film industry to comply with the Production Code by removing controversial content, particularly overtly graphic depictions of sex and violence, from all films. Until the 1950s the Code controlled screen content, demanding respectful treatment of those in authority (particularly law enforcement officials and politicians), of religious faiths of all denominations, avoidance of socio-political themes and overt depiction of sexual behaviour. Compensating moral values were demanded in the plots of all films where any character indulged in crime or 'illicit' sexual activity.

In the more liberal climate of the 1980s and 1990s films featuring powerful dynastic families and their connections with international crime syndicates and illegal business continue to provide raw material for spectacular real-isation on the big screen. Based on the successful combination of the traditional gangster format of official corruption and mob violence with the epic family saga established in films such as *The Godfather* (1972), filmmakers continue to make films which, on the one hand, claim verisimilitude in the antecedent realities of criminal syndication and gang violence, and on the other exploit the potential for real-isation of abundant displays of wealth, material consumption and extreme violence. The remake of *Scarface* in 1982 begins with a plausible claim to the reality of antecedent events through its use of what appears to be 'authentic' newsreel footage of the communist leader Fidel Castro talking about the forcible extradition of criminals from Cuba, claiming that he is ridding society of undesirable elements. This grainy black and white 'news' footage is intercut with colour documentary styled sequences of the hazardous journey undertaken by the outcasts as they sail to the United States seeking political asylum. The refugees are shown landing in Florida, where they are interned in an immigration camp and questioned by American officials. It is at this point that the film abruptly shifts from using the observational camerawork associated with documentary to classical conventions of continuity: a questioning session between a refugee and immigration officials becomes the focus of narrative interest through the use of medium close-ups and shot/reverse-shot editing which dramatically reveals the scarred face of one of the refugees. Instantly recognisable to gangster film fans, Al Pacino is a star well-known for his tough persona and criminal roles.

The story that follows is identical in almost every aspect to the plot of *Scarface* (1932), updated by altering its contextual background from the Prohibition era of the 1920s to the illegal drugs trade in Florida in the early 1980s. Notably missing from this version of the story however is any reference to the press or a public discourse of protest that accuses the media of sensationalism. Instead, the film suggests a rather different public agenda, one that starts from a narrative premise of 'undesirable others' entering the United States, situating the Cuban immigrants as a corrupting influence who, in their desire for money and success, resort to illegal activities and violent behaviour. The price exacted for pursuing such a path once again emphasises the overweening hubris of personal ego envisioned through the spectacle of material consumption and scenes of spectacular violence. Towards the end of the film, Scarface is dwarfed by the material sumptuousness of his surroundings in a manner reminiscent of the vast empty spaces of Xanadu occupied by the ageing Kane, an image redolent of isolation and moral bankruptcy. Locked behind the steel doors in his fortified mansion, he sits at a huge desk, a vast mountain of white powder in front of him, his expression vacant, his mouth and nose covered with the substance that is the source of his wealth, his power and his downfall. Here the mise-en-scène serves symbolic and narrative ends, underlining the moral of the film and its anti-drugs stance, in spite of the scenes of graphic violence which constitute much of the film's action. Once again, the spectacle of excess supports the moral message, that the wages of sin is death. If this moral meaning can be read from the film's symbolic associations, a realist reading confronts an ambiguity at the heart of the film's politics: it seems critical of an over-liberal establishment that can no longer distinguish between political dissidents and exiled criminals from nearby Cuba, the communist thorn in the flesh of the American liberal state. Given public concern and debate at the time on questions of immigration, border control and the drug problem, linking these reference points to its narrative schemata through the use of documentary newsgathering techniques undoubtedly gave the film a contemporary frisson which is now lost. In contrast to this use of realism to reference antecedent events, the use of expressionist technique in the form of a symbolic mise-en-scène emphasises individual character psychology; Scarface is not only a product of social and environmental factors such as poverty and exclusion, but a weak character with a tragic flaw.

By the 1980s and 1990s, the gangster film's roots in any antecedent discourse of social reality is largely obscured by 'high concept' aesthetics that foreground stylistic excess, its entertainment value articulated through accrued layers of generic self-reflexivity and intertextuality. Jim Collins proposes that this self-reflexive 'genericity' appears in two forms in contemporary cinema, one based on parody, the other a nostalgic re-creation of traditional styles termed by Collins 'the new sincerity' (Collins 1993). The stylistic pot-pourri of contemporary filmmaking practice is characterised by using generic codes and conventions as a dominant part of a film's system of motivations: artistic motivation and intertextuality have become inseparable. Collins's second category, the new sincerity, is of particular relevance, not only because it draws on audience pre-knowledge of the forms and themes of popular genre cinema, but because it uses this knowledge to claim verisimilitude for its own status as a 'truthful' representation. One example will serve to illustrate the point in more detail. *Sleepers'* (1996) marketing strategy and its cast, headed by Robert De Niro, Dustin Hoffman and Brad Pitt, seems to promise a contemporary twist to the 'dead end kids' saga in the tradition of *Angels with Dirty Faces* (1938). Based on a best-selling controversial autobiographical novel, the film was billed as 'a tense drama of four friends growing up in a notorious area of downtown New York whose futures are determined by a juvenile prank that changes their lives for ever'.[19] The content of the story and the manner of its telling are indicative of the 'mix and match' techniques of contemporary big budget filmmaking: a 'true story' of the problems of growing up, a staple of American made-for-TV movie formats, is given the high concept values more commonly associated with contemporary gangster and romance fictions.

The film opens in the nostalgic, playful mode of coming-of-age films established by *American Graffiti* (1973), constituting its period setting through the use of a Beach Boys sound track. Voice-over narration provides the continuity for a series of cameos of life in Hell's Kitchen, an area of New York notorious for its criminality. Domestic violence is rife, divorce non-existent, we are told, because the Catholic church maintains a vice-like grip on personal morality. Eschewing the grainy shooting style often associated with depicting 'low life' poverty and criminality, the film is shot in soft focus using colour tones of warm browns, reds and yellows; the style unashamedly seeks to reflect the rose-tinted memories of the narrator who tells of an innocent boyhood where the only temptation is a career in crime. Generic intertextuality is omnipresent, constructing character types and actions through a diegetic public memory that repetitively references 1930s gangster films: Father O'Brien (De Niro) is an unashamed recreation of the priest made famous by the actor Pat O'Brien in *Angels with Dirty Faces*; 'Little Caesar', the adopted name of a contemporary drug baron, refers to the character played by Edward G. Robinson in an early 1930s gangster film. The boys are told stories about the great gangster heroes of yesteryear by an older generation who see in these old movies the only public recognition of the history of their lives. Black and white footage accompanies these stories, fictionalised images of characters such as Al Capone (*Scarface* 1933) performing a documentary function; within the film's diegesis film history becomes 'real' history.

The lengthy depiction of idyllic childhood innocence ends abruptly when the boys are sent to prison reform school for a petty crime that misfires. As the prison doors clang shut the soft pink and brown hues of nostalgia abruptly end, replaced by colder blue, green and grey colour tones and a lens with a harder focus. A bleak depiction of daily life, characteristic of the prison genre, is intercut by short black and white sequences of expressionistic montage to indicate horrific scenes of rape and torture inflicted on the boys by their guards. A walk down a long dark corridor ends in a montage of acutely angled close-ups of terrorised faces and naked body parts, a recurring symbol of the boys' journey from innocence to experience that indicates not only the brutality and sexual abuse they experience

but its shattering psychological effects. The simple dualities of good
and bad that govern neighbourhood morality are violently over-
turned by the authoritarian regime of the prison. Entry to the symbolic world of manhood is literally and metaphorically one of
subjugation to their male captors, representatives of state law and of
symbolic law, the patriarchy and the Lacanian Law of the Father.
    Ten years later: a violent shooting in a bar catapults the film into
its third generic mode, the legal thriller. Two of the boys have followed a life of crime and are now professional killers and hopeless
drug addicts; in a bar, they recognise one of their former captors and
kill him. A third boy, Michael (Brad Pitt), has found a way out of the
ghetto and become an assistant district attorney; he is assigned to
prosecute the case. The fourth boy (now identified as the narrator)
is a newspaper reporter. Together, they decide to rig the case in the
interests of vengeance on those who abused them and, with the help
of their old neighbourhood contacts, take revenge on the remaining
three abusers. Surprisingly, in terms of plot motivation and expectation, the revelations of abuse that emerge at the trial serve only to
provide a hook for narrative suspense: will Father O'Brien (Robert
De Niro), knowing the circumstances that motivated the shooting,
lie on the witness stand to defend the two killers? Needless to say,
he provides the necessary alibi and the film concludes as it began,
awash with nostalgic sentimentality as the boys, all together for the
last time, celebrate their victory. In this context, the final narrated
coda that tells us what happens to the characters seems oddly out of
place, a claim to a pre-known diegetic reality formally unconstituted
by the film's generic codes and rationales. The re-emergence of the
narrating voice completes the circle of story logic but by breaking
the conventions of the legal drama in implausible ways, the film has
lost its anchor in generic verisimilitude. Because generic intertextuality cannot finally reconcile character motivation at the level of
narrative plausibility, this highly emotive film is unsatisfying at a
number of levels. As a depiction of a contemporary social issue, the
psychological effects of rape and sexual abuse on young males in
institutional care, it raises fundamental concerns about contemporary masculinity, male power and control and the relationship
between individual acts of brutality and institutionalised violence,
the keeping and breaking of rules and laws, questions of justice and
revenge. The spectacular depiction of sexual abuse becomes a substitute for the ritual violence normally associated with the gangster

movie, transforming the film from action picture to male melodrama, but the excessive stylisation of these sequences within the film's mise-en-scène, in a similar way to the perceived excess of violence in 1930s films in their day, serves to sensationalise and sentimentalise the issues raised by the film rather than confront them. But unlike the 1930s films, with no anchor of plausibility in a public diegesis (in this case the trial), the signifying codes of the film become hermeneutically sealed and cannot connect, other than at the level of emotional empathic response, to wider debates on the topic circulating in the public sphere. Unable to resolve the various expectations created by conflicting visual styles and generic formats, the film can only finish as it began, awash with nostalgic memory.

Sleepers is a good example of the kind of filmmaking practice embraced by the term 'high concept'. Issue-based content, of itself, cannot anchor a film in realism. Realism is a system not only of narrative logic but of mise-en-scène, characterisation, situation and event motivated by various forms of antecedent and generic referentiality, some of which we have touched on here. In spite of commercial demands for films based on 'high concept' marketing formulas, and the continual predictions that big budget spectaculars will squeeze other types of filmmaking out of the market place, the segregation of the mass audience into numerous taste cultures has so far ensured the continuing production of films that seek not only to entertain, but to engage in social and political issues of contemporary relevance and debate. Social problem and social issue films are subject to the same terms of narrative engagement and adjustment as other genre films, but they foreground particular sets of prototypes and procedural schemata, using cues, patterns and gaps that draw heavily on pre-knowledge of the social world. It is through their use of shared assumptions of aspects of daily life found in, for example, gender role schemata, social attitudes and cultural conventions, that these films are accused of perpetuating dominant ideological norms, but it is equally possible to suggest that they have the potential to engage our perceptions of the social world in ways which can be illuminating. We take up these issues in Chapter 5 and Part II of the book, but before we proceed to a more detailed examination of social problem and social issue films in the 1990s, we want to draw together some of the formal aspects of realism that continue to inform contemporary films and summarise some of their principal characteristics.

Notes

1 Justin Wyatt (1994) offers a critical definition of the aesthetics of 'high concept' in *High Concept: Movies and Marketing in Hollywood.*
2 For a full account of classical style, see D. Bordwell (1985: 1–70).
3 On science fiction and genre, see, for example, James Donald (1989) and Annette Kuhn (1990).
4 For particular examples of this approach, see Noel Carroll (1996) and David Bordwell and Noel Carroll (1996).
5 In an audience study of why people enjoy watching violent films, Hill concludes that viewers are testing the boundaries of their own response to depictions of screen violence. See A. Hill (1997).
6 See, for example, Barker and Brooks (1998) for an account of audience responses to the film adaptation of the cartoon character Judge Dredd.
7 For a full account, see S. Bach (1986).
8 The concerns about the costs of *Titanic,* with production costs in excess of $200 million, created a fever of anxiety; failure at the box office might have created a different climate for film production into the new millennium. For a critical account of the effects of this success on independent film production in a British context, see Sally Hibbin (1998).
9 See, for example, Tom Gunning (1990b) on the relationship between spectacle and the avant-garde.
10 We discuss perceptual realism in more detail in Chapter 5.
11 Wyatt points to this tendency in the professional discourse of the industry trade journals, where the term 'high concept' is often used to suggest creative bankruptcy within Hollywood. See J. Wyatt (1994: 13–15).
12 See, for example, Tasker's comments in *Spectacular Bodies: Gender, Genre and the Action Cinema* on the equation of realism with the sensibilities of liberal critics (1993: 100–5). We take up this issue in more depth in Chapter 6.
13 See, for example, Jonathan Romney, 'Terminated', *Guardian,* 21 December 1997.
14 For an account of AIP in the 1950s, see M. Jancovich (1996: 198–218).
15 See R. Maltby and I. Craven (1995: 153–7) for a succinct account of the development of widescreen systems as an example of the links between technological and economic forces in shaping the appearance and realism of Hollywood movies.
16 Edward Dwight Easty, *On Method Acting,* 1st edn., New York: Allograph Press 1966, quoted in R. Maltby and I. Craven (1995: 257–63).
17 See Steve Cohan (1992) and Jackie Byars (1991) for accounts of gender and sexuality in *Rebel Without a Cause* (1955).
18 See A. Acker (1991) and Annette Kuhn (1988) for the effects of censorship on the narrative structures of early films aimed at female audiences.
19 Video cover, *Sleepers* (Levinson 1996).

Chapter 4

The epic of the everyday: notes towards a continuum

Realism can express the gritty, the mundane, the horrific, the dramatic across a range of photographic, cinematic and televisual aesthetics. The development of audiovisual technologies has been driven not so much by a realist project as by an illusionary *one. The illusion of the real has had to be made more convincing and the spectacular has had to be made more realistic. The second-hand has to become first-hand, the vicarious has had to be made vivid. Audiovisual technologies have had to make illusions realities.* (Hayward and Wollen, 1993: 1–2, emphasis in original)

Kaminski films all of it in faded, grainy, newsreel-quality footage, so that we all know that this is the way the war really looked.[1]

In an age where 'the real' can be simulated through computer modelling without the need for material objects or events to generate the image, a conception of realism as a representation of reality seems outmoded. It seems more appropriate to think about how realist aesthetics mediate our conceptions of everyday realities both past and present, for it is this ordinary, everyday aspect of realism that dominates Western audiovisual culture in the late twentieth century. In his writings, Raymond Williams frequently returned to questions of realism, an interest that was motivated not by cataloguing the codes and conventions of realist works, but in exploring the complex relationships between the shapes and forms of artistic expression and their adequacy to describe social experience. For Williams, the abiding shifts in late eighteenth- and nineteenth-century drama – social extension, the use of contemporary settings and an emphasis on actions and events in the present, and (in Williams's view, most importantly) an emphasis on secular action, which is associated with rationalism and of scientific and historical attitudes towards society – become frequently conventional by the

latter part of the twentieth century, but the contexts in which drama
is created, produced and viewed have changed beyond all recognition. Whereas dramatic and literary realism were once attributable
to a white, middle-class bourgeois sensibility and a belief in rationality and scientific progress, today that cultural link is stretched and
inextricably entwined with the daily lives of those who consume fiction films and drama on television as part of their everyday, lived
experience. Tracing a history of realism and film in Chapter 1, we
noted the ethical concerns brought to bear on filmmakers by citizen
groups who saw themselves as responsible for the moral health of
American society, reflected in the growth of numerous reform movements who sought to infuse the developing film industry with a sense
of social and duty and moral purpose. Critics of popular culture
have always tended to regard Hollywood cinema as a conventional
and conservative system of organising narrative fiction that relies on
a mimetic, rather than a referential system of organising logic and
plausibility. In terms of 1970s ideology critique, Hollywood constructs false (idealised, utopian) constructions of the real world
which are validated through mimetic (realist) strategies. In contrast,
social-democratic and Left-leaning filmmakers, often as part of an
agenda to construct a national aesthetic, have stressed the referentiality of realism, incorporating a suitably existential and moral seriousness into their treatment of everyday life.

In Chapter 2, 'Realist Moments', we examined how issues of realism have inflected political and nationalist discourses about cinema
throughout much of the earlier part of this century, culminating in
the post-war period in the harnessing of realism to a 'progressive'
political agenda that sought to show people how things 'really are'
by applying Williams's principles to new forms of filmmaking practice in the context of growing competition for the audience from
television. Since the 1970s, there has been little critical interest in
addressing the continuing uses of realism in film or its ongoing, if
somewhat diminished, potential to critically engage with contemporary social and political issues. Currently, realism is conceived as
'everywhere', the dominant media aesthetic of late twentieth-century Western societies, but at the same time critically it is 'nowhere',
except in the writings of those traditionally excluded from mainstream representation. Some African-American filmmakers and critics, for example, as we noted in Chapter 2, continue to view realism
as a potential tool in their fight against the homogenising tendencies

of Hollywood film production. As their work testifies, realism continues to inform a range of filmmaking practices that invoke both
ethical and political concerns. In this chapter we aim to identify
some of the modes of contemporary realist film practice currently in
use. Examples of such a practice are identified by critics in neorealist films such as *Bicycle Thieves* (the Italian context) and *Saturday
Night and Sunday Morning* (the British context). Films such as
Straight Out of Brooklyn and *Menace 11 Society* are similarly concerned with existential issues, moral seriousness and an emphasis on
their referentiality to external social realities. If realism can be said
to have an abiding legacy, it is one of a dual commitment to ethical
and political principles and a refusal of conventional, mimetic (classical) frames of reference. However, we will suggest that referentiality and moral seriousness cannot straightforwardly be separated
from the mainstream paradigm in contemporary filmmaking practice. This is, in part, a consequence of economic determinations. The
relationship between independent and mainstream production is by
no means clear cut, with convergence of funding, distribution and
exhibition between all sectors of the film and television industries
increasingly prevalent. The financing of films is increasingly dependent on co-production deals and distribution across a range of exhibition 'windows' or outlets. As Wyatt has noted, this has
undoubtedly affected the range of aesthetic strategies used by filmmakers seeking to address large audiences. We examine the aesthetics of films that tackle local issues while addressing the globalising
tendencies of the industry in more depth in Chapter 7. Here, importantly, it must be pointed out that the 'moral seriousness' which has
traditionally accompanied alternative modes of realist filmmaking
practice is not necessarily regarded as a positive factor in the current
socio-political cultural climate. The terms on which disaffection
from Williams's conception of a politics of progressive incorporation are often articulated (and sometimes subsumed) are those of the
postmodern condition, a structure of feeling which often, falsely,
attributes a lack of critical meaningfulness to all forms of filmic and
televisual texts, when it is perhaps a rather simplistic notion of 'progressiveness', rather than the forms of expression themselves, which
has become exhausted.

The films chosen for examination here have all been dubbed 'realist' in one way or another by the reviewing establishment and are
indicative of the breadth of definitions currently in play. Here, we

attempt to systemise the codes and conventions of these texts in more detail and construct, for heuristic purposes, a typology of the range of strategies employed in pursuit of referentiality and an ethical standpoint on social and political issues. Popular film has moved out of the cinema and into the home at the same time that it has continued to seek spectacular differentiation from television's familiar modes of address. The aesthetics of high concept, by weakening the relationship between causal narration and character motivation and creating a strong match between image and soundtrack through the use of extended montage sequences, foreground the artifice and construction of spectacular real-isation. Lifestyle modelling and character quotation obviate the need for in-depth development of character psychology, shifting the focus of the narrative away from delineation of character traits and causal chains of narrative events towards a more aggregated style of entertainment. In contrast, television dramas (particularly in Britain) continue to emphasise how both characters and their situations are 'just like us' through their construction of the televisual world as a parallel everyday reality, while various forms of docusoap, surveillance and participant observation programming inform much of television's factual output. Films that seek to address contemporary social and political issues are rarely produced according to 'high concept' formats (although *Sleepers*, a story of institutional sexual abuse of young offenders, is, as we discussed in Chapter 3, exactly this kind of film). Rather, they rework classical Hollywood conventions and/or adopt frameworks which use codes and conventions associated with televisual immediacy to position characters and their situations in relation to everyday life. Within this context, a conception of realism as a hybridised continuum of signifying conventions operating across a wide range of production practices seems more appropriate to an analysis of contemporary films than the neoformalist and ideological models of realism currently on offer in film studies, briefly outlined in Chapter 1. The continuum is an interpretative framework that uses formalist analysis to indicate the shifting modes of mimesis and referentiality that are continually in play as filmmakers attempt to mediate a significant relationship between viewers and the antecedent facts and experiential realities which inform the fiction. Rather than suggesting that any of these strategies are inherently more 'realistic' or 'progressive' than any other, this inclusive concept of realism allows us to examine the codes and conventions deemed 'realist' by popular criticism and consider, in Part II of the book, the contribution such films can make to contemporary debates on contentious social and political issues. We do not claim a privileged space for realist aesthetics within this imaginary, only an acknowledgement that realism continues to negotiate antecedent realities in ways which may still have the potential to be provocative.

The formalist distinction between the *fabula* (the raw material of the story) and the *syuzhet* (the ways in which this raw material is shaped and transformed by artistic procedures) is a useful one in this context: how is story material shaped and transformed to create plausible framings of pre-filmic, anterior socio-political situations and events that correspond to current conceptions of realism as an aesthetic of everyday life? For heuristic purposes, films attempting to engage with social and political issues can be divided into three groups based on their narrational relationship to antecedent reality factors. These we have labelled:

a) *Expositional realism*, where an episodic or picaresque narrative structure aims to explicate the relationship between characters and their environment. This has close associations with neorealism and is similar to Bordwell's formulation of 'objective' realism, but often includes, in its contemporary form, elements which he would consider 'classical', such as an emphasis on the psychology of the principal character(s).

b) *Rhetorical realism*, where an argument is presented to convince the audience of the truth of the film's proposition. Rhetorical films are sometimes expositional, but more frequently they adopt the conventions of classical narrative and melodrama through an emphasis on an individual's heroic actions within the context of a personal socio-political dilemma.

c) *Spectacular realism* uses large budgets and high production values to create epic biographical narratives about characters whose lives are enmeshed in a matrix of socio-historical events. This is a common practice in classical narrative cinema but, within the context of post-classical high concept aesthetics, becomes more intentional as a sign of commitment to a particular ethics of filmmaking practice and style.

In practice, the three types share many similar features: both spectacular realism and expositional realism can be rhetorical, expositional realism can be used in spectacular films, and expositional films arguably spectacularise actorly performance and the everyday environment. A further link between the three types is their relationship to antecedent reality factors; fictional content is invariably drawn from factual reportage and eyewitness accounts of known events, autobiographical and biographical sources as well as official histories. In order to establish a recognisable relationship with these antecedents, many films use a range of codes and conventions associated with the reality claims of other contemporary media forms, particularly documentary and newsgathering techniques, but including more personal forms, such as camcorder footage, home movies and video diaries. Rather than suggesting that any of these formal techniques necessarily offers a more 'truthful' account (indeed, it is often claims to veracity which excite controversy and debate amongst commentators), we prefer to think about their codes and conventions as a signifying continuum that extends from the documenting functions of the camera and microphone used as tools of surveillance and observation to the highly wrought artifice that constitutes the spectacular realism of the epic film.

Within the signifying continuum, it is possible to break down the use of codes and conventions into four groups through which the relation to the real is activated.

a) First of all, through mise-en-scène, various modalities of referentiality are signified. Some of these we have already pointed out in our chapter on genre: they can be summarised as authentic recreation of setting through use of location, the furnishing of sets and locations with objects that are narrationally obsolete, a use of costume and set furnishings that correspond to popular and officially perceived notions of authenticity, and the use of actors (or non-actors) whose body type, facial characteristics and speech correspond with recognisable schemata drawn from everyday life. This physical verisimilitude is an essential element of realist aesthetics and is invariably accompanied by a soundtrack design in which underscore is absent or minimised: the use of diegetic sound is favoured, with characters uttering forms of speech that correspond to their social situation, location and circumstances.

b) Second, there is the organisation of the characters and objects within the frame; classical filmmaking takes great care to position characters and objects in balanced compositions. The lexicon of standard filmmaking practice favours character-centred compositions that emphasise the face of the character who is speaking, or focus on the reaction of the character who is being addressed. The organisation of screen space serves narrative ends; camera movements such as reframing and refocusing support character centred motivation and causality. In contrast, films that claim a referential relationship to antecedent experiential realities often subvert these paradigmatic classical codes, favouring techniques associated with television factuality genres such as documentary, surveillance and newsgathering forms. Primarily, these consist of observational, static camerawork that creates the impression of raw, unmediated footage or 'hand held' camera work that creates an unsteady image and the impression that the operator is a participant observer, caught up in the thick of action and events. Here, the claim to veracity is deferred rather than direct, the referential link relying on the signifying veracity of modes of filmmaking associated with the use of the camera and microphone as recording instruments.

c) Third, editing organises shot sequence: the paradigmatic text uses the 'invisible' or unnoticed codes of continuity editing. In contrast, expositional practices favour the use of mid-shots and long shots, use longer shot lengths and cut to a different scheme that tends to favour, for example, two-shot compositions of character interaction rather than the field/reverse-field shooting patterns of continuity editing. In practice, the combination of shooting and editing techniques used in contemporary films is far less rigid than this, as we will discuss in more detail below.

d) Fourth, the distinctive use of technology to 'real-ise' fantasy sequences, as discussed in Chapter 3, can also be used in spectacular realism to create both historical and contemporary authenticity in the service of a broad referentiality to antecedent factors. This has less to do with anchoring the text in physical verisimilitude and mimesis than securing viewer engagement to a socio-historical matrix and is primarily epistemological rather than ontological in character, aiming to engage general knowledge of place and events rather than specific, embodied experiences. It is rarely used in low budget productions, hence our designation of this technique as a particular feature of spectacular realism.

Definitions of the realist film have historically depended on a style of filmmaking practice that has close associations with Bordwell's concept of the 'objective realism' found in neorealist art cinema: films with a location shot mise-en-scène; acting that corresponds to a recognisable plausibility of motivations and responses, both psychological and physical, in everyday life; and events and situations that are credible not only in terms of the film's loose, episodic narrative structure, but in terms of antecedent, factual credibility (Bordwell 1988:217). Expositional films combine looser, episodic narrative structures with location shooting and observational or participant/observer camera techniques, but, unlike 'objective realism', create detailed character-centred studies of lifestyles and events that are often the subject of social concern. British films such as *Secrets and Lies* (1996) and *Nil by Mouth* (1998) exemplify this form of filmmaking practice, emphasising dialogue and performance as a focus for viewer engagement rather than action and events. At the other extreme, spectacular realism can weave a discourse of social concern into the generic framework of popular formats such as the legal drama, the police procedural, the coming-of-age youth movie and the bio-pic to create a parallel fictional world. *Do the Right Thing* (1989) uses the conventions of the coming-of-age youth movie to tell a story of racial conflict; *Philadelphia* (1993) uses the conventions of the legal drama to tell a story about AIDS. Within these narrative frameworks, codes and conventions are variously combined to suggest a range of engagements with antecedent reality. One of the most popular narrative strategies is to construct an argument, to make a case for social or political justice based on a controversial topic or known instance of public debate. *Ladybird, Ladybird* (1994) argues for the rights of a mother to rear her children by presenting her story through a combination of observational camerawork and character-centred narration. *First Do No Harm* (1996) criticises the blinkered attitudes of the American medical establishment and its culture of drug-dependent treatment through a more conventional use of omniscient narration and star-led character-centred action.

Expositional realism: space, place and characterisation

Expositional films explore social issues through character-centred narration but have looser, less predictable plot structures than classical films, emphasising the locatedness of characters in particular environments. These films explore the milieu of characters who lack motivation in the conventional sense, people who are often alienated from themselves and their social world, driven by internal anguish and despair, such as Johnny (David Thewlis) in *Naked* (1993) and Hubert and his friends in *La Haine* (1995). Alternatively, expositional realism can present minority lifestyles and identities as a positive option to conventional life under patriarchy: *Go Fish* (1994), for example, celebrates the lives and loves of a community of women who share same-sex preferences. Exposition can also afford a privileged view of characters conventionally positioned as outcasts or villains within the classical structure. *Henry, Portrait of a Serial Killer* (1986), as the title suggests, depicts the everyday life of a murderer without explicating any causal motivations for his actions. Broadly speaking, expositional films explore the private worlds of individual characters or groups; visually, the films construct social space as a character-centred environment, giving the films something of the flavour of contemporary ethnography.

The realist strategies adopted by these films are closely related to many of the conventions found in the post-war European art cinema. These include characters without clear-cut motives or goals who are less constrained by the chains of cause-and-effect motivation typical of classical films, more dependent on chance meetings and the chaos of uncontrollable events. The films depict relationships between characters and events without providing external motivations to drive the action; events happen, they are not always explained, their purpose and significance serving to reveal character psychology rather than drive the plot. In *Naked*, Johnny's aimless wandering around London has no motivation other than his desire to leave the claustrophobic environment of the flat he is staying in. *La Haine* features the aimless wandering of three friends subjected to constant harassment from the police who are seeking the perpetrators of the previous night's rioting. The time frame in both films has no causal relationship to character action and events, but is imposed by external constraints that accentuate, particularly in *La Haine*, the characters' lack of control over existential factors. Closure results from chance meetings: in *La Haine* with yet another confrontation with the police, which this time ends in violence; in *Naked* with Johnny continuing his random wanderings. Sometimes the characters are the victims of social circumstances beyond their control: in *La Haine*, unemployment and urban riots generate the boredom and aimless activities of the three main protagonists. Johnny in *Naked* is similarly driven by a sense of anomie, his nocturnal wanderings around the streets of London a series of chance meetings and accidental encounters. Bordwell calls this form of narration 'the boundary situation'; the film's causal impetus derives from the protagonist's recognition that she or he faces a crisis of existential significance (Bordwell 1988: 208). In expositional realism, unlike in art cinema or modernist narration, the contrast between 'objective' and 'subjective' verisimilitude with its corresponding disruptions in space and time is limited. These films are sparing in the use of techniques conventionally associated with depicting internal mental states such as dreams, memories, daydreams and fantasies. *Bad Lieutenant* (1992) is a good example of such a limited use, but even here the sequences which depict the character's visions are logically motivated by his drug-induced state, itself a result of existential loneliness and personal guilt which cannot be assuaged by a frantic ingestion of narcotics and alcohol.

Expositional films often use space and time in ways that are superfluous to classical realism. Cross-cutting between different locations is infrequent, creating a sense of ongoing temporal and spatial immediacy; cutting within sequences is motivated to depict details that reveal character psychology rather than driven by the effects of character action. Characters are often shown interacting in two-shot, rather than field/reverse-field shooting; direct point-of-view shots are reserved for particular purposes. This style of shooting is often described as an observational form of *vérité* or fly-on-the-wall documentary, but the analogy does not withstand close analysis. 'Documentary realism' has become a standard term for referencing a broad range of conventions associated with the 'gritty' look and sound of film texts rather than their narrative conventions. Maintaining a static observational camera, or alternatively following a character as if capturing their actions and interactions as they occur, extends the reality effect by an apparent lack of directorial control over camera and audio-visual input. Although expositional films are invariably location shot with 'wild' or found sound audio tracks, a limited use of continuity editing invariably sustains the character-centred narration of the classical film.

The depiction of actions regarded as redundant by conventional narrative standards is often perceived as a hallmark of realism. In *On the Waterfront*, a 1950s film about corruption in the American labour unions, the central protagonist played by Marlon Brando conveys his mental turmoil and confusion through his actions, facial expression and voice; he fumbles and drops small objects, averts his gaze in conversation, hesitates and mumbles incoherently. Today, such characterisations seem excessively contrived, but at the time this 'excess' of acting endeavour was perceived as realist because of its attention to detail considered redundant in the narrative economy of the film. In contemporary expositional films, the revelation of a character's psychological state often becomes overt through the accumulation of small but significant details. *Spanking the Monkey* (1995) uses close-ups to accentuate a growing awareness of sexual desire between a teenage boy and his mother, confined to bed with a broken leg after an accident. Their awkward but developing intimacy is depicted through close-up shots of the boy's hands engaged in physical contact with his mother's body. Aspects of daily washing, foot and thigh massage, lifting and carrying his mother to the toilet are shown in close-up and mid-shot amidst long shots of the other routine tasks of daily life – preparing food, shopping, walking the dog and continuing his study. Tension is generated in this film by restricting the use of the close-up (usually used to show a character's facial expression and reaction or to direct viewer attention to narrationally significant cues) to actions that have no apparent significance until the film nears its climax. It is only when the sexual desire between mother and son is consummated that the clues divulged by the shooting and editing techniques become apparent.

Observation of a character performing routine tasks takes precedence in spatial and temporal terms to the demands of narrative action and progression. Viewer engagement rests on a preparedness to accumulate the numerous visual details provided by this apparently extraneous camerawork, without knowing which details will necessarily become significant to an interpretation of the narrative. This disruption of classical conventions was used by feminist filmmaker Chantal Ackerman in her portrayal of the daily life of a 'respectable' Belgian housewife who works as a prostitute, *Jeanne Dielman, 23 quai du Commerce 1080 Bruxelles* (1975). Ackerman provides an intimate picture of Jeanne's everyday life in a long film (approximately four hours), during which time the minutiae of her monotonous daily activities are recorded by a static, observational camera. Amidst the welter of repetition of insignificant and extraneous narrative information, a change in the smallest of details becomes noticeable; a button left undone on a blouse, a task not fully completed takes on narrative significance. Slowly, Jeanne Dielman's tidy life painfully disintegrates, the loss of control of her immediate environment an outward symptom of interior breakdown that eventually culminates in an extreme act of violence, the murder of her client stabbed to death with a pair of household scissors.

Since the construction of everyday life depends upon an apparent stripping away of artifice, choices about lighting and film stock aim to replicate the appearance of genres closely associated with the everyday and the ordinary. There is often a self-conscious imitation of camcorder actuality images or of home movie footage shot on amateur formats, which aims at the flat, less vivid and slightly grainier quality typical of video footage or cheaper production formats such as 8mm and 16mm film. Lighting is rarely overt, its noticeable presence often confined to sources within the diegesis, such as windows and lamps. Characters are not lit to stand out, but disappear into the background. In *Naked*, much of the shooting takes place at night: characters are illuminated by the lights from office buildings and shop windows. Colour is often muted or drained from the image, tending towards the use of a particular spectrum to depict certain situations: blues, greys and browns tend to predominate in films often described as 'gritty' depictions of urban life, such as *Naked*; soft browns, greens and yellows in 'natural' rural environments, such as *Spanking the Monkey*.

Choices about film colour reference a range of audio-visual and filmic realities; *Go Fish*, a low budget feature film set in an urban environment, combines a grainy textured black and white image with stylised shooting techniques. The clichés of 'kitchen sink' realism are avoided by the frequent use of an aerial shot of the head and shoulders of three women, the crowns of their heads touching at the centre of the image, talking and joking about their experiences. In *Go Fish*, the narration is episodic, the collectively experienced lifestyle of the group depicted through the device of multiple narrators who, between them, reveal individual aspects of their communal life. The shooting style of much of the film has strong connotations with 'fly on the wall' *vérité*: unknown actors deliver performances that play to each other rather than to the camera. Instead of classically situating characters within the frame or creating a point of view for the viewer from the fourth wall of the fictional space, the camera fits in with events happening around it, creating an apparently unstaged visual style that roams around the space following whatever events appear to capture the interest of the camera operator. Interruptions, partially heard sentences, meanings obscured by accent, dialect and the use of slang emphasise the locatedness of characters in their physical environment and their varied social identities. The fluctuating intensity of the soundtrack adds to the film's credentials as a low budget independent feature. Produced outside the mainstream for a specific audience, Go Fish flaunts the conventions of its own construction in the interests of staking a claim on the authenticity of its representation, aiming to present a more truthful mediation of the everyday lives of a socially marginalised group.

Acting in expositional realism can entail the kind of low-key ensemble performance seen in Go Fish, but equally the focus on character can lead to virtuoso performances; in Britain, a focus on the performing abilities of actors is commonly associated with the films of Mike Leigh.[2] Characters are constructed according to researched and observed behaviour of similar character types and developed through improvisation. Improvisation is often used to generate a sense of emerging character traits that reveal, little by little, more about the psychological make-up of the characters. Sometimes such a production strategy involves placing actors in particular situations to gain the necessary experience to be convincing in their role; sometimes actors are chosen because they have worked in a similar milieu to the one they are recreating. Ken Loach, for example, a director noted for his political commitment and preference for realism, often uses unknown actors who have had experience of being the characters they are representing. In Riff-Raff (1991), a film about the illegal employment of labourers on a building site in London, Loach sought actors who had experience of the building trade. Body type and appearance are a key element in casting: performers have to look the part to be convincing. Using unknown actors breaks the conventional codes of lifestyle modelling and physical attractiveness that rule the star system and paradigmatic depictions of standard 'types', such as villains. But typecasting of supporting characters and subsidiary roles still has an important function; actors who can look and sound authentic within the setting are often selected to complement a sense of place.

The content of contemporary expositional films tends towards the revelation of social taboos, violence and non-conformist behaviours, often in graphic detail. *Henry, Portrait of a Serial Killer* depicts Henry and his friend Otis raping and murdering a family. The sequence is revealed as home movie camcorder footage shot on video, relayed to the viewer via the television screen in Henry's lounge. Using realism to depict taboo aspects of social and sexual behaviour has a long history, one that can claim a close relationship to the empirical environmentalism of nineteenth-century literary realism that aimed to 'show life as it is' through stripping away artifice and convention. Contemporary exposition attempts a similar 'effect of the real' by adapting the visual codes and conventions associated with actuality footage and home movies. Often offering no obvious point-of-view structure to encourage alignment with characters, viewers are situated outside the fictional diegesis in a position that invites fascination with watching the 'other' that is reminiscent of the viewing relations associated with screening ethnographic films. They offer a voyeuristic view, an observational look at characters and their lifestyles, presented as objects, as a spectacle for the viewer's gaze. We are reminded here of a common Liverpudlian colloquialism, 'don't make a show of me'; contemporary expositional films often 'make a show' of characters absent from the generic repertoires of mainstream cinema, taking as their subjects the socially excluded, the dispossessed, the marginalised and the 'aberrant'. Here, fictional entertainment is granted artistic status through a stylistic revelation of taboo behaviours and psychological states that often tends to sensationalise 'others' and their lifestyles rather than elucidating causes or mapping the broader matrix of social relations in which they are enmeshed.

Rhetorical realism

Rhetorical realism is a mainstream strategy used to re-present contentious social and political issues, employing argument as a central feature of its narrative structure. It is often used in 'true story' films centred on biographical experiences of historically recognisable figures or living individuals to strengthen the truth claim of the fiction and make the case for an unpopular or minority viewpoint. In rhetorical realism, the information content calls on public knowledge of contemporary issues and events, often presenting a potentially contentious interpretation of those events in the interests of stimulating public interest and debate. The contemporary genres chosen are often domestic melodramas, the legal drama, sometimes the political thriller and occasionally the historical epic; many are hybrid variations that combine elements of a wide range of generic formats.

Rhetorical realism favours characters who have to overcome adverse circumstances in order to achieve their aims and ambitions. The adverse circumstances often hinge on questions of social (in)justice or ethical and moral issues. In *The Accused* (1988) Sarah Tobias (Jodie Foster) battles with her female lawyer (Kelly McGillis) who has accepted (without her client's knowledge or permission) a reduced plea of reckless endangerment rather than rape. Sarah persuades her lawyer to reopen the case; the lawyer finds a way to prosecute (for criminal solicitation) those who watched her humiliation and did nothing to intervene. Based on a notorious gang rape some years earlier, the film poses questions about the thin line between sexual provocation and assault, and observation of and participation in crime. Like most legal dramas, *The Accused* uses a standard dual narrative structure, in this case the effects of the rape on Foster's personal life and the lawyer's investigative and persuasive strategies, to provide human interest and narrative drive. The cause-and-effect story structure follows a classical pattern of disruption (the rape), followed by attempts to resolve the disturbance that involve the characters in acts of investigation and retribution that finally, after a number of setbacks, result in successful resolution of the central dilemma, in this case the verdict of guilty passed on those who cheered and provoked the rapists. Character motivation is provided by Foster's demand for justice and retribution and the lawyer's search for witnesses.

Rhetorical realism foregrounds character motivation as its principal strategy: it is through the plight of the central character, sometimes played by a star known for their sympathetic portrayal of particular character types (in this instance a feminist and lesbian icon, Jodie Foster), that audience empathy is elicited for the character's situation. In *Serving in Silence* (1996), a fictional depiction of Margarethe Camermyer's fight to remain in the army despite her declared lesbianism, Glenn Close, a star known for her acting ability rather than her beauty, fights a legal battle with the American Army in a case that, at the time the film was completed, remained unresolved. Meryl Streep, a star similarly renowned in the early

1980s for her acting abilities, played Karen Silkwood in a controversial biographical drama that examined the circumstances surrounding the death of a nuclear worker who dies in mysterious
circumstances on her way to a meeting where she plans to reveal to
the media the slipshod working methods and poor safety record at
the reprocessing plant where she works (*Silkwood* 1983). Based on
a true story, Silkwood's death in 1974 was officially ruled an accident, but widespread public concern about nuclear safety in the
early 1980s gave the film contemporary significance and a controversial edge. Rhetorical realism often uses sympathetic central characters based on real people and events, heightened to achieve
dramatic effect by the use of stars, structured narration and a film
style tending towards melodramatic effect through its use of music
to underscore meaning. The central character's progress through the
film is marked by personal change; complex moral decisions have to
be made that involve a displacement of personal concerns in favour
of abstract concepts such as 'truth' and 'justice'. In order to achieve
their goals, the characters of rhetorical realism take control of their
situation rather than accepting the *status quo*, often at the expense
of their own safety, reputation and personal life. The lawyer in *The
Accused* risks losing the case and her professional reputation when
she agrees to reopen the brief to fight for the rights of a woman less
privileged than herself; Gerthe in *Serving in Silence* risks personal
exclusion from her family and professional expulsion by making her
love for a woman public knowledge; Silkwood loses her life in an
attempt to reveal corporate corruption to the public. All these transformations, elicited by a personal response to events, involve characters sacrificing their private lives to engage with the social world
and its bureaucratic structures. Public acts of personal bravery are
the mainstay of one strand of 'true life' stories.

The construction of heroic individuals is part of a broader discourse of rhetorical realism found in autobiographies and biographies of accomplished lives great and small, novels, news events
and popular infotainment television programming, such as the
British rescue reconstruction drama *999* and even public service
medical dramas such as *Casualty* (BBC 1985 to date). These
dramas are perceived within known schemata for resolving problems that correspond to possibilities for action within the social
world. This type of film is invariably considered ideological by left-
wing critics; the solution to injustice is presented in individualistic

terms, the system critiqued from within rather than challenged from without. Yet they can flag up the constraints and limitations of existing social practices, without necessarily providing utopian resolutions. Although the lawyer in *The Accused* succeeds in her aims, the perpetrators of the rape escape full retribution for their crime. The film takes issue with social attitudes that claim women who dress or act in certain ways are asking to be raped. The final rape sequence may, as some commentators claim, undermine the film's interrogation of these conventional social attitudes, creating gratuitous entertainment by depicting the abuse and humiliation suffered by the victim, but such arguments cannot deny the context in which the violent sequence takes place. Situated at the end of the film as part of Foster's testimony, it is a very different scenario from the violence perpetrated in many a mainstream genre film, which depicts forced sexual intercourse as pleasurable for women, or from the graphically real-ised depictions of rape in expositional films such as *Henry* and *Naked*. *Silkwood*, similarly, cannot effect the usual happy ending typical of the investigative thriller; the antecedent factors of the case on which the film is based deny any simple narrative resolution to the cause of Karen Silkwood's death. Since this death is the subject of the film's interrogative narrative structure, the conclusion reached fits not only a satisfying generic solution of cover-up and conspiracy, but serves to confirm rather than deny public suspicion and accusations of industrial espionage and corporate corruption. *Serving in Silence* is similarly unable to resolve its central narrative dilemma since homosexuality is still deemed illegal in the American armed forces at the closure of the film's narrative, with Gerthe's case still under investigation. The emphasis in all these films is on depicting private battles with public institutions in the interests of social justice.

Cinematic time and space are constructed in all legal dramas around the processes of investigation, disclosure and the eventual trial; the trial deadline constructs the investigative timespan of the film, which can take place over several days or several years. Narrative information is delivered through the usual continuity structures of the classical film. Excess detail is pared away, leaving only material which will prove instrumental to character decision-making and eventual resolution. Devices such as parallel editing are used to depict the development of events in spheres beyond the immediate knowledge of characters, creating an omniscient narration which can be used to build tension about the possible outcome of events, particularly where these are publicly unknown. Spatially, the mise-en-scène constructs an environment based on antecedent reality factors such as contemporary clothing, settings and props which furnish a sense of the real by including paraphernalia associated with the lifestyle of the type of character depicted. Foster in *The Accused* lives in a trailer park and works as a waitress; the comparative poverty of her material life stands in marked contrast to the comfortable lifestyle of her lawyer. Gerthe is a successful career woman, a nurse at the top of her profession who owns her own house. Karen Silkwood is comparatively poor, separated from her husband and children and sharing a house with other women, one of whom, Dolly (Cher) is passionately devoted to her. Such settings correspond to viewer knowledge about lifestyles and characterisation in various ways – either directly, through their own experiences, and/or indirectly through knowledge of a range of texts about American life. All three films depict subjects usually ignored in contemporary mainstream films – poor working-class white women and lesbians.

The spectacular real

The spectacular real-isation of stories of individual heroism and bravery played out against a background of historical events of world-shattering significance is classical Hollywood's preferred mode of presenting history as entertainment. Such films, invariably constructed according to classical conventions, continue to form a significant corpus in the repertoires of mainstream production, providing a counter-balance to the use of high concept aesthetics but sharing a close relationship to their development. Arguably, this spectacular style of real-isation is often nostalgic, recreating the form and style of an earlier era of epic filmmaking in which the films of David Lean (*Bridge On the River Kwai*, (1957), *Dr Zhivago*, (1965), *Lawrence of Arabia* (1962), are often considered exemplars. In formal terms, these epic films aspire to create a film canvas equivalent in scale and scope to the realist novels of the late nineteenth century. Highly dramatic personal stories of great heroism, love, intrigue, hatred and revenge are played out against a vast landscape of social upheaval – war, natural disasters, revolution and political intrigue.

There are significant variations in the ways which realism's codes and conventions can be used spectacularly rather than narrationally within these epic productions. The first of these is identified as a characteristic of the British 'New Wave', when the camera lingers on place and characters in the landscape, creating a gap or lull in the forward drive of narrative action that turns place into spectacle. This is a characteristic of some forms of low budget expositional realism, but it is also found in big budget features such as *Kundun* (1997) and *Seven Years in Tibet* (1997) which create exotic ethnographic spectacles of people and places. *Kundun* claims authenticity of characters and their environment through the use of unknown (possibly Tibetan) actors and aestheticising the landscape as mysterious, beautiful and romantic, creating a real/ideal known/unknown antithesis. Spectacular realism tends to be visually and temporally extensive covering large-scale events, vast landscapes or a range of locales, long timespans and a rich panoply of characters. Sometimes based on a literary work, narratives tend to be episodic rather than causally driven, their characters often at the mercy of known historical situations and events. Great attention is paid to authentic depiction of detail, which is often rendered exotic through lavish evocation of place, period and character milieu. Films such as *The Sheltering Sky* (1990), set in post-war North Africa and *The Last Emperor* (1987), an epic of twentieth-century Chinese history, are typical of this approach. The acclaimed adaptation of Michael Ondaajte's award-winning novel *The English Patient* (1996), with its sumptuous cinematographic treatment of the desert landscape and intricate flashback narrative structure, was heralded as exactly this kind of a film event, winning numerous Academy awards. The opening shots invite an appreciation of the film as a serious work of epic aspiration and intention. The desert forms a spectacular backdrop to a tempestuous adulterous love affair, the camera treating the landscape as raw material of light, shade and motion, the shifting sands and desert storms creating an excess of expression critically regarded as a hallmark of melodramatic affect. Aerial shots of the desert in the opening sequence accentuate the relationship between landscape and the female body, the soft planes and curves of the image and the warm honey hues creating an age-old Western analogy of woman and nature, the desert as the exotic body of the female Other. A real/ideal familiar/exotic antithesis is created, setting the scene for a passionate love affair that ends in disaster and death.

The opening sequences of the film focus on the effects of war on a group of privileged young people working for the British government tracking the advance of enemy forces, but this aspect of the story is underplayed in favour of a focus on their interpersonal relationships. Much of the story is revealed in a series of morphine-induced flashbacks recalled by 'the English patient' (Ralph Fiennes) from his sickbed as he lies dying in a deserted farmhouse in the Italian countryside, cared for by a young nurse. Paralleling this story in the diegetic present is another romance between the nurse (Juliette Binoche) and a young Indian soldier who is an explosives expert. Their haltingly shy love affair, with its respect for protocol and cultural difference, stands in marked contrast to the bored indulgences of the British colonial class, living out the last days of a system of imperial government soon to be displaced by the vicissitudes of war. Although war is the background against which the romances are played out, creating an epic backdrop to both stories, its intrigues play a secondary role to the love affairs that dominate the narrative. The film was heralded as a 'masterpiece' of old fashioned filmmaking values, critically acclaimed and showered with awards, but it failed to ignite similar passions amongst the filmgoing public.

The use of character(s) constructed as eyewitnesses to or participants in (established) historical events is the most obvious dramatic device for claiming 'truth' status for the events and situations depicted on the screen. This is a fairly common technique and by no means exclusive to spectacular realism, but it is invariably a component of the category. Although from very different generic families *Casino* (1995), *Sleepers* (1996), *Titanic* (1998), and *Saving Private Ryan* (1998) have unknown fictional but plausible 'eyewitness' narrators who focalise history as a personal story. On the other hand, the life story of an existing individual or a known historical figure often forms the core of the narrative structure of films depicting political events: obvious recent examples are *JFK* (1991) (which is also rhetorical), *Malcolm X* (1992), *Michael Collins* (1997) and *Nixon* (1995), but autobiographical accounts such as *Born on the Fourth of July* (1989) can be included within this very broad remit. To recreate the life of a character is the most obvious way to stake a claim on a referential link with antecedent events. But not all the above named films necessarily create realism as spectacle, as an outstanding element of their signifying system; often it is taken for granted, a 'transparent' value of the film's narrative economy that establishes an epistemological framework for action and events.

Expositional narrative structures can be used to accentuate the spectacular real-isation of place in some Hollywood films. *Casino*, for example, is episodic in structure and includes sequences that emphasise the environment rather than character action. Hence the long opening sequence with its voice-over narration aims to reveal the backstage processes of managing a casino, revealing the lives of those who work there by a technique that formally has some similarities with docusoap. Narrative structure and point of view stake a claim on the authenticity of everyday experience, the focus on a protagonist's routine activities often revealing important narrational information about that character's psychology. Expositional narration can also be used to thwart conventional narrative expectations. In *Born on the Fourth of July*, the filmed autobiography of Vietnam war veteran Ron Koviks, a long episodic sequence tracks his slow return from self-loathing and disgust to the point where he comes to terms with his physical impairments. By depicting small but significant details, the psychological changes in his character that are the key to understanding his later actions as a political activist are slowly revealed. Eschewing the trite heroics of paradigmatic images of disability, the film shows Kovics, through his experiences, achieving neither heterosexual harmony nor physical enablement, but the political consciousness that enables him to become an anti-war activist.

For realism to become foregrounded as visual spectacle, there have to be iconographic elements which centre attention on the performance of realism as a signifying value within the film's narrative structure. The opening of *Titanic* performs this function, the exploration of the wreck establishing a contemporary realist context for the melodramatic story attributed to the fictionalised survivor. *Saving Private Ryan* is a paradigmatic example of such a use. The film breaks free from its generic intertextual frame, the Hollywood combat movie, through its spectacular use of realism in the long battle sequence that follows the opening of the film. Part of the fascination with this sequence is the gory depiction of the detail of battle (dismembered limbs, intestines spilling from blasted bodies) but it is the sense of being in the thick of the action, a feeling intensified by the soundscape of the film (bullets whistling through the air as if close to your ear, inarticulate cries and shouts, deafening explosions) which excites many of the film's viewers.[3] The spectacular staging of the battle sequences are not the overt cause of the excitement and acclaim with which the film has been greeted: this is reserved for the intimate view of the battlefield constructed by using a handheld newsreel camera, its lens splattered with blood and water, to create a sense of total immersion and chaotic immediacy within the heart of the action. At the end of the battle, however, there is a more typically generic shot of the beach: bodies remain whole, with no heads or limbs littering the place, no-one still screaming in agony. Death is still quick and ultimately clean. With its contemporary associations of news footage, the bleached colour and handheld camerawork is emblematic of a style of 1940s newsreel realism that typified the documentary war work of well-known studio directors such as John Huston. Located in a narrative structure which vacillates between the meandering search for Private Ryan and the highly motivated, character-driven causality of the need to fight to survive, this spectacle of realism is incorporated within an intertextual generic framework that reminded at least one critic of a composite of every combat movie Spielberg was likely to have seen.[4]

The codes and conventions of the classical film are still the preferred forms of choice for many filmmakers who wish to articulate their viewpoints on social and political issues, whilst also ensuring a good return at the box office. Steven Spielberg is but the latest in a long line of Hollywood filmmakers to seek recognition as a serious filmmaker by turning his attention to American historical themes. In pre-release publicity interviews Spielberg claimed that his attempt to enshrine official history in popular memory is motivated by civic intentions and public duty, but, as in other projects, the highly publicised scenes of graphic action are offset by patriotic images of flag-waving, a juxtaposition that provides a moral corrective to other war movies whilst simultaneously guaranteeing sales at the box office. Highly acclaimed in some quarters for its 'intensely realistic' depiction of the D-Day landings on Omaha Beach in June 1944, the historical events on which the film is based are remembered both for the numbers who died in the offensive and as the beginning of the invasion that eventually led to the Allies' victory. This is not the first film to be made about the D-Day landings (see, for example, the star-studded *The Longest Day*, US 1962) but it is the first film about the Second World War to be made in an era where filmmakers have at their fingertips the technological armoury to create the arsenal of special effects characteristic of blockbusters such as *Jurassic Park* and *Titanic*.

Saving Private Ryan epitomises a critically contentious trend that is currently becoming apparent in contemporary Hollywood fictions that engage with social and political issues, the intertextual referencing of film style as part of a film's claim on the truth of its depiction of antecedent realities. High concept films are rarely criticised for quoting film style in this manner: their form/content relations revolve around questions of postmodernist aesthetics, consumerism and intertextual irony rather than issues of realism, history and popular memory. The pressure on official historical accounts exerted by films such as *JFK* and *Schindler's List* is sufficiently provocative to create a frisson of anxiety amongst diverse communities of critical intellectuals and journalists, who accuse the films of blurring the distinctions between fact and fiction, official history and popular memory. These issues are explored in greater depth in Chapter 6, but here we want to flag up three ways in which realism turns history into spectacle that seem to lie at the heart of these critical concerns. The first of these, 'period referencing', refers to the replication of filmmaking techniques (including the use of visual style and musical underscore) associated with a particular era in order to signify that period. *Saving Private Ryan* references 1940s newsreels and pre-existent generic formulations of the combat movie in its signifying structure. *Schindler's List* is also an obvious example, its interior shooting style informed by the classical framing and lighting typical of the studio period, its exterior sequences owing a debt to Italian neorealism.

The second of these, 'intertextual referencing', refers to the use of films as reference points for historical events rather than external antecedent sources of information. *Sleepers* provides a lighthearted example of this form of quotation at the point where family history is articulated to the younger generation by showing 1930s gangster films, because they provide 'the only recorded history of our lives'. Far more controversially, *JFK* uses the home movie footage of Kennedy's death to lend status to its own claim to truth, as well as reconstructing documentary footage in the style of 1960s television newsreels. Finally, antecedent realities are perhaps most readily evoked when the locations used in the film are imbued with the resonance of events that are known to have happened in the very place where the pro-filmic action is being enacted. *Schindler's*

List provides the most emotive example of such an ontological use, filmed in Krakow and outside the gates of Auschwitz – the actual sites of the atrocities that are the source of the film's story. *JFK* has a similar ontological link to the events that are the focus of the film, but this time the link is a deferred, mediated one: the controversial Zapruder home movie footage that captured the event of the shooting. In *JFK* the actual location of the shooting provides the set for the numerous re-enactments and re-viewings that frame the structure of investigation. Filmic reality in these latter examples is rooted in mediated public knowledge, but also in remembered experience, creating what one critic has described as 'a fantasy of witnessing' in which the use of place as location recreates history as a public spectacle of remembrance.[5]

In this chapter we have explored some of the ways in which public reactions to filmed fictions are activated by the films themselves, examining the codes and conventions used by films that seek to establish a relationship with antecedent situations and events. These attempts are based on the iconicity of the film image coupled with an acoustic soundscape that privileges diegetic sound, an episodic character centred narration that foregrounds revelation of psychological states and the use of deferred referentiality through the use of codes and conventions associated with televisual and camcorder aesthetics.

The legacy of the linguistic turn in film studies, that film is a language with its own codes and conventions, is increasingly challenged by approaches from other disciplines which seek to locate the interpretation of films within frameworks that attest that the reading of audiovisual texts is closely associated with the interpretative processes of everyday life. If this is the case, then cognitive theories offer film studies a framework for engaging with realism that remains unexamined in contrast to the cine-psychoanalytic paradigms that have dominated the discipline in recent years. We explore this avenue more fully in the following chapter.

Notes

1   Vladimir Zelevinsky on *Saving Private Ryan*, *The Tech*, 118: 30, MIT Press, at: http://www-tech.mit.edu/V118/N30/spielberg.30a.html, visited October 1998.
2   Notable examples include *Naked* (1995) and *Secrets and Lies* (1996).

3   The film has excited commentary from viewers around the world on the
    Internet, most of whom have high praise for the 'realism' of this
    sequence. See the listings of more than five hundred responses at:
    http://comments.imdb.com/CommentsShow?120815/us17.imdb.com,
    visited October 1998.
4   See Jonathon Rosenblaum's article in *Chicago Reader* at: http://
    www.chireader.com/movies/archives/1998/0798/0798/07248.html, visited
    October 1998.
5   See Gary Weissman (1995: 17, 293–307).

Chapter 5

Discerning viewers: cognitive theory and identification

'*I know its only fiction but these things are happening somewhere*'. (Viewer of *Oranges are Not the Only Fruit*, quoted in Hallam and Marshment 1995: 11)

'*One film I can't watch is* Outbreak *because to me it is a real threat which affects everybody. I find that disturbing and difficult to watch.*' (Participant 3 – FG4, quoted in Hill 1997: 61)

All fiction is, of course, an illusion. The hallmark of a good book or play is its potential, in the words of Coleridge, to suspend our disbelief. Another way of thinking about this is to argue that all filmic works of art depend upon a willingness to play a game of make-believe when we engage with them. As consumer participators, we know that the fictional world is not the real world, and that our responses to it are imaginary, no matter how our reactions seem equivalent to that which we might experience if the situation were actually happening to us. This notion of game playing is central to cognitive theory, where a work cues engagement with a set of propositions in ways that are similar to our engagement with real world situations and events. It is a somewhat different conception from thinking of filmed fictions as inducing various forms of illusionism in the spectator through their unique type of signifying practice. Christian Metz has argued that the experience of film spectatorship depends upon a conception of belief in the reality of the fiction; during the process of viewing the credulous spectator (who believes in the reality of the fiction) takes over from the incredulous spectator (who knows the action is a representation). This process of disavowal, of knowing/not knowing, accords with psychoanalytic concepts of the development of subjectivity and is a foundational concept in theories of cine-psychoanalytic identification. As will be argued in more detail below, for our purposes this construct of the spectator is not the most useful one for a discussion of viewer engagement with popular films and their uses of realism. In this chapter, constructivist cognitive theory is used to examine viewer engagement with such texts and re-examine the concept of 'identification', drawing on recent work that theorises the relationship between characters and emotion. The first section of the chapter outlines Bordwell's neoformalist interpretation of cognitive psychology; part two presents Murray Smith's theory of character engagement; part three makes a case for viewers engaging not only with characters, but with their situation. This latter position is an important consideration in assessing the social and political impact of films on individuals and their varied viewing constituencies.

Cognitive theory

In what ways is it possible to speak of viewer engagement with realism and popular cinema within the contexts of contemporary film studies? Realism is not a fixed group of textual attributes but a continuum of signifying potentialities, a range of strategies used by filmmakers to mediate information about characters and their situations in reference to dominant conceptions of what constitutes reality. Realist films are those which combine these formal and thematic properties in combinations that are labelled 'realist' by the discourses of criticism, critical reviewing, promotional literature and advertising. In discussing the realistic effect of films, Barthes states: 'verisimilitude is never anything more than the result of opinion; it is entirely dependent on opinion, public opinion' (Barthes 1978: 131–5). Arguably, the organs of the press and popular reviewing are one aspect of the mediation of what is considered at any one time 'public opinion', not because they are necessarily indicative of a wide range of value judgements from a broad spectrum of the viewing public, but because they help constitute the climate of interpretation that surrounds the popular reception of a film or media text. Since most professional reviewers draw on paradigms of classification acquired through their education and professional training, their interpretations tend to remain wedded to the conceptual frameworks that continue to inform humanistic study.

In what sense, however, are non-professional viewers using the term when they describe a fiction film as 'realistic'? Empirical research on audiences suggests both that viewers are well aware of the fictional status of fictional texts and that they assess a text's realism in terms of their own idea of what constitutes a plausible fictional world. Plausibility is a key term in the discursive construction of an aesthetics of realism. Characterisation and dialogue, mise-en-scène and the way a film is put together to support a notion of diegetic plausibility is a defining feature in Bordwell's analysis of classical Hollywood films, where 'classical' refers to the unity or harmony of the work. A fiction film may be considered realistic, even if the characters, setting and situation are unfamiliar to a viewer, provided the totality of the fictional world is considered to be a convincing portrayal of the characters and the world they inhabit. In making this judgement, viewers will, of course, draw upon their own experience of what constitutes reality, including their knowledge of others' realities.

In her study of viewers of the 1980s US television serial *Dallas*, Ien Ang introduces the concept of 'emotional realism' in order to account for what she sees as the contradiction between some viewers' judgement of the programme as realistic and her own and other viewers' opinion that its content does not correspond empirically with the realities of everyday life in America. Ang suggests that the realism of *Dallas* is connotative rather than denotative; that it is situated not at the cognitive, but at the emotional level: 'what is recognised as real is not knowledge of the world, but a subjective experience of the world: a "structure of feeling"' (Ang 1985: 45). *Dallas* fans are well aware of the untypical, 'unrealistic' aspects of the text (such as the family's wealth), but they find the characters and their relationships realistic in the sense that they recognise them as similar to those they encounter or have knowledge of in their own lives. In this sense, when responding emotionally to the text, they are perhaps treating it as a catalyst, as cathartic in the Greek sense, because it enables a release of emotion comparable to that experienced in real life situations. This is clearer from the words of her respondents that she quotes than from Ang's own analysis, which reinforces a divide between empirical and emotional realism and corresponds rather too closely to notions of male objectivity and female subjectivity, whereas her respondents, well aware of the constructed nature of *Dallas* as fiction, nevertheless insist on its plausibility. It may be that critics and researchers have been unwilling to allow for the elements of tragedy, complication, coincidence and even melodrama in the lives of many viewers.

The notion of plausibility has implications for thinking about and analysing popular films because the legacy of film theory has tended to favour paradigms that stress that film is an illusion, that it creates a fantasy world, a false reality. But if we take the highly constructed nature of the film text as the end point of a creative, productive process, it then becomes possible to ask questions about how codes and conventions are used to mediate (rather than represent) reality – to create 'believable fictional worlds' across the filmic spectrum, from what is now often termed the grainy or documentary realism of fly-on-the-wall *cinéma vérité* – in Bazin's terms the 'degree zero' of signification – through variations on the classic realism of mainstream genre texts to the highly stylised worlds associated with particular generic forms such as science fiction and horror.

Bordwell provides a useful approach to questions of plausibility and rationality in film texts, maintaining throughout his various studies of film art that the viewer is always in their senses. This accords with Kendall Walton's premise that all representational artworks involve a form of game playing; the work acts as a cue for stimulating the imagination (Walton 1990: 180–6). Bordwell's work engages with cognitive theories that are interested in exploring how we make sense of our physical and material world; he argues that we use the same processes to make sense of films, because the perceptual physiological processes of hearing and seeing remain constant irrespective of whether we are engaging with actuality or mediated constructs of actuality.[1] This throws greater emphasis onto the form/content relation than purely formal/textual theories; at root, it is a theory of psychological engagement with the text that emphasises familiarity and recognition – it maintains that viewers engage with narrative films in ways similar to those in which they engage with everyday experience. Realism articulates a relationship between the conscious, perceiving individual and the social world, activating a mental mise-en-scène of memory, recognition and perceptual familiarity. Culturally embedded knowledges of characters and events held by individual viewers, defined by constructivist cognitive theory as personal schemata, recognise similarly coded behaviour of characters and events represented on the screen, facilitating processes of identification and comprehension. This active process of engagement is the basis of an approach that situates meaning as interactive and in process, accepted or rejected by viewers as they piece together the informational cues given by the film.

In *Narration in the Fiction Film*, Bordwell uses constructivist cognitive theory to explain the sense-making activity of viewers as they engage with the sounds and images emanating from the screen. Viewers are cued by the text to form hypotheses about the next event as the film proceeds in an ongoing, interactive engagement with its narrative trajectory. Hypothesis formation in this model is largely automatic. Viewers use the same set of assumptions to structure the input of information they are receiving from the film that they use to construct meaning in their everyday realities. Bordwell identifies three key areas of cognitive activity that are brought into play when we watch a film: our perceptual capacities, our prior knowledge and experiences and the material and structure of the film itself (Bordwell 1988: 32–7). Our perceptual processes, such as our ability to perceive colour and to construct a three-dimensional space on a two-dimensional plane through depth cues, are the same perceptual processes that we use to shape our visual and auditory experience of everyday life. Perception is an active process of hypothesis testing. The organism, tuned to pick up information from the environment, frames expectations based on prior experience about what it is receiving. It checks this information against an existing perceptual hypothesis, which is confirmed or modified. A distinction is made between 'bottom-up' perceptual processes, such as perceiving a moving object, which operate in fast and involuntary ways and 'top-down' processes which are more overtly based on assumptions, expectations and hypothesis generation. When we watch a film, bottom-up perceptual processes automatically come into play because they are based on the capacity of our physiological apparatus to perceive light and movement. The retina of the eye is limited in its ability to perceive changing light intensities; at more than fifty flashes a second, light appears constant, a phenomenon known as flicker fusion. Secondly, the eye perceives a series of still images as apparently moving if the images are projected at sufficient speed. This combination of flicker fusion and the illusion of motion constructs a coherent moving image from a series of stroboscopic fixed frames. Top-down perceptual processes generate schemata, organised clusters of knowledge that guide our hypothesis making. Bordwell uses the example of searching for a friend in a crowd as a model of top-down perceptual processes in action. As we scan the crowd, the probabilities of past experience – our memory of the person's face, previous searches for people we know in crowded places – frame our assumptions, expectations and hypothesis formation. Schemata involve different types of sense-making activity that allow the mind to process the vast amount of sensory data it constantly receives. This patterning gives shape and structure to our understanding by providing the interconnections and elaborations that enable us to extract meaning from sensory data.

When we watch a film, we draw on a wide range of schemata based on this prior knowledge and experience of the everyday world; these schemata shape the processes through which we learn to interpret representational forms of all kinds including books, magazines, television, art works and fiction films. In Western societies, narrative comprehension of films is a learnt social activity that encourages us to create a meaningful story out of the sense-generating material presented on the screen. Bordwell emphasises that the form and structure of narrative film texts encourage the viewer to execute storymaking activities by presenting cues, patterns and gaps that shape the application of schemata and hypothesis testing. Narrative comprehension depends on several types of schemata. Prototypes are schemata that involve identifying classes of objects according to understood norms, which applies to the identification of protagonists, actions and locales. For example, films aiming to address social issues and concerns draw on existing prototype schemata through which we make sense of social life. Watching *Boyz N the Hood* (1991) involves applying personal schemata of young black males and their experiences of racism, violence, drugs, inner city life, families, friendship networks, unemployment, poverty and crime. Viewers' schemata are shaped by their individual experiences which in this case may be close to the 'person schema' of the characters on the screen if they are young black males living in similar circumstances, may be shaped by personal or professional contact with people in similar situations, or framed by mediated factors such as accounts of young black male behaviour, drug-taking and contemporary urban life televised in documentaries, narrated in novels and reported in newspapers. Pre-knowledges and existing schemata are of particular importance in ascribing degrees of 'realisticness' to film texts and assessing their 'truth' to experience.[2]

Part of recognising an elderly person, for example, as a realistic character in a fiction lies beyond the mimetic capacity of sound and image technologies to reproduce a recorded physical and aural likeness, a copy of a real person. The filmmakers and the actors draw on

cultural knowledge of elderly people in the real world to construct
a particular type of elderly person, a gendered individual who is
racially distinctive with particular personality features who is
embedded in the social fabric of an environment at a particular point
in time. To varying degrees, viewers will recognise this person
schema as one they are familiar with (or not), employing the same
schemata that they use to construct their impressions of elderly
people in everyday life. As Christopher Butler puts it, 'we must see
the text, at least initially, as mimetic, since our knowledge of the
meaning of its expression is so largely drawn from experience'
(Butler 1984: 53, quoted in Smith 1995a: 54). In this sense, realism
in popular narrative films is a template of the familiar drawn from
experiences of social life as well as a template of narrative form
drawn from cultural knowledge of story structures.

Prototypes operate within larger structures or cognitive frameworks called templates, which involves classifying events and relating them to broader systems of organisation. In fiction films,
research has suggested that perceivers relate story information to a
particular pattern or master schema that creates an interpretative
framework for understanding, recalling and summarising a narrative. When recalling stories, certain structural elements act as reference points aiding the intelligibility of the narrative which is then
filled in by the viewer extrapolating and adjusting what they can
remember. The most common story template for narrative films in
Western cultures is the familiar format identified by Bordwell in the
classical Hollywood film. Typically, a story begins by introducing the
characters and setting and explaining the current state of affairs
(exposition); actions and events follow that complicate existing relationships and disturb the *status quo*. Work then takes place to
resolve the problems and resolution is eventually successful leading
to a satisfactory conclusion in the establishment of a new equilibrium. Bordwell focuses on the narrative template in his model of
narrative comprehension, ascribing the management of deviation to
procedural schemata, whereby a viewer will adjust their template
schemata if the film does not proceed as expected. (For a full
account of these processes, see Bordwell 1988: 30–47.)

The advantage of the cognitive approach to questions of viewer
engagement with filmic texts is that it proposes neither a 'transcen-
dental' subject controlled by their unconscious desires, nor a 'vol-
untarist' subject in full control of their desires and motivations.

Many of the processes of patterning are automatic, beneath our conscious control in that they are performed quickly and unreflexively, but they are conscious in that they are available to reflection (Smith 1995a: 48). Schema theory is informed by a constructivist epistemology which neither sees the mind as a blank *tabula rasa* passively accepting the imprint of a meaningful world, nor as an idealism which posits the mind as unconstrained in its construction of 'reality'. Cultural schemata are learned and sustained within given cultural environments; their automation is like a reflex action, something we do not have to think about within that context. Everyday communication is full of such reflex responses. We do not think consciously about how to greet our friends, although we may to need to revise our schemata if we are meeting a person in a position of power or authority that we wish to impress. Using the telephone provides a good example of how schemata of greeting change according to patterns of everyday use and social protocol. Many older people still answer the phone stating their location and number, a response acquired when domestic phones were less common and answering etiquette more formalised. This schemata is uncommon among younger people accustomed to using the telephone as part of their daily communicative activity, generating a far more casual pattern of social use and response.

Murray Smith argues that schema theory can be used in a theory of the mental representation of social practices, beliefs and values, and to elucidate the relationship between imagination and ideology. In the cognitive model, both general cultural and specifically ideological beliefs and values can be conceptualised as automated schemata and therefore apparently ingrained in the mind. Schema theory posits ideology as a network of automised beliefs which allows for the constraining nature of ideology, but also for the ability of individuals to move within and beyond these constraints. Automised practices are beneath consciousness, but they are not repressed: they are assumed, the vehicle rather than the object of thought. In certain contexts, they can be brought to consciousness and we can reflect on them. Feminist theory is a model of such a practice, requiring us to reconsider and reflect on the position of women in society as gendered subjects in order to change the way we conceptualise our schemata of women as social subjects, bringing our automated responses to our conscious attention (Smith 1995a: 48–52). If it is possible to bring our automated responses to consciousness in this way, to expand and adapt them by new experiences, there is no reason to doubt that fictional representations can play a part in this process. The changing status of women in some fictional representations is a particular case in point here. In the 1980s and 1990s, popular films have exploited common generic expectations of the action hero as a male character. In films such as the *Aliens* quartet, *Thelma and Louise* (1991) and *Terminator 2* (1991), women have occupied narrative positions conventionally held by male heroes. These films subvert the usual patterns of expectation commonly held about who can be active in the action genre, but they also activate what are called 'default values' in schema theory, beliefs and values commonly circulating about, in this case, gendered identity. Women are traditionally represented in roles and functions through codes and conventions that ascribe subjectivity to male protagonists. Arguably, a shift in the usual pattern of expectation offered by popular films is indicative of a change in the default hierarchy of the prototypical case, a shift from female protagonists as passive objects of the (male) gaze and (male) desire to active, dynamic, controlling subjects.[3] Importantly, we want to note here that our engagement with popular films is predicated on our experience of the world, but films themselves can alter the ways in which we understand and experience the world, potentially introducing alternative social and moral schemata, different possibilities of acting and being, albeit often couched in terms which foreclose these possibilities even as they pose the problem. The criticism of popular films is that they reinforce dominant attitudes and beliefs, but such a conception ignores both the multifaceted personal schemata of the film viewer and the potential capacity of films to engage with pre-conscious and automated viewer responses, perhaps bringing them to conscious awareness.

Emotional engagement and identification

The cognitive approach increasingly emphasises a holistic approach which resists the rationality/emotion split characteristic of the neoformalist and psychoanalytic approaches in contemporary film theory. For the last thirty years, psychoanalysis has provided the dominant paradigm for understanding emotion in films, but the dualistic structure of the psychoanalytic paradigm – the battle between the id and the superego for mastery (the term is used advisedly) of the human subject – creates a binary battlefield between the forces of desire with the rational order and the law of the Father. Within this model, emotion has been conceptualised as repressed and perceived as a negative rather than an integrated facet of human behaviour. But cognition is not independent of emotion and the needs of the body; new holistic work in film theory is attending to the strategies of emotional engagement and its relationship to cognitive perception cued by the characters, filmic narration and music.[4] Here, we want to focus on one aspect of this work, the question of identification, because as Murray Smith argues, 'character structures are perhaps the major way by which narrative texts solicit our assent for particular values, practices and ideologies' (1995a: 4).

In everyday, lay discussions about fiction (film or otherwise) identification is frequently used as a value-judgement to comment on the experience of fictional engagement. The inability to identify with a central character is often proffered as a negative evaluation – I couldn't identify with her/him – implying a lack of emotional and/or moral engagement with the fiction and its content that prevents enjoyment of it. Conversely, a positive evaluation suggests that pleasure and engagement were felt, suggesting that for many viewers identification with the characters and their concerns is a deciding issue in the enjoyment of fictional texts. Assuming that people are more likely to be convinced by the arguments (implicit or explicit) of a text they enjoy than of one they experience as disagreeable, then the degree and nature of identification felt is likely to be an important factor in the success of a film that seeks to communicate a 'message'.

The psychoanalytic school of film theory attempted to account for audience identification with characters in film through concepts of psychic identity: loss of ego and adoption of the perspective of the other was used to explain not only audiences' emotional engagement and pleasure in film, but their 'suturing' into the narrative so as to create for them a 'subject position', an identity that stitched them into the ideology of capitalism.[5] Although the underlying psychoanalytic premise of these theories raises problems for cognitive theory, the relationship between engagement, pleasure and ideology remains a challenge to film theory, and the psychoanalytic attempt to explain it is in many ways suggestive as the following analyses will demonstrate.

Noel Carroll is perhaps the most influential theorist to critique the psychoanalytic approach. His rejection of the concept of identification in favour of that of 'allegiance' rests in part on an exaggerated notion of what is involved when spectators are said to 'identify' with a character. He claims that 'the concept of identification is incorrect' because 'very often spectators do not have or share the identical or same emotions of the characters in question'; this 'logical asymmetry', he claims, 'makes it impossible to characterise the relation [between spectator and character] as one of identification' (Carroll 1996: 116). In relation to psychoanalytic claims of 'loss of ego' and 'subject positioning', Carroll's critique undoubtedly has force. The implication of these claims, that spectators' psyches are helplessly transformed into those of the fictional characters, is clearly incredible. One may recall Dr Johnson's commensensical critique of academic insistence on the theatrical unities, 'that the audience is always in its senses'. But everyday concepts of identification rarely deny this. What is claimed is not an identification *as* a character but an identification *with* a character. The dictionary definition of identification cites as its second meaning: 'associate oneself with; regard oneself as sharing characteristics with (another person)'.[6] In this sense, viewers clearly *do* identify with characters and their situations. Of course, they do not have *the same* experiences as characters: but then, in a fictional film, the characters are not having any experiences for the obvious reason that the figures on the screen are actors pretending to have these experiences. They are fictional. For Carroll to object that identification is an inaccurate term because 'normal viewers do not believe that they are about to be crushed by a train, pushed off a building, knifed and so on' (Carroll 1996: 116) ignores the obvious point that neither do they believe that the actors on screen are about to suffer these fates.

And yet, to harness another time-honoured concept of literary analysis, they can suspend their disbelief to the extent of associating emotionally with the characters' situations, feeling on their behalf, say, fear, anger, grief, joy and so on. For many purposes, Carroll's concept of 'allegiance' may well be a perfectly adequate, and as he says 'less mysterious', way of dealing with the phenomenon. However, the intensity of response that may be involved does present us with a *prima facie* paradox: our ability to simultaneously experience something as a fiction and feel real emotions in response to it. This paradox, as well as underlying many Western concerns with the morality of fiction (from Plato onwards) is also commonly felt to be a problem. During a small study of viewer responses to *Oranges are Not the Only Fruit* (BBC2 1991), one of the respondents

commented on her husband's disparagement of her emotional
engagement with fictional texts, especially those where she 'got
upset'. Her justification for this emotional response was that she
knew that 'these things are happening somewhere' (Hallam and
Marshment 1995: 11). This is, in fact, not only a valid justification
of her response, it is also a fairly adequate explanation of it. At one
level, her response is no different from the empathy she feels for
people in real-life situations. She does not have to experience the
same situations to empathise with these people: she can imagine
how she would feel if she did experience them. Obviously – *pace*
Carroll – she does not have identical feelings, but empathy does not,
fortunately, depend on this. It depends on the ability to imagine
what others' feelings might be, and to feel sympathy, anger and so
on, with them, on their behalf.

Whether we call this allegiance or identification with a character
may not be very important, but for our purposes the finer distinctions are useful. In his analysis of the varieties of emotional response
to characters in film, Murray Smith distinguishes between recognition, alignment and allegiance in defining the relationship between
spectator and character. According to his schema, recognition is the
initial process by which a spectator recognises a set of cinematic
signs as a character in a fiction through mimetic reference to human
beings as they exist in the real world. Alignment describes the
process 'by which spectators are placed in relation to characters in
terms of access to their actions, and to what they know and feel'
(Smith 1995a: 83). Both these processes involve the spectator in
understanding the character, without implying any moral or emotional involvement. For the latter, Smith uses the term 'allegiance' in
a similar way to Carroll, as approximating to what is usually called
'identification': he sees it as pertaining to the process whereby the
spectator evaluates and responds 'emotionally to the traits and emotions of the character, in the context of the narrative situation'
(1995a: 85). These are, according to Smith, the components of what
he calls 'the structure of sympathy' of a film. But he extends Carroll's usage to 'pertain to the moral evaluation of characters by the
spectator' (1995a: 84). This is an important distinction, implying a
level of support for certain characters, a matter, so to speak, of
taking sides; yet the word 'moral', despite his attempt to extend the
reference of the term, cannot simply imply a particular kind of
judgement. His schema embraces rather than distinguishes the

processes of emotional engagement that spectators might feel with, or on behalf of, a character or characters. Smith tends to assume that all these processes depend on the uniquely important relationship between spectator and character, whereas we prefer to recognise ways in which spectators are positioned in relation to films that do not only privilege their relationship to particular characters, but include the possibility of a relationship between situation and event.

'Alignment' seems the most useful term to work with since it can be used to describe a textual process without implying any necessary response on the part of the spectator. We suggest that a distinction between different kinds of alignment can illuminate the finer distinctions between the various relationships that film and television fictions construct between character(s) and viewers. This has the advantage of recognising that these different kinds of alignment overlap and slide into one another, and even that they might not be focused on character. When critics refer to identification (in a non-psychoanalytic sense), they usually mean to suggest that the spectator is invited to share the character's emotional response to events. This is problematic in several respects. First, it implies that this is a desirable situation, asking for a successful, convincing fiction. To some extent, we would agree with those critics (both of the Left – psychoanalytic school and the moral majority) who are suspicious of the automatic desirability of being induced to identify emotionally with characters. More important, however, we think that, powerful as cinematic representation appears to be, emotional identification with characters is not necessarily the most important source of this power. Murray Smith recognises this in defining his category of 'allegiance' in terms of 'moral evaluation' rather than emotional engagement. Much as we sympathise with his project to reintroduce moral perspectives into film criticism, and, while his extended reference for the word 'moral' makes for a useful approach to questions of alignment, it is still too broad a category for our purposes. Instead of 'allegiance', a further series of types of 'alignment' reveals a range of possibilities open to the spectator. These are specified as: intellectual alignment, interest alignment, concern alignment, moral alignment, aesthetic alignment and emotional alignment.

It could be argued that the first of these is not only common to almost all films, and therefore the ground upon which many of the others are based, but also, in very many cases, the dominant mode of the work. By intellectual alignment, we mean those processes of information, reasoning and understanding which the spectator is positioned to receive from the text. Because so many filmic narratives employ a central character to lead the spectator through the narrative, this information, reasoning and understanding may more usually be mediated through the psychological construction of and/or the activities of the central character. But this is not inevitable. An omniscient narration, with or without a central character(s), can also align the spectator with particular knowledges, reflections upon and conclusions from them. Nor is it inevitable that intellectual alignment will necessarily involve moral or emotional alignment.

Interest alignment arises from the positioning of particular characters at the centre of the narrative. This inevitably focuses the spectator's interest on their fate: we want to know what happens to them. This is a simple matter of curiosity and is related to what we might call the 'narrative imperative'. It seems that the briefest of narrative situations can arouse our curiosity about 'what will happen next', so that it takes little to induce us to be curious about the future of characters with whom the narrative has already familiarised us. This is not the same as *caring* about what happens to them – which is our next category, concern alignment. Here the text positions the spectator to invest a certain hope and/or fear in relation to the fate of the character(s). This is not necessarily directed towards hoping for the character(s) to prosper although the positioning of positive, morally validated, characters at the centre of a narrative is perhaps the norm in popular narratives, so that concern alignment *will* induce spectators to hope for them to prosper. But there is no shortage of anti-heroes or villains as the narrative focus, which would invite spectators to be concerned for their downfall.

This brings us to moral alignment; this category concerns the text's evaluation of the character, which the spectator is aligned to share. A text may present the character(s) and their concerns as deserving of validation or condemnation, as ambiguous, as posing a dilemma, and/or as a challenge to accepted moral criteria. If the text endorses the moral position of the protagonists(s), whether or not this is a challenge to what we can assume as accepted morality, then it is a relatively simple matter to analyse how the spectator is positioned to share, or come to share, this (perhaps developing) moral position. When the text distances itself from the protagonist's moral position, we have to deal with distancing strategies such as irony.

This is a crucial strategy for realist texts presumed to be attempting radical intervention in socio-political issues.

Our last two categories are perhaps the least scientific because they would appear to be so open to the subjective responses of spectators, but they feature prominently in both popular debates about the power of the media and its effects and in academic discourse. Aesthetic alignment invites the spectator to *enjoy* the character(s). Perhaps the most common strategy here is through the body. A character is presented as conforming physically to the dominant culturally sanctioned norms of beauty, offering the spectator an aesthetic pleasure that not only offers the pleasure of spectacle but also invites an alignment with the character. Contrary to psychoanalytic criticism, we do not see this as necessarily relating to issues of sexual desire. What is important is that the spectator should recognise the character as conforming to the culture's norms of beauty and/or attractiveness. Individual spectators do not need to share these norms to understand the meaning of the fiction, although they might be influenced in the degree of their alignment with the fiction according to whether they share them.

While physical beauty – including the face – is important in aesthetic alignment, it is by no means the only factor. Aspects of personality feature just as importantly, and may even work towards defining the aesthetics of the body. Among these personality features we might mention, for example, competence, kindness, wit, energy and sincerity. Like physical attributes, these are culturally defined, so, while there will be considerable space for individual judgement, we can assume certain criteria that are socially shared. The aesthetic construction of a character may conflict with other categories of his/her construction, and be a fruitful source of narrative ambiguity or conflict in the reading of the text.

The last category is emotional alignment. This is the process whereby spectators are positioned to share the emotional response(s) of character(s). This is frequently assumed to arise automatically from alignments in previous categories, but it is important to identify it separately. It is quite often the case that spectators are aligned with a text on a variety of levels – intellectual or interest alignment, even concern or moral alignment – without being emotionally aligned. That said, it is most unlikely that emotional alignment can occur without at least one of these categories of alignment being brought into play. It is important to note, however, both that

these other alignments will not necessarily lead to emotional alignment, and that emotional alignment can, in fact, be constructed
without them. This is because emotional engagement in a fiction is
not primarily premised upon a character, but on their situation.

Alignment, situation and event

Suspense provides a useful point through which to examine the
processes of alignment because the anxiety that suspense provokes
in the spectator is necessarily *on behalf* of a character and/or their
project. It therefore requires us to ask what the nature of this identification is and how it is being produced. Noel Carroll defines suspense in film as occurring when the moral outcome, the
consequence that the spectator is likely to hope for, appears to be
the unlikely result of events (Carroll 1996: 94–117). Thus viewers
experience anxiety that, for instance, the heroine will not be rescued
or that the hero will not survive because the narrative has stacked
the odds against these outcomes. Carroll cites Hitchcock as a director who deliberately breaks the rules, creating suspense where the
morally desirable outcome appears to be the unlikely one, so that
audiences are invited to feel anxiety about whether the undesirable
result will actually be achieved. This exception suggests not only that
Carroll is probably right in thinking that 'desirable' rather than
'moral' is the more appropriate term for defining suspense, but also
that the process of creating this suspense deserves closer attention.
We would like to link this point to the one Carroll makes about how
the 'moral' (in his sense) quality of characters may conflict with the
acceptability of their ethical position. His argument is that protagonists 'will be regarded as right in the moral system of the film' provided they 'are presented as possessing some virtues' (Carroll 1996:
105). We think this is not an adequate account of how the relationship between spectator and character is created.

   The example Carroll cites is from Hitchcock's *Strangers on a Train*
(1951) (Carroll 1996: 111–12). The following analysis is of a similar
scene from *Dial M for Murder* (Hitchcock 1954). In this sequence, a
hired killer arrives to murder the wife of the man who has hired him
so that he can inherit her money. The audience has already witnessed
the hiring, and the details of their plot, whereby the husband is to
telephone home at 11.00 p.m. to lure his wife from bed to the phone
by the window, where the killer will be concealed behind the curtain,

conveniently positioned for strangling her from behind. We ourselves, and all viewers we have asked (mostly students of film and/or
cultural studies), experience the sequence as suspenseful. The suspense is created fairly conventionally by means of a series of obstacles to the fulfilment of the plan, with the action cutting between the
husband at a business dinner and the killer in the flat. First, the killer
is shown arriving on time, finding the key left for him under the stair
carpet, letting himself into the flat and hiding behind the curtain. But
the pre-arranged phone call doesn't materialise. The wife continues
to sleep peacefully in her bed. Then, the husband discovers his watch
has stopped and he has missed the 11.00 p.m. deadline. The shot of
the watch at 10.40 and the information that it is past 11.00 p.m. creates a frisson of anxiety in the spectator. The action cuts to the killer
preparing to leave: a second frisson of anxiety. The husband arrives
at the hotel phone booth, to find it occupied: another frisson of anxiety. Another cut to the flat, where the killer is tiptoeing towards the
exit door and another frisson of anxiety. When the husband is able
to use the phone, we are shown the mechanics of the call – his fingers
dialling one number after another, the telephone exchange making
the connection – which creates a sense of further delay. Finally, he
succeeds; the wife gets out of bed to answer the call, the killer has
returned to his hiding place, the tension subsides and the audience
can sigh with relief: the murder can commence.

   The suspense-anxiety felt by the spectator is obviously at odds
with a morality that condemns the cold-blooded murder of a wife
for money, and viewers we have talked with express a sense of
extreme unease, not to say shock, at the focus of their anxiety. This
might have satisfied Hitchcock, if Carroll's account of his purpose in
such scenes is correct, but we will return to this point. What is
important for us initially is that it is not possible to explain this suspense as arising from any positive qualities in the characters who are
the perpetrators of the planned crime. On the contrary: the wife is
already known to viewers as a sympathetic, beautiful, good woman
and loyal wife. During the scene she is shown innocently sleeping
and then sleepily and innocently rising to answer the phone. The
killer is depicted as a seedy, immoral character, and is coded visually
as a conventional villain. The husband may be handsome, but has
been shown to be, as he continues to be, cold and ruthless. It is certainly not to any personal qualities in the characters that the spectators' involvement in the suspense is harnessed.

So we must seek its origins elsewhere. We may begin by attributing it to the construction of the narrative, which, as we have seen, conforms to the pattern of such suspense sequences. In addition, it conforms to the gender imbalance identified by Mulvey in the representation of subjectivity in classical Hollywood films, whereby we share the male protagonist's view of events, but not the female's (Mulvey 1975). Whether or not this applies universally, it does apply in this case. The audience is party to the plans, hopes and fears of the male characters, so that, even if they do not approve of them, they do share them. Whereas, during the scene in question, they are only witness to the female character's position: they do not share her perspective on events, so that they do even experience anxiety *on her behalf*. This is reinforced by the camera's sexualisation of her as she rises from bed in a translucent nightdress that displays her body, the positioning of her prone body beneath her assailant during the murder attempt and the post-orgasmic expression on her face after she has survived and killed her would-be murderer; all of which distance the spectator from her experience by presenting her as 'something to be looked at', an object of spectacle, rather than someone to be identified with.

There is a further point to make. The sequence has been framed within the point of view of the husband. The spectator encounters the scene aligned with his knowledge and his hopes, and is therefore positioned to relate to his frustration and fears during it. At its closure, the spectator does not share the woman survivor's perspective on events, but the husband's. This is mostly a question of alignment of knowledge. The woman does not know what the spectator and the husband do know: that he tried to have her killed. The spectator therefore identifies more with his disappointment than her ... well, we do not know what she feels, as there is no alignment with her perspective on events. (This is a turning point in the film; the spectator's knowledge of the husband's disappointment combines alignment with his disappointment and satisfaction that his evil plan has been thwarted. From now on, the spectator is invited to identify with the wife's plight – though initially from a position of more knowledge than she has.)

The question of framing of sequences is a matter of narrative structure, whereby individual scenes are read within the perspective of the already established protagonist. Years of teaching Mulvey's thesis about the 'male gaze' have shown us that, on the one hand, attention to precise camera movements can reveal structures of looking that are, indeed, about the relative power positions of the characters and what they represent (not only in relation to gender, but also to race, class, generation, sexuality etc.), which may contradict the apparent direction of the narrative and dialogue. An example of this occurs when the police interview the Gloria Grahame character in *In a Lonely Place* (1950), where her narratively powerful position as the witness to a murder is undercut by the way the camera consistently places her under the gaze of not only the investigating policeman, but the curious (and narratively vulnerable) suspect of the crime, played by Humphrey Bogart, so that she appears visually (and therefore ideologically) vulnerable in ways that are by no means supported by the narrative.

On the other hand, there are many instances where a scene would be read, *à la* Mulvey, as supporting a hypothesis of a 'controlling male gaze' within the context of the film as a whole, that do confirm this reading in isolation. For example, the first meeting between the male protagonist of *Double Indemnity* (1944) and the seductive woman played by Barbara Stanwyck would be likely to be read in context as one where the man is in a position of power over the woman. When they first meet he is already known to the spectator as the protagonist: his point of view is pursued into the house where he, fully dressed, sees her covering her state of undress with a towel and subject to his explicitly desiring gaze; her reappearance is shown via a shot of her legs descending the staircase, apparently from his point of view; and the whole sequence is contextualised within his voice-over, before, during and after the scene. The Stanwyck character is presented as confident and self-contained, so that the averagely competent viewer might anticipate plot developments contrary to the protagonist's values and aspirations, in spite of his central narrative position, voice-over and controlling perspective. These suspicions might be aroused by the visual language of the scene, in which the camera position alternates between his and her points of view, making it unclear, during an uncontextualised viewing, who occupies the position of power, either visually or narratively. However, even here, the issue is one of ambiguity: the scene does not assert the Stanwyck character's power in contradiction to the narrative in the way that the Bogart character's power is asserted against the logic of the narrative in the scene from *In a Lonely Place*. Laura Mulvey may have overstated her case, but what these examples demonstrate is that she did have a case, and that what compromises it, most importantly, is the context of the narrative and overall point of view.

The most significant implication of both Mulvey and Carroll's (very different) conceptualisations is that they acknowledge the power of film to invite and confirm specific perspectives on represented events. This has important implications for assessing the power of film, both to reinforce ideological positions of the *status quo* and to challenge those same positions. If, through engagement of the spectator's sympathies with particular characters and/or situations in a fiction, film can moderate our responses towards a fictive situation, then securing this engagement will be an important strategy in certain types of realist fiction.

One final example will serve to sum up and concretise the points made in this chapter. There is a scene in *Thelma and Louise* (1991) which provides a clear instance of the distance between fictional and real-life responses, but also of the relation between them. This is the sequence near the beginning of the film in which Louise shoots the man who has attempted to rape Thelma in the car park. Louise has already prevented the rape by threatening the would-be rapist with a gun and he has conceded defeat. But he resists this defeat in his verbal aggression towards Louise. When he verbally insults her ('Suck my cock'), she shoots him dead. The spectator's pleasure in this rests simultaneously in the dramatic surprise of Louise's morally satisfying ability to respond to this insult adequately (she kills him) and identification with the ability to deflate his (sexist) arrogance – he didn't expect that, did he? Most viewers who find this episode pleasurable for these reasons would not, in fact, applaud the death of a man on these grounds. It is pleasurable because it makes a symbolic statement about the importance of the insult in the everyday experience of women: insult is symbolic of the contempt in which men hold women. A recent report on the experience of women in the British police force, for example, cites the practice of male police officers referring to *all* women as 'tarts' as a 'minor' example of sexism. It is not hard to see Louise's killing of the man in the car park as an act of revenge on behalf of all women who have been insulted in these 'minor' ways. We may not actually want to see the perpetrators of these insults dead, but we would like them to realise just how profound the insult is, and that *we* realise just how profound they intend the insult to be.

Notes

1   Bordwell takes a theoretical stance; for an empirical approach to these questions, see Paul Messaris (1994). Messaris argues that visual literacy depends more on the physiological processes of perception than most current theories allow for. We do not have to learn a 'vocabulary' of visual depiction in the way that we have to learn a vocabulary of language. For a philosophical approach to the same issue, see Gregory Currie (1995). Currie explores the relationship between depiction and perception through a concept he terms 'perceptual realism': 'For naturally generative systems of representation work by exploiting our visual capacities to recognise the objects represented, and so the experience of recognising a picture of a horse is in an important respect like the experience of recognising a horse when you see one' (1995: 90). Similarly, Stephen Price claims that computer-generated special effects anchor created 'pictures of objects in apparent photographic reality by employing realistic lighting (shadows, highlights, reflections) and surface texture detail ... which structurally corresponds to the viewer's audiovisual experience of three-dimensional space ... Perceptual realism designates a relationship between the image or film and the spectator, and it can encompass both unreal images and those which are referentially realistic. Because of this, unreal images may be referentially fictional but perceptually realistic' (1996: 32).

2   Hence the fierce critical debates generated by films that engage the politics of identity. See Chapter 7 for a more detailed discussion of the potential positionings available in these films.

3   This gendering of the cinematic look and conception of the spectator as male has been challenged by feminist and lesbian theorists. See, for example, Clare Whatling (1997), particularly Chapter 3, for an excellent analysis of the complexities of lesbian desire, identification and popular film. Many feminists are sceptical about the role of women in action movies, claiming that the incorporation of women into action roles formerly occupied by men in films such as *Terminator 2* and *Blue Steel* does little to alter patriarchal values; see, for example, Deborah Cartmell and Imelda Whelehan's (1998) introduction to their edited collection *Sisterhoods*.

4   See, for example, Torben Grodal (1997).

5   See 1970s apparatus theories, in particular Daniel Dayan (1974) and J. L. Baudry (1974).

6   *Concise Oxford Dictionary*, 1982.

Part II

Chapter 6

Re-visioning history: realism and politics

> To 'make a film politically' one must forget theory and be realistically
> aware of one's audience and how they can be reached – the form of
> address to which they might be expected to attend. If you wish to
> address, not just a tiny revolutionary elite, but a vast and heteroge-
> neous general public, then you make Salvador ... (Robin Wood
> 1990/1: 16)

The 1990s have seen a shift in concern amongst Anglo-American
film critics and theorists around the depiction of politics and
history in popular films. The legacy of 1970s *Screen* theory, which
favoured creating new visions of social life using Brechtian techniques of distanciation through the use of formal strategies in order
to create a radical text and a politicised viewer, remains pertinent,
but with the integration of many these techniques into mainstream
film and video practice, it has become increasingly apparent that
formal strategies alone cannot guarantee either a radical or a politically 'progressive' text nor a politicised viewer.[1] Brecht's contention that conventional (realist) dramatic forms produce a
crippling empathy with characters that fatalistically reconciles
spectators to social ills rather than encouraging them to intellectually engage and challenge them, is, as Murray Smith suggests, one
of the most tenacious arguments of twentieth-century aesthetic
theory.[2] The widespread teaching of Brecht's ideas, in terms of
their application to theatrical practice and their formal appropriation by film theory is undoubtedly responsible, both directly and
indirectly, for the prevalent use of an extensive range of inventive
formal strategies in a range of popular media forms encompassing
pop videos, television commercials, documentaries and some
mainstream films. This teaching has flourished, somewhat ironically, in a climate in which the foundationalist thinking underlying

Brecht's recommendations for practice, the class politics of Marxism, has been systematically undermined by feminist, gay and anti-
colonial politics which have not only challenged the blindness of
Marxism to issues other than class, but have themselves been seen
in some versions of postmodernism as redundant 'grand narratives'.[3] There is, of course, considerable debate about the efficacy
and/or desirability of postmodernism, both as a theory and a cultural practice. Some Marxists and feminists continue to insist on
the importance of class and gender as structures of inequality which
need to be challenged; others have embraced a postmodern politics
which rejects the singular focus and linearity of these perspectives.

As well as calling into doubt the foundational premises of a politics of identity based on singular categorical definitions of self-hood
such as 'working-class' and 'woman', postmodernism draws attention to the difficulties of developing forms of critical emancipatory
discourse. Any attempt to discuss the politics of a popular film text
in relation to realism as a mode of representation is problematic in
the face of such theoretical challenges. First, because it is now less
clear what does and does not constitute the category of 'politics': if
the personal, the cultural and the social are all included within the
political, as feminist and post-Marxist critiques suggest, then all
texts are political in some sense and none are specifically so. But
such an all-embracing notion of the political, while theoretically sus-
tainable, is too broad to serve the aims of this chapter, which takes
a far narrower, more common usage of the term in order to examine the cinematic representation of socio-economic systems, governments and their actions. This has the advantage of distinguishing
a particular group of film texts with an explicit address to political
issues from others, as well as according with the general understanding of the term in journalistic reviewing practice.

Secondly, and perhaps more crucially, if there is no longer a progressive 'grand narrative', if images are trapped within an endless
hermeneutic circle, then there is no overarching aim in view, no
requirement for emancipatory or critical thought, and no criteria for
establishing whether a text can challenge dominant conceptions of
the *status quo* since all viewpoints are equally valid. It would seem,
therefore, that the task of discussing realism in relation to the politics of a film text is an impossible task and bound to fail. But it is not
necessary to eschew a postmodern position in order to ask how realism operates as a political strategy in popular film. What might

'being political' imply for both producers and consumers in such a climate? Without seeking to make judgements on whether or not a text is (or can be) 'progressive' in a social and political sense, it is possible to ask whether it raises questions about the actions and nature of governments or socio-economic systems which might lead viewers to shift their personal schemata, to alter their 'templates of the familiar' to accommodate interpretations of political and historical events different from the commonsensical views that they are ordinarily familiar with.[4] In the 1990s, there is a widespread understanding that popular film and television mediate not only dominant perceptions of the *status quo*, but also construct images of the recent and more distant past through a range of codes and conventions broadly termed 'realism'. We agree with Ryan and Kellner (1988: 268) 'that it might be more important to accept the viewing assumptions of narrative realism in order to be better able to change the dominant figures of thought, value and action that are the substance of society'. The rupture of paradigmatic narratives through formal techniques of distanciation is not the only way to re-vision change; projecting different characters, using alternative plot strategies, tropes, actions, situations and events within conventional narrative frameworks are formal interventions that remain potentially accessible to audiences for popular films. A focus on these uses of realism in political films serves to illustrate both the diversity of approach and the range of limitations that mark the mediation of political critique through popular forms of cinematic expression.

Political themes and popular forms

There are two principal ways in which a popular film can attempt to disturb conventional depictions of the *status quo*: it can represent alternative views in a positive light, or it can expose the evils of the present system. Many political films, of course, do both. Whichever strategy is adopted, and whether or not its narrative is based on specific historical events, the political film is likely to be judged in terms of its overall accuracy (i.e. its fidelity to officially sanctioned representations of historical reality as well as attention to the details of period and setting) and its 'fairness'. Historical inaccuracy is invariably criticised, as is political 'bias', even when inaccuracy is not alleged. Perhaps because narrative film is perceived as primarily entertainment, or maybe out of a belief that historical situations can rarely be subject to unambiguous judgements, or perhaps because certain ideological positions are so deeply embedded that challenge to them is found very uncomfortable, a film is usually severely judged if it adopts a critical political position.

In practice, this mostly applies only to texts espousing a left-wing politics. The commonsense political discourses in contemporary capitalist societies span a range of positions from libertarian (especially with regard to such issues as gender and sexuality) to authoritarian, and permit a considerable amount of disagreement over, and criticism of, specific governments or government policies. What is excluded from these commonsense discourses is a rejection of either democracy (interpreted as a system of government involving an elected parliament) or capitalism *per se*. This renders any film advocating alternatives to Western democratic systems of government or capitalism as a radically political text.[5] Obviously, such radicalism could be either left- or right-wing. However, while left-wing alternatives such as communism or anarchism are commonsensically regarded as ranging from the evil to the idealistically naïve, and therefore in certain contexts capable of relatively sympathetic, if critical, representation, right-wing alternatives are too closely associated either with historically unacceptable forms such as German Nazism or Italian Fascism or with contemporary Islamic regimes (a currently perceived threat to both democracy and capitalism) for them to receive anything but outright rejection. To date, we know of no popular Anglo or American texts advocating such positions.

On the other hand, the authoritarian end of the spectrum of commonsense political discourse can be, and frequently is, represented in terms of conventional definitions of heroism, masculinity or public safety. Mainstream genres such as crime fiction, adventure stories, gangster movies, science fiction, horror films and war films all commonly involve the validation of undemocratic, violent resolution of conflict. Narratives where the villain is identified to the audience – as an enemy army, a criminal or a supernatural threat – preclude any questioning of the actions of the hero in his (usually) heroic mission to defeat it. In this sense, very many films – perhaps the majority of output in these genres (and they account for a considerable percentage of mainstream film production) – are political in import, and their politics is undoubtedly one that confirms the *status quo*. But such films are not usually considered to be about politics. While agreeing that they are of significant political importance ideologically, as has been amply demonstrated by, for example, Ryan and Kellner (1988), we will, for the purposes of this chapter, employ a narrower definition. As a result, for us, as for most film reviewers, a political film is not only one directly concerned with recognised political power structures, but is also likely to be, at least on the surface, critical of those structures; in brief, a political film is likely to be considered as left-wing, and qualify perhaps for Lukacs's definition of critical realism.[6] This is an interesting comment on how politics is defined in our society in many contexts: sexist, racist or homophobic behaviour may be defined as unpleasant, even unacceptable, but it is anti-sexist, anti-racist and anti-homophobic behaviour that is seen as political. To fight for one's country in war is merely a patriotic norm; to be a pacifist is a political act; and so on.

It is important to state that what constitutes a commonsense political discourse is not stable over time. The mainstream of the 1950s in Britain, for example, with its 'never had it so good' conservative agenda of social conformity that masked underlying homophobia, racism and sexism is clearly not the mainstream of the late 1990s, with its New Labour emphasis on stakeholding and avowed respect for difference. It is our contention that popular film is one of many modes of representation that has contributed to these changes. It may be that film, together with other representational forms, is only capable of mediating already existing changes, but it is certainly able, along with other media, to represent these changes in popular narratives that give them currency and perhaps shift the regimes of representation in crucial ways. In this chapter, we explore the extent to which, through popular realist narratives, film can shift regimes of representation in relation to political issues.

If the political film, as we have defined it for heuristic purposes, is most usually a form of 'critical' realism, it is possible to identify two principal modes in which this criticism is conducted. The majority of such films are, as we have suggested above, rhetorical. They aim to persuade audiences of particular political perspectives. A second category of political film, however, is more interrogative; these films explore issues in ways which challenge political orthodoxies, but without necessarily coming to a conclusion that is clearly recommended to the audience. Such films work in ways similar to some of Brecht's better known plays, such as *Mother Courage* or *The Good Woman of Setzuan*, and, we will argue, do succeed in revealing contradictions. It is interesting to note that a summary of the narrative of these plays by Brecht clearly points to the contradictions exposed by them, and does not depend on non-realist formal strategies of production. But whereas MacCabe's thesis suggests that the realist text cannot show contradiction, we will suggest, on the contrary, that 'critical' political films expose contradictions not merely within the text but through the text, by stimulating a struggle for control of the meaning of the text within the 'body politic' at the discursive levels of reception. The textual strategies employed in presenting a political message are much the same as those used in any genre film. However, while mise-en-scène, camerawork and sound may all be significant factors in a political film, we will focus specifically on three elements that, as we argued in Chapter 5, have a particular importance because of their potential to engage viewers with alternative perspectives on events and situations. These are narrative, characterisation (including casting) and alignment.

Narrative structures

There are three types of narrative which, while not specific to political films, are characteristic of them. The first of these is the biography of an historical political figure. The 'biopic' is a recognised Hollywood genre, which may be more or less faithful to the known facts about an historical personage. Many earlier 'biopics' were thinly disguised as fiction, for example, *Citizen Kane* (1941), widely believed to be about the newspaper tycoon William Randolph Hearst, although the character has a different name in the film. The fictional disguise allows for more licence in the construction of character and events without laying the film open to accusations of misrepresenting history, an ongoing issue in relation to the filmic depiction of historical events and personages. Later examples, such as *Lady Sings the Blues* (1972) (based on the life and times of Billie Holiday) and *Chaplin* (1992) present themselves as historical accounts with actors (Diana Ross and Robert Downey Jr respectively) playing the parts of real people. This is inevitably the form that the political biographical film takes, from *Young Mr Lincoln* (1939) to the more recent *Nixon* (1995). The subject of this type of film is often a hero of the people in conflict with the authorities who is represented as a sympathetic and usually heroic person. Like Rosa Luxemburg, Malcolm X and Michael Collins in the films named after them, these political heroes usually meet an untimely, violent death at the hands of their enemies, which distinguishes them from most popular Hollywood films, especially the action genres, where heroism is not only rewarded, but almost defined, by the hero's success. Such films are therefore not only tragedies, but rhetorical in mode, if not without a critical perspective on the protagonist, as well as the authority he or she represents. Two exceptions are *Nixon* and *Schindler's List* (1993), the latter of which is discussed below as an example of a more interrogative film. Assuming the audience has at least a basic knowledge of the history, which, in many cases, is informed by advance publicity for the film, this genre lacks the element of narrative tension, since the outcome of events is generally well known. The interest is, therefore, more on the process of the character's development, together with an explication of the ideas he or she embodies and the forces ranged against him or her.

A second narrative structure characteristic of the political film is the conspiracy. These films are structured as thrillers, in which the enemy is the State, or a faction of the State, plotting secretly in its own interests against at least a section of the people, and responsible for breaking the law, not excluding murder. Probably the most noted example of this genre is *JFK* (1991), with its thesis that President John F. Kennedy was the victim not of a lone resentful psychotic, as the official version has it, but of a conspiracy by the military-industrial complex in the United States. Political conspiracy dramas became prevalent in Hollywood films in the 1970s, beginning with *Executive Action* (1973) which depicts a right-wing plot to kill President Kennedy. Ryan and Kellner argue that the success of the genre in that decade speaks to a generic assent between films and audiences of growing distrust with the processes and practices of government as liberal political agendas became increasingly out of step with conservative economic realities. The in-built contradictions of an individualistic liberal ethos in American society make it difficult to define social reform in anything but individual terms (Ryan and Kellner 1988: 95–105). The almost paranoid sense of state-corporate conspiracy in Hollywood's political films rests on turning the systematic concealment of capitalist power structures into personalised accounts of struggle against monolithic institutions whose power seems hidden and insurmountable. Other films of this type include *Missing* (1982), *Silkwood* (1983), *Hidden Agenda* (1990) and *In the Name of the Father* (1993), all of which accuse Western governments in capitalist societies of violence against their own people. The heroes in these conflicts are either the victims themselves, or the investigators of the conspiracy, often caught up involuntarily before realising its extent. Again, these heroes are rarely successful. The state proves too powerful, and heroism and truth are defeated. So, while the narrative depends, like all thrillers, on the tensions involved in solving an enigma, these tensions are not the dominant pleasure of the film: they serve to communicate the political critique which is the point of the film. Interest is rarely in narrative tension, since again the outcome is probably known to the audience, although focusing on the activities of the investigators may allow for some tension concerning their fates. These films are often rhetorical, their tactics of interrogation only serving to underline their polemical message, as in *Hidden Agenda* for example, but in some cases they interrogate events and circumstances without suggesting a political solution as in *JFK*, discussed in more detail below.

The third type of narrative may be either rhetorical or interrogative. It is set within an historical situation of political importance, but deals with the experiences of one or two individuals, more or less central to the situation, in such a way as to comment on and/or raise questions about the logic or morality of that situation. This type of narrative, focused on the fate of individuals, is the familiar structure of most popular films, but the difference here is that the fate of the individuals in a political film is explicitly determined by their relationship to political events. This category would include films as different as *Reds* (1981), *A World Apart* (1987), *Cry Freedom* (1987), *Schindler's List* (1993), *Land and Freedom* (1995) and *Some Mother's Son* (1996). The appeal of this strategy is that audiences are used to narratives which focus on a few individuals; alignment with character(s) personalises the conflict and facilitates an understanding of the situation. Here, the outcome is not necessarily known, especially if the characters are fictional, so that the usual narrative pleasures of anticipation and enigma are present. The problem with using this strategy, of course, is that allegiance with particular individuals will overwhelm interest in the general issues being dealt with, creating 'the dangerous mesh of empathy' that Brecht and others considered an anathema to any understanding of the underlying political implications of the situation. This is particularly the case when these individuals are either attractive or successful.

Certainly this accusation was brought against *Reds*; the film depicts the lives of John Reed and Louise Bryant, played by Warren

Beatty and Diane Keaton, two early twentieth-century journalists and left-wing radicals who become involved in the momentous historical events of the Russian Revolution. Beatty and Keaton might be expected to secure audience sympathy for the revolution through their support of revolutionary action but at the expense of glamorising the historical event. Given that the scene depicting the storming of the Winter Palace is intercut with Reed and Bryant making love, there is a suggestion that the revolution is forming a background for their romance, rather than taking centre stage. But it might equally be argued that, enacted to the rousing strains of the 'Internationale', it succeeds in informing revolutionary politics with a set of positive orgasmic emotions – feelings which some analysts suggest are too all often absent from left-wing political films with their sober, moralistic messages.[7] In comparison, consider *Schindler's List*. Spielberg's selection of Schindler's narrative through which to tell a story of the Holocaust that has a happy ending – the fate of those Jews saved from the death camps by Schindler – conforms to the requirements of a mainstream feature film. But the fate of this group is constantly located within the overall atrocity of the Holocaust: we are never allowed to rejoice at the survival of Schindler's people, because of the overwhelming presence of mass murder in the film. This makes Schindler's achievement both heroic and pathetic, as he himself admits at the end of the film. It is possible to perceive this in the scene where Schindler's people, mistakenly sent to Auschwitz, are rescued from certain death by a countermanding order. As they leave, the camera draws back from the group of saved Jews, to reveal the general scene in the camp – of those many, many more Jews, destined to die. The effect is to deny the audience any sense of elation: even relief is muted, since advance publicity ensured that the public knew the group would, in fact, survive. A similar example can be found at the end of *Cry Freedom* when, after the successful escape of Donald Woods (the white British journalist who has befriended the murdered black activist Steve Biko) from South Africa, the film ends with a scene of conflict in a Johannesburg 'township'. With the camera sited among the inhabitants, the police appear as aggressors from the audience viewpoint – a marked difference from the usual newsreel footage, which is invariably shot from behind the police lines. The previous alignment with the converted outsider character, whose story is satisfactorily resolved, is placed within the overall political situation in

which the people of South Africa continue to be oppressed. The success of this strategy was confirmed by collectors for anti-apartheid
outside cinemas in the UK, who reported cinemagoers leaving in
tears and donating generously.

Characterisation
The issue of characterisation is obviously crucial in enlisting audience involvement in, and sympathy with, the politics of a film
through alignment with the characters. That characters representing
unpopular political positions will enlist such alignment more successfully if they are attractive and personable individuals almost goes
without saying; so it is not surprising to find figures like Malcolm X
and Steve Biko represented by handsome actors, in order to persuade audiences to feel well disposed towards their views and activities. This is a standard practice in casting: but whereas in films
informed by a mainstream ideological position this attractiveness
confirms expectations by presenting a congruence between ethics
and aesthetics, in the political film it constitutes a challenge to commonsense expectations, and is all the more important as a strategy.
A mainstream film can afford to take risks and create new definitions
of attractiveness through casting actors with unconventional appearances in roles that assume their appeal, but employing the strategy
of casting an attractive actor in an unpopular social role, such as a
political activist, is a safer option, although, as noted above, it lays
the representation open to accusations of glamorisation. One effect
can be to play down the fate of those others who are not depicted as
attractive or as successful – a criticism, examined in more detail
below, levelled at the representation of the Jews in *Schindler's List*.

There are, however, more subtle effects available through characterisation and casting in communicating a political message. Consider, for example, the casting of Peter Postlethwaite in the role of
Gerald Conlon in *In the Name of the Father*. It is not only through
the narrative information given to the audience about this character's innocence of terrorist activities that the injustice of his conviction is asserted: his screen presence conveys the impression of a
well-meaning, decent, but definitely unadventurous man. As the
narrative proceeds, his physical presence continues to insist on the
incredibility of the official definition of him as a terrorist and therefore on the injustice of his imprisonment, potentially engaging both
concern and moral alignment with his situation. A rather different

effect is produced by the casting of Helen Mirren as the mother of an IRA hunger striker in *Some Mother's Son*. Known to audiences in Britain through her role as a competent, if embattled, police chief in the television series *Prime Suspect*, she has a reputation as a serious actor which lends weight to her role in the film as a woman who campaigns on behalf of the hunger strikers (who were allowed to die without widespread protest in Britain) and is faced with the dilemma of whether or not to authorise her son to be saved from death.

Point of view

A final consideration is point of view. Audience alignment with characters and events can develop a viewer's allegiance to the political message conveyed. In the biographical films, alignment is generally with the leading protagonist, so that, whatever the degree of criticism of that character, there will be a tendency to understand, if not completely sympathise with, the historical figure, which may well conflict with conventionally accepted views of him or her. This is presumably why such films are often controversial, regardless of historical accuracy and/or the presence of a critical perspective. To make people like Michael Collins, the Birmingham Six, Rosa Luxemburg or Malcolm X attractive, sympathetic figures challenges official historical constructions of them (as 'terrorists' or 'loony left' revolutionaries) and necessarily fails to show 'the other side of the story'. The latter is an obsession with film reviewers with regard to political films; war films, crime fictions, adventure stories and so on, even romances, all have 'another side to the story', but we rarely find them accused of omitting to do justice to the point of view of the enemy army or the criminals. In the development of Hollywood cinema, shifts in the construction of point of view have, of course, occurred – as with the ideological rehabilitation of Native Americans in the western – but the question does not usually arise with respect to individual films. *Some Mother's Son*, for example, was accused of being a one-sided view of events, although it is hard to see how a narrative about the dilemma of a Catholic woman confronted with her son participating in a hunger strike could have included a Unionist perspective. In fact, this film is interrogative rather than rhetorical; the hunger strike is the setting and cause of the mother's dilemma, which in itself questions both the efficacy and the motivations of the strike as a political strategy, and interrogates the role of the IRA and the hunger strikers themselves, as well as that of the British Government.

In the other types of political film there are two possible align-ment positions for the audience: either with the participants them-selves or with an outsider whose character serves as a point of alignment in relation to a situation with which they are assumed to be unfamiliar. The former is the less common, and since the tech-nique is similar to that of the biographical film, the focus here is on the latter. The assumption seems to be that audiences need a point of entry into a situation which is provided by a character more like themselves than the subject of the film. In most cases this outsider character is of the same nationality as the target audience (i.e. Amer-ican or British in the films we are concerned with) when the subject and their situation is located outside that nation. Thus, the story of the South African Steve Biko and his struggle against apartheid is told by Donald Woods, a white South African (English) journalist. *Missing* (1982) portrays the events in Chile following the overthrow of the Allende government by Pinochet with the aid of the American government through the experiences of a white middle-class Amer-ican, played by Hollywood star Jack Lemmon. He is initially incred-ulous of his left-wing daughter's suspicions of the horrors following the coup and of American participation in them, but is persuaded by events to accept her interpretation of the situation. Here American audiences are encouraged, through alignment with the Jack Lemmon character, to alter their perceptions and to be persuaded to criticise their own government.[8] A similar narrative strategy is used in *Salvador* (1986), where an American journalist is persuaded of his government's collusion with the death squads in that country, but in this case he is a less sympathetic character, an arrogant bully only interested in furthering his own interests. During the process of events, he starts to question his motivations and actions as he becomes increasingly aware of the extent of American involvement in El Salvador and its opposition to the popular movement for non-military self-determination. His own transformation provides a pos-sible point of alignment for viewers who share a similar perspective initially, but might be persuaded to become critical of government policy. In conspiracy films, the main protagonist is inevitably the inquirer into the conspiracy: the lawyer in *JFK*, convinced that Kennedy was assassinated by the American military; the journalist in *Hidden Agenda*, who uncovers the British Government's 'shoot to kill' policy; the journalist again in *The Killing Fields* (1984) who investigates American government involvement in the bombing of Cambodia. Journalists and lawyers are obviously well placed to investigate conspiracies, so this makes for a plausible narrative, but the effect is also to align the audience with a middle-class, invariably white figure, as with most outsider narratives of this type. *Land and Freedom* (1995) is an exception in pursuing the experiences of a working-class man's participation in the Spanish Civil War, although he too is partly an outsider in that conflict.

It would seem that, on the whole, filmmakers are somewhat timid in their assumptions about the scope of audiences' willingness to align themselves with unfamiliar or unpopular characters. In other genres this has not proved an obstacle to popularity. Although those films that challenge traditional views of Native Americans in the western usually employ strategies aimed to align viewers with a white male character – as in *Dances with Wolves* (1990), for example – gangster movies from the beginning featured criminals as heroes, and the more recent spate of violent films such as those directed by Tarantino have had ruthless criminals as leading protagonists. Arguably, the extension of the range of social roles with which audiences have been invited to align themselves in order to represent the lives of independent women, gay people and black people, in spite of the tendency to recuperate difference and represent 'them' as 'just like us', has been a major contribution to shifting stereotypical regimes of representation in popular moving image dramas.[9] It might seem that the effort required of audiences in making such alignments (assuming a shift to be necessary for the majority audience) is not less than that required to align themselves across lines of class and nationhood.

The evaluation of political films frequently situates them within wider debates about modernism and postmodernism, indicative perhaps of the deep suspicion of popular culture still harboured by many intellectuals. In the subsequent sections of this chapter, three films act as catalysts to explore these issues. Within this context, questions are raised concerning the responsibilities of filmmakers in relation to artistic licence, the representation of historical 'facts' and the role of films in creating popular memory, questions which, as we pointed out above, continue to be asked of popular films that adopt critical political positions.

Direct intervention: *Cry Freedom*

It seems apposite to begin our discussion with a film of the mid-1980s which now seems very moderate in its politics, but at the time constituted a radical intervention in British representations of the apartheid regime in South Africa. Richard Attenborough's *Cry Freedom*, made in 1987 and distributed by an American studio (Universal/MCA), was the first mainstream film to deal directly with the issue of apartheid. It did so with an unambiguous denunciation of the white South African regime and equally unequivocal support for its black opponents. Today, with a black government in South Africa whose former president Nelson Mandela is a hero world-wide, and apartheid universally condemned, the film's stance seems unexceptional. But only a decade or so ago British attitudes towards apartheid were less focused and more equivocal. Opposition to apartheid in Britain, which gathered some momentum in the 1960s, was generally perceived as a left-wing activity alongside opposition to nuclear arms and the Vietnam War, rather than as a popularly accepted 'commonsense' ethical position. General press coverage of South Africa did not necessarily mention apartheid as a system of racial exclusion, or if it did, tended to compare the situation of its black inhabitants with the plight of those in other African countries, not always in favour of the latter, while fictional representations, in films such as *Zulu* (1964), represented African people, or rather African men, as savage threats to civilisation.

In many respects, *Cry Freedom* was accurately perceived as a timid film politically. Left-wing critiques of it pointed rightly to its selection both of a white British protagonist as the figure for audience alignment to the exclusion of a black perspective, and of a non-violent political activist as the representative of the black community's opposition. Despite the long history of non-violent opposition to apartheid both in South Africa itself and in Britain, press and television coverage would probably have given the British public an impression of that opposition as characterised by violence, at least in the sense of disorder and illegality. So the characterisation in *Cry Freedom* of Steve Biko as a reasonable, ethical man committed to justice and non-violence, and also with an attractive appearance and personable presence, who is murdered by the South African police, constituted a significant intervention in mainstream representations of the conflict.

The film is based on two books written by the exiled liberal journalist Donald Woods about his relationship with the former leader of the Black Consciousness Movement, Steve Biko. A very brief outline cannot encompass either the complexity of internal South African politics in which Biko was involved, or the events that lead to his death and their aftermath; but by the time of Attenborough's film in 1987, world opinion was beginning to turn against the official regime in South Africa. In 1970, at the age of 23, Biko was the first President of the South African Students Organisation (SASO) and a major figure in the Black Consciousness Movement. The Movement was informed by a black separatist revolutionary ideology that had little time for white liberalism;[10] not wanting to be banned and imprisoned like the leaders of the ANC, Biko and his colleagues were careful to obey the law, confining their activities to philosophical and political speeches and social work. Nevertheless in 1974 he was placed under a 'banning' order, prevented from any political activity and restricted to moving only amongst his family and meeting with one other person. In 1977, in the aftermath of the Soweto riots, he was arrested and subsequently died in police custody. Woods, a newspaper editor and a known associate, was placed under a banning order for five years, permitted neither to write nor publish. A month after Biko's murder at the hands of the security forces, the South African Government declared all black consciousness movement organisations illegal. Ten years later, world opinion on the South African regime had changed to the extent that some foreign banks, concerned about the possibility of civil war, were beginning to curb their South African investments. Commonwealth heads of state were determinedly pressing the British government to impose crippling economic sanctions. *Cry Freedom* opened in America the day before President Reagan and Margaret Thatcher were due to meet to discuss what, if any, new steps should be taken to increase the pressure for majority rule. The US Congress was debating the implementation of new world-wide trade embargoes, with Reagan and Thatcher leading the opposition against any further trading restrictions. Politically, the film's intervention was a timely one.

Cry Freedom was released in Britain to a barrage of criticism from the press; pronouncements on the film varied from 'worthy but dull', to a denouncement of it as propaganda. Much of this criticism was undoubtedly due to the film's narrative structure; although Attenborough adopts the conventions of the Hollywood epic, the film forgoes action in favour of words, development of character in favour of polemic. Structured around three massive set pieces at the beginning, middle and end of the film, the first half depicts the developing friendship between Woods and Biko. The film opens with the bulldozing of the Crossroads settlement near Cape Town by the white authorities before people have time to gather their meagre possessions; amidst clouds of choking tear gas, they are driven away or crushed in their homes. Later that morning, a white radio station describes the success of the police in peaceably dispersing squatters from an illegal township. This opening sequence, filmed as dramatised documentary, sets the scene of oppression, but this larger vision is not maintained. Whilst there is much talk of oppression and violence in the first half of the film, little of this is shown, although there is a slow build-up of harassment from the authorities, eventually leading to Biko's arrest. The detail of Biko's imprisonment and eventual death is sparse; instead, there is a lavish set piece funeral, a scene that required something in excess of fifteen thousand extras. This orchestrated spectacle is followed by an account of the Woods family's attempt to flee South Africa, culminating in their eventual escape. The shift in narrative attention away from Biko to the Woods family was a source of disquiet to reviewers in the liberal press, who might have been expected to enthusiastically support its oppositional message.

Adam Mars Jones in the *Independent* commented that the film 'does nothing to refute Biko's belief that white liberals often used the black revolutionary cause to further their own ambitions'[11] while the *Village Voice*, accepting that the film was well-intentioned and indignant, found it self-righteously paternalistic: 'Attenborough's speciality is presenting Third World liberation as inoffensive to First World moviegoers'.[12] Critique in these reviews hinged on the presentation of Woods as 'champion of the black cause' to the detriment of focusing on Biko and the complexities of South African politics. The casting of Denzel Washington in the Biko role was a further source of consternation, in spite of Attenborough's claims that he had screen tested numerous African actors for the part, before deciding on an American to play the role. Biko, introduced as a young black demagogue, shot through the leaves of a tree and brightly backlit in beatific white light, is rather thinly characterised as an intellectual leader, leading to accusations of political bias and inaccuracy among numerous reviewers – a common occurrence, as we noted above. The film's strongest champions were found in the right-wing press, which heralded the political commitment of the Woods family,[13] and, despite its intellectual and historical paucity, praised its 'triumphant emotional polemic'.[14]

In America the film failed to attract an audience, perhaps because of its ponderous, polemical style.[15] In South Africa, the film opened to packed houses in thirty cinemas nation wide, only to be seized and confiscated by the police. Three years later, in the wake of measures designed to end white majority rule, it reopened without controversy. In an interview with *The Times*, Attenborough claimed that although a failure in America, the film was well received in Germany, Japan, Sweden and throughout Europe: 'Even if the film will never make it into the Box Office Top 500 in *Variety*, I'm very proud of the fact that we made it. The statistics of the anti-apartheid movement show that wherever it has been shown recruitment has rocketed'.[16] Such attributions of cause and effect are, of course, impossible to verify, but the film undoubtedly contributed to the debate on apartheid in Britain at a time when the government regarded the ANC and their president Nelson Mandela as 'terrorists'. Attenborough is right to attest that, whatever the merits of the film, it remains as a record of the existence of apartheid; the final credits are a roll call of those who died in police custody with the official explanations of their death – self-strangulation, suicide, slipped in the shower – a chilling memorial to an oppressed people's fight for change.

Challenging 'the settled bodies of history': *JFK*

If *Cry Freedom* presents itself as a radical intervention (at least from an establishment perspective) in the representation of apartheid, *JFK* challenges the official version of the past, accusing the American government of conspiracy and deception. Oliver Stone is one of the few successful Hollywood filmmakers to have continuously produced films which intervene in the contemporary politics of American society. More than any other Hollywood movie, it is Stone's prodigious production *JFK* that has engaged (and enraged) critics with questions of artistic licence and the responsibility of the cinematic historian to the representation of political history. The film re-presents not only a historical narrative but a hypothesis, arguing that the Warren Commission's investigation of President John F.

Kennedy's assassination was a cover-up of immense proportions. According to the film, Kennedy was a cold war liberaliser whose stance on Vietnam provoked a vast conspiracy within the US government that aimed to eliminate him, thereby staging a *coup d'état* and installing a president more sympathetic to entrenched American military, industrial and economic interests. The film generated an intense interest in US public affairs and demands from across the political spectrum for the government to open up its records for public scrutiny.

The film's producer and director is no stranger to courting controversy. Earlier films such as *Salvador* (1986), *Platoon* (1986), *Wall Street* (1987) and *Born on the Fourth of July* (1989) had similarly taken issue with the government's relationship to the triple forces of imperialism, militarism and capitalism: what Eisenhower famously referred to as the power of the military-industrial complex and its domination of American civic life. *Platoon* and *Born on the Fourth of July* reopened debate on the Vietnam War for a new generation, placing the experiences of those who fought in the war and their treatment by the US government at the centre of public consciousness. *JFK* can be seen as a continuation of Stone's interest in raising the spectre of Vietnam, a result of his own experiences as a Vietnam veteran and consequent disillusion with American foreign policy. In interviews, however, Stone has explicitly denied that he is motivated by political objectives: 'I consider first and foremost my films to be dramas about individuals engaged in personal struggles, and I consider myself a dramatist before I am a political filmmaker – that's what links all my films – stories of an individual in struggle with his identity, his integrity, his soul ... I do not believe in the collective version of history'.[17]

This perhaps goes some way to explain Stone's preference for filmmaking strategies that aim to forge a strong involvement between viewers and events depicted on the screen. He is the antithesis of a Brechtian filmmaker, favouring a character-centred classical narrative structure that focuses on a single male protagonist. In all the above films a young male is forced to choose between competing ethical values often embodied in contrasting portrayals of older, more experienced men: the two sergeants in *Platoon*, for example, and the two father figures in *Wall Street*, one the protagonist's own father, the other a corrupt stockbroker. Stone's 'bad father' figures embody the negative aspects of American values enshrined in capitalism and imperialism; the good father embodies various possible alternatives which are never effective.[18]

The narrative trajectories of Stone's films play out this oedipal drama of masculine development against a background of political events, but unlike in most classical melodramas, in these films political events are integral to the development of character, emphasising that the construction of American masculinity is deeply implicated in the social and political organisation of society. At one level, the narrative structure of *JFK* continues to engage these concerns. Garrison (Kevin Costner) is depicted as an all-American family man, a good father and a good husband, who refuses to be corrupted or swayed from what he believes is the truth. The casting of Kevin Costner as a Capra-esque reincarnation of James Stewart in *Mr Smith Goes to Washington* (1939), a character well-known as a common man who tries to uphold the virtues of traditional American ideals of freedom and democracy but meets resistance from powerful corrupt politicians, encourages viewer alignment and moral allegiance with Garrison's quest for truth. President Kennedy is presented in a similarly positive light, as a loyal family man and a model statesman dedicated to serving his country with no hint of the scandals concerning his associations with Marilyn Monroe and the Mafia tarnishing the 'golden king' image. This iconic portrait is substantiated by home movie footage and news clips of the handsome, youthful president with his elegant wife and two young children, emphasising his popular appeal. Positioned in Manichean opposition to this romanticised portrait of a more innocent age are the Secret Service and those who control it, a malevolent but unseen force that pervades all aspects of public life. The only visible manifestations of this evil are the small-time collaborators and informers Clay Shaw, David Ferrie and Willie O'Keefe. These three men are depicted as Fascist, sexually promiscuous and mentally unbalanced homosexual characters, sustaining a deeply conservative traditional Hollywood image of 'perverted' male sexuality as the visible face of corruption within the body politic.[19] Similarly, the depiction of Garrison's wife as a politically naïve woman whose only concern is the effect of the investigation on their family life seems somewhat at odds with contemporary definitions of what might constitute a 'radical' text. But perhaps part of the strength of the film lies within this very conventional use of classical filmic depictions of gender and sexuality, which is not to condone their use but to suggest that this conservative social dogma, while an affront to both feminist and gay critics, viewers and sympathisers, made it more difficult for right-wing critics of the film to discredit Stone as a left-wing anarchist whose only purpose is to undermine the dominant *status quo*.

Attempts to discredit both Stone and the film appeared before the film was completed and were sustained for seven months in an attempt to create a political climate that would prevent the film ever reaching the public. While still in its first weeks of shooting, Jon Margolis of the *Chicago Tribune* claimed the film was 'an insult to the intelligence'.[20] In the *Washington Post*, George Will claimed the film was 'an act of execrable history and contemptible citizenship by a man of technical skill, scant education and negligible conscience'.[21] James Petras argues that these attacks on the film's politics, months in advance of its release, by commentators who had neither viewed the film nor read its screenplay 'speaks to the knee-jerk political reflexes that have become so much part of the mass media's sub-servient defence of the American political elite' (Petras 1992: 16). In an article published just days after the opening of *JFK*, the *New York Times* columnist Bernard Weinrab attacked both the film and its maker, renewing calls for studio censorship of films that question official accounts of historical events.[22] Throughout the furore, Stone staunchly defended the film; in an address to the National Press Club, he challenged the failure of his critics to interrogate those implicated in the assassination, defending the right of filmmakers, journalists and writers to question 'settled bodies of history' (Stone 1992: 23–4).

The historical target of Stone's cinematic investigation is the report on the assassination compiled in its immediate aftermath by the Warren Commission, which, as far as Stone and numerous crit-ics and historians are concerned, fails to provide a satisfactory explanation of not only why the President was killed, but who was implicated in the murder. The film recreates the investigation insti-gated by the officially discredited New Orleans district attorney Jim Garrison, focusing on his examination of the evidence and the col-lection of testimony from eyewitnesses and known associates of the convicted killer Lee Harvey Oswald, who was himself murdered before he could be brought to testify. Although the structure of the narrative conforms to well-worn generic conventions in its overall investigative trajectory, the interrogation of the evidence is matched by real-isation of the events depicted in a complex internal narrative structure which flashes both forwards and backwards as conflicting points of view and speculation are played out against each other, using a range of realist forms of depiction, such as news footage culled from television reports, photographs and recreated *vérité* documentary. For some critics, 'the montage is the message', the film's fragmented style of narration presenting competing versions of 'the truth'; testimony is re-viewed and contradicted even as it is stated.[23] *JFK* builds the case for conspiracy using both real and recreated TV news and documentary footage shot on 16mm, home movies shot on 8mm, models, diagrams, press photographs and reconstructed photographs woven together through the agency of Garrison and the more familiar trappings of the mainstream investigative thriller. This mixing of factual material that inscribes or documents original events with re-enactment sequences laid the film open to charges of 'fictionalising' history and distorting the past, with the subsequent result that viewers (and young people in particular) would unquestioningly believe this unofficial version of events. Stone was accused of fostering paranoia and undermining faith in the practices and processes of government. The rapid editing style of the film was considered by some to be particularly aggressive in this respect, delivering the film's message 'in a pummelling style, a left to the jaw, a right to the solar plexus, flashing forward, flashing backward, crosscutting relentlessly, shooting "in tight", blurring, obfuscating, bludgeoning the viewer until Stone wins, he hopes by a TKO'.[24]

The assumption here is that viewers are tricked and beaten into submission to accept the film's conspiracy thesis, rather than being convinced by the logic of narration that the film presents a plausible interpretation of events. But this assumption ignores both intertextual and extratextual factors. In terms of the latter, evidence suggests that a large proportion of Americans already believed in some form of conspiracy before the film's release.[25] In terms of the former, Stone claimed his editing strategy was analogous to reading the Warren Commission's Report, twenty-six volumes of undigested fragments that contradict themselves. For some viewers, watching the film was reminiscent of unfolding layers of a story as it was experienced at the time, a series of disconnected and contradictory fragments absorbed from television news reports, radio announcements, documentaries, newspaper articles, home movies, books, whispered rumours and shocked announcements from friends and family. The

contextualising montage of historical footage and dramatic re-enactment that opens the film embeds Garrison's investigation in a seemingly disassociated cluster of 1960s political iconography that
includes news footage of the Cuban revolution and the Bay of Pigs
fiasco, Kennedy's declaration that the fight in Vietnam is
unwinnable, footage of Martin Luther King and the Civil Rights
movement and the dramatic re-enactment of a woman thrown from
a moving car. Only later does this montage become suggestive; for
Pat Dowell, the editing of *JFK* 'is an epistemological assertion about
the world, what we know and can know … Every cut produces only
one conviction, that the past we thought we shared is a mosaic of
conflicting histories, a History just this side of chaos'.[26]

For some film critics and historians, *JFK* is seen as a postmodernist
work of cinematic history which presents all of its events as if they
were equally 'historical' and 'really happened'. Hayden White argues
that, 'Everything is presented as if it were of the same ontological
order, both real and imaginary – realistically imaginary or imaginar-
ily real, with the result that the referential function of the images of
events is etiolated' (White 1996: 19). White suggests that the criticisms levelled against Stone – in particular, the accusations that the
film blurs fact and fiction – need to be understood in the context of
the difficulty experienced by present generations of coming to terms
with the meaning of historical events that prior to the twentieth century could not possibly have occurred. Two world wars, the Holocaust, nuclear destruction and pollution, the use of scientific
technology to wreak mass destruction on human life, the Depression, poverty and hunger on a world-wide scale defy explanation in
simplistic narrative form. He insists that it is not the facts that are at
issue, 'but the different possible meanings that such facts can be construed as bearing' (White 1996: 21). None of these events can be
understood through the actions of individual human agents who can
neither discriminate between the causes of events nor their short- or
longer-term effects. Any attempt to understand the Kennedy assassination has to cope with a potentially infinite number of details and a
context that is equally infinitely extensive. For White, these problems are respectably resolved through storytelling (fabulation)
because the historical event by definition is a past event and cannot
be represented as an object of knowledge with any certainty: 'The
issues raised in the controversy over *JFK* could be profitably set
within a more recent phase of the debate over the relation of histor-

ical fact to fiction peculiar to the relation between modernism and postmodernism' (White 1996: 24).

Janet Staiger disagrees with White on some fundamental issues, one of which is that the mixing of fact and fiction within filmic texts is necessarily a contemporary phenomenon – re-enactment has been a common practice since the earliest days of filmmaking. But more germane are her comments on *JFK*'s reception: Staiger claims that the critics and spectators of twentieth-century histories are knowledgeable readers, in that they have learned the rules of representation and read the film as a dramatic narration.

> It is not the formal properties of the editing strategies that makes the movie (post)modern; rather, it is the reading strategies of the viewers who recognise that the movie is a subjective version of the past, created by shots put together by some agent. What is undecidable, finally, is who is appropriately authorised to fill in the missing narrative material. (Staiger 1996: 52)

Equivocation amongst the viewers and reviewers of the film is less a product of the film's internal structure than a continuing search for a satisfying narrative resolution because the assassination remains an 'unsolved mystery'. The internal contradictions presented by the text are representative of a common feeling among many American viewers, exposed by the text rather than a product of the text. By bringing together a number of competing conspiracy theories and suggesting links between them, it unified common feelings of dissatisfaction with the official account of events and activated a political response that led to calls for increased public accountability and access to official records.

Enscribing popular memory: *Schindler's List*

The critics of *Schindler's List* are similarly preoccupied with questions of who can author popular history, but for rather different reasons. The film occupies an altogether more ambiguous cultural and political ground than either of the two films discussed above. Although it is not the first film to attempt to convey the horrific magnitude of the Holocaust, it is the first Hollywood 'blockbuster' made by a Jewish director to engage a mass audience with the Nazi practices of ethnic cleansing and mass genocide.[27] Not only does the film presume to represent events so horrific that they have been deemed by many artists and critics beyond all forms of expression, but it does so from the point of view of an exceptional German Nazi, Schindler, using the stylistic conventions of the historical epic. The film achieved popularity on a world-wide scale, creating controversy and debate wherever it was shown. In doing so, it constructs a popular memory of the Holocaust through the existing codes and conventions of mainstream film, a language that many critics and commentators consider a totally unsuitable form of expression for the collective 'remembering' of horrors that are deemed by many beyond representation. The discussion here will draw on these criticisms to suggest that for many of the critics an underlying current in their evaluation of the film is a modernist opposition to the commodification of culture and history and an accompanying hostility to the film's eclectic (postmodern) style.

Made by the most financially successful individual director in the history of Hollywood, *Schindler's List* achieved success on a global scale, becoming a media event of epic proportions that generated extensive media coverage and debate. For many watching the film, the events of the Second World War are well known through the mediations of social and political history represented in books, magazines, film and television, and increasingly through museums and theme parks. The film contributes to and extends this history, entering popular consciousness when eyewitness survivors of the Holocaust atrocities are diminishing in numbers as they gradually die of old age. The collective desire to preserve the memory of the Holocaust – and to consume that memory – occurs at the very moment when the personal testimony of the witnesses is becoming history.

> The film reifies the fragile moment of transition in historical consciousness from lived, personal memories to collective, manufactured memory. Furthermore, this moment signifies the victory of collective memory as transmitted by popular culture over a memory contested and debated by professional historians. (Loshitzky 1997: 3)

The story of the Holocaust, as recounted in *Schindler's List*, is one that celebrates salvation of the few rather than focusing on the mass death of the many, marking a generational shift in sensibilities and Holocaust narrative tropes; it is a film about survival rather than death, redemption rather than annihilation. As such, it challenges 'the limits of representation' erected around the Holocaust by

'making the unimaginable imaginable, the unrepresentable repre-
sentable' (Loshitzky 1997: 2).[28] A taboo on explicitly representing
the Holocaust was advocated and practised by artists of the generation of survivors as a mark of dignity and respect for the millions of
people who were killed, but with the waning of this generation, the
taboo is loosening its moral grip. Loshitzky suggests that what matters to American Jews such as Spielberg (and the American Jewish
community at large) is not death but survival; the mourning for the
six million Jews annihilated in Europe is symbolically transformed
into a celebration of the lives of five million Jews living in America
today. By desacralising the taboo on imagining the Holocaust, the
memory is 'colonised' by a diasporic American Jewish culture, dis-
placing not only the personal testimony of the older generation but
also the European sensibility which, to date, has structured the cinematic imagination of the Holocaust (Loshitzky 1997: 4).

The making of the film coincided with the opening of the Holocaust museum in Washington DC, itself emblematic of the growing
centrality of the Holocaust to debates about Jewish identity in the
multicultural struggles that partition the ethnic landscapes of contemporary American society. In this context, Spielberg was transformed from a maker of light-hearted fantasy entertainment to a
'serious' filmmaker, from Hollywood's greatest showman to its finest
artist. Accounts of the film stressed its factual authenticity and its use
of documentary strategies, in contrast to the technical wizardry and
action-packed intensity of Spielberg's usual products. The assumptions were that Spielberg had transformed himself into a non-Holly-
wood filmmaker, one who had achieved a more objective (truthful)
style of storytelling. This transformation was interpreted by the
American press as a process of maturation ('Fantasy Merchant
Steven Spielberg Grows Up and Tackles the Holocaust'[29]), sometimes
linked with his developing role as a father to his five young children.
But primarily Spielberg's rebirth as a maker of serious movies was
articulated through his own comments concerning his developing
Jewish consciousness and self-realisation as a Jew. In interviews,
Spielberg claimed that he himself had encountered anti-Semitism as
a child; that for many years, he had denied his ethnic background,
and that 'The movie is a result of what I went through as a person'.[30]
This personalisation became integral to Spielberg's widely quoted
quest to 'tell the truth' about the Holocaust; he supported a popular
discourse that claimed him as a documentary filmmaker, hoping his

use of the camera would 'generate the aura of a CNN news report'.[31] This reconstruction of Spielberg as Jewish rather than Gentile and as a maker of 'faction' rather fiction was intimately connected with the question of who has the authority to speak, to construct the popular memory of an historical event that had been considered 'beyond representation'.[32]

For European filmmakers, a deconstructive form of documentary that avoids the clichés of popular modes and interrogates events rather than representing them is the only mode deemed suitable to bear witness to such unimaginable horrors. The film that is held up as respecting the taboo of transgression by refusing to represent any direct (mimetic) reference to the past is Lanzmann's *Shoah* (1985), which combines interviews with numerous witnesses (survivors, perpetrators, historians and bystanders) to give testimony but rejects the use of any actual footage of the events. *Shoah* is praised for 'its uniqueness, its rigorous and uncompromising invention of a filmic language capable of rendering "imageless images" of annihilation' (Hansen 1997: 84). In contrast, *Schindler's List* uses the iconic power of filmic images to construct a coherent fictional world; it is a paradigmatically classical film that tends towards an epic, spectacular reconstruction of the historical events it claims to depict although it contains elements of Italian neorealism in its conception. This is most apparent in the first section of the film, but even here there are overtones of Hollywood stylisation. The use of location settings, the lack of well-known Hollywood actors, the use of black and white rather than colour and a shooting technique that favours hand-held cameras combined with an episodic narrative structure creates the superficial appearance of a documentary. But the opening scene, shot in a cabaret/lounge setting and carefully lit, seems more akin to the shots of decadent social life associated with émigré German expressionist directors in Hollywood such as Joseph von Sternberg[33] and the Hollywood studio film of the 1930s and 40s than an 'authentic' recreation of setting and location.[34]

For critics such as Loshitzky, these shifts in style, which range across documentary and fictional forms garnered from European and American traditions of filmmaking, create a postmodern pastiche because the transitions from one style to another are barely visible. There is an unvoiced preference here for a Brechtian film style, one that calls attention to itself and makes the film's construction as artefact apparent. But perhaps more important to the film's inscription within a tradition of 'realist' film are Hansen's comments on its 'reality effect'. Hansen is less concerned with its unremarked use of a range of stylistic devices than its recycling of images and tropes garnered from other Holocaust films, particularly European documentaries, which are used 'without quotation marks', as if it were telling the story for the first time. Hansen poses the question of whether, in adopting this strategy, the film 'follows the well-worn path of nineteenth-century realist fiction, or whether it does so in the context of a postmodern aesthetics that has rehabilitated such syncretistic procedures in the name of popular resonance and success' (Hansen 1997: 82). Again, it is the form of the film that critics find disquieting; but if Spielberg is quoting from the European documentaries as suggested by Hansen, the limited circulation of these films has not brought these tropes and images of the Holocaust to the notice of a broader public. It is therefore unlikely that the film will recall or suggest other tropes and images to many in the audience in quite the manner suggested. The complexities of the film's 'reality effect' are rooted not only in its use of filmic references but, as we will discuss in more detail below, in its ontological relationship to the history it aims to depict.

In addition to seamless quotation of filmic tropes and styles, the narrative structure of *Schindler's List* is a further source of disquiet to the film's critics. The initial episodic structure of the work soon becomes classically centred on the figure of Schindler, deflecting attention from the film's ostensible subjects, the Jews who are saved by his heroic actions. The second half of the film is dominated by two presences, the camp commander Goeth, the 'bad' Nazi who kills, and Schindler, the 'good' Nazi who saves. As Hansen points out, this Manichean structure of opposites enacts a melodramatic battle between the forces of good and evil that is predicated on a masculinist hierarchy of gender and sexuality, played out through Goeth's subjugation of the Jewish housemaid Helen Hirsch and the restoration of Schindler as a family man who, by returning to his estranged wife, renounces his promiscuity. This narrative structure is, of course, a secular echo of the Christian world view: the resolution (saving the anonymous Jewish masses) hinges upon the heroic actions of the Gentile rescuer and the restoration of familial forms of subjectivity encapsulated in the figure of Schindler as a superfather to the (childlike) victims he rescues (Hansen 1997: 81). Closure is achieved through a restoration of Schindler as 'fully human', a good man, an emotional catharsis enhanced by the image of the saved Jews walking towards the horizon (the Promised Land) accompanied by a rendering of 'Jerusalem of Gold' on the sound-track, a tune which ironically symbolises not only the euphoria of the Israeli victory of 1967 but the ensuing occupation and repres-sion of others that heralded the formation of the emergent Jewish state (Bartov 1997: 45). This finale, fully in tune with the film's (and Spielberg's) Hollywood sensibilities, is not the final image; it is fol-lowed by a contemporary sequence of actors accompanying sur-vivors and their families as they file past the grave of Schindler in a Jerusalem cemetery, each depositing a pebble (on the grave) in honour of his memory. Shot in full colour, this Brechtian quotation both underlines the film's status as a fictional representation whilst authenticating its status as dramatised documentary. The obviously staged homage to the Gentile Other serves to situate the film within a collective popular memory that securely locates its genesis with the Jewish survivors. Somewhat surprisingly, this final image is rarely remarked on by the film's critics.[35]

In some ways, the Schindler character can also be read as a Brecht-ian figure; he is a crook who, like Mother Courage, seeks to profit from war but at the same time undermine the authority of the 'legal criminals' with whom he associates. His profits are put to a moral use as he seeks to save at least some of the people he has exploited; the result is personal material impoverishment but spiritual success because of the innocent lives he has saved (Bartov 1997: 43). Nonetheless, he is an Aryan: as played by Liam Neeson, he towers above those depicted as Jewish who perpetuate a racial stereotype of the Jew as a weak, feminine character in need of protection by a strong, male Christian/Gentile – a Good Samaritan. Some critics of the film claim that the Jewish characters are anti-Semitic generic stereotypes, money-grubbing victims incapable of engaging audi-ence alignment or concern. Judith Doneson points to dominance of this stereotype in popular films about the war that have appeared since the end of the Second World War, irrespective of their country of origin.[36] If Schindler provides a point of alignment for Gentiles at the expense of Jewish subjects, the character of Goeth points to a further cluster of concerns. As Hansen points out, alignment with Goeth's point of view in shots that show his pursuit of victims through the telescopic sight of his gun accords with cine-psychoan-alytic models of identification that claim subjectivity is formed unconsciously: identification strategies depend on the mediation of meaning through flashbacks, voice-over and optical point of view (Hansen 1997: 83). If this is the case, it is equally possible that spec tators will identify with Goeth's murderous intentions and desires in spite of their coding within the film's moral discourse as depraved and repugnant. As we have indicated, however, emotional identifi cation with a character is more likely to depend on various levels of alignment that depend on viewer biographies and sensibilities than on textual features alone.[37]

Finally, Spielberg is the first mainstream Jewish filmmaker to explicitly break the taboo of imaging the horrific metaphor of the gas chamber by following a group of women into the showers. The construction of tension and suspense in this sequence worries a number of critics because it might be used to support the argument of Holocaust deniers that the gas chambers did not really exist. Sara Horowitz, for example, suggests that the scene immediately preced ing the shower sequence, an argument among the women about the existence of the gas chambers that takes place in the women's bar racks at Plaszow, affirms the claims of the deniers because the women's fear that they will perish is refuted by the spraying of water, seemingly denying the reality of the gas chamber (Horowitz 1997: 129). Allied to this critique is the accusation that the film's close resemblance to reality eroticises the Jewish woman as a figure of voyeuristic contemplation for the spectator, linking sexuality with violence in order to provide a perverse viewing pleasure. The shower scene is pornographic not only because it depicts naked and terrified Jewish women, but because the image of the gas chamber becomes a device for provoking suspense and anxiety in the specta tor. Horowitz claims that the scene 'titillates with the promise of a kind of kinetic wax museum of horrors. The anticipated enactment of genocide is thrilling because it is forbidden and at the same time permitted because it is artifice' (Horowitz 1997: 128). Undoubtedly Horowitz has a case here; the implications of using techniques inevitably associated with thrillers and horror movies where naked women are the victims of sadistic acts for the purposes of entertain ment seems particularly inappropriate in this instance.

For Horowitz, Spielberg transgresses a moral boundary, one that Gary Weissman identifies as a skilful balancing act 'between *showing too much* and *not showing enough*' (Weissman 1995: 294, italics in original). In an astute analysis of the pre-publicity that heralded the production and release of *Schindler's List*, Weissman argues that it is Spielberg's desire, as reported in *Entertainment Weekly*, to 'bring truth to these impossible images' (cited in Thompson 1994: 16), an aspiration to capture the horror of events 'much too obscene to picture' as scenes in a movie that motivates the film's relationship to historical events. The desire to represent that which is deemed by many to be beyond representation risks 'showing too much', creating a vulgar scenario available for voyeuristic pleasure, but to 'show too little' would be to hide from the truth of the Holocaust and the events that preceded it. This complex negotiation between remaining within the perceived boundaries of taste and decency by not *showing too much* and providing a deficient account of the obscene realities by *not showing enough* blurs the line between the film and the history that is its reference point, fostering what Weissman terms 'a fantasy of witnessing' (Weissman 1995: 293–5).

Banned from filming in Auschwitz by the World Jewish Congress, Spielberg filmed the façade of the still standing symmetrical guardhouse at the entrance to the camp as if it were the back, the view from the interior of the camp, creating an inversion or mirror image of the actual spatial relations. To quote Weissman:

> it seems that fifty years after approximately 1.3 million Jews were gassed and incinerated at Auschwitz-Birkenau, Catholic Poles, hired as extras to play Jews, climbed into cattle cars which were backed into the death camp by locomotive; then the train was filmed as it pulled out of the camp, coming to a stop not too far outside the gates, where the Poles exited the cattle cars and assembled on a reconstructed, relocated ramp. (Weissman 1995: 299)

The main gate is an ontological boundary, the 'sensitive line' that separates the real from the re-creation, the film from history. But Weissman emphasises that this boundary is not a secure one: 'it is breached from both sides: re-creations incorporate the actual site, and the actual site (preserved as a mausoleum, a solemn memorial to mass extermination) incorporates re-creations' (Weissman 1995: 299). Neither the memorial site nor the film can recreate the reality of the events that took place although both attempt to convey it: 'the real adheres neither at the actual site nor in the re-creation, yet the two rely on each other to create the special effect of the real' (1995: 300).

This 'special effect of the real' is the source of morbid fascination for critics and audiences alike, creating what Weissman terms 'a fantasy of witnessing'. The critics in the popular press that Weissman singles out for attention are caught up, not in a web of deception or illusion created by the transparency of realist depiction, but by their own fascination with both the realism and the artifice of Spielberg's extravagant re-creation. Part of the key to this fascination is the use of authentic locations: Krakow itself, and Auschwitz, which as one reviewer commented 'is only forty-five minutes away' (Perlez 1993: 17). Production stories emphasise the emotional impact on the cast and crew of recreating 'violent', 'brutal' and 'painful' scenes, as if their experience and their journey to the past brings the audience to '"the same awful place", where the difficulty of looking authenticates the experience of witnessing' (Weissman 1995: 302). The film's strict adherence to verisimilitude in its recreation of atrocities while refusing to depict the grossest of deeds divided the critics, who tended to greet the film with uncritical acclaim for its realism or critical disdain for its refusal to depict the actual details of atrocity. Weissman suggests that both approaches stem not from the historical distance created by time, which leaves the film open to counter claims on its veracity, but, in the light of subsequent events, on the lack of impact the Holocaust has had on our collective consciousness and self-understanding. A fascination with the barbaric events and the transgression of moral limits – of showing too much and not showing enough – masks the underlying moral quandary that Yoshifa Loshitzky points to when she discusses the nostalgic impulse that has motivated the Holocaust memorial in Washington. The dictum that we must 'Never Forget' is captured in *Schindler's List's* re-creation of the Holocaust as a spectacle that can be captured and mourned, creating the opportunity for viewers of the film to engage with the film in complex ways, in a fantasy of witnessing past events, or of bearing witness to the cultural absence marked by the film 'as exemplary of our current relation to an absent reality' (Weissman 1995: 306). Weissman emphasises that these two kinds of engagement do not exclude each other – and can be a source of vacillation, wavering between present and past, blurring the distinctions between the film and the actual historical events that took place.

In creating a Hollywood movie from what is undoubtedly one of the most (for many people *the* most) horrific acts of inhumanity perpetrated in recent history, Spielberg took a calculated risk. Epic films on contentious historical events are not always popular at the box office in spite of the Hollywood publicity machine, as some producers/directors have discovered to their cost. The price of failure may be the end of a career, as Michael Cimino discovered when his revisionist history of the American west, *Heaven's Gate* (1980), failed to ignite the popular imagination. Some of Spielberg's critics claim that he has commercialised the Holocaust in the interests of lining his own pockets, perhaps ignoring the fact that profits from the film are donated to the establishment of the Survivors of the Shoah Visual History Foundation, which aims to videotape and archive the testimonies of the remaining thousands of Holocaust survivors. Spielberg insists that the film is 'a document, not entertainment'; accompanying educational materials are provided to assist teaching about the Holocaust in schools, evidence of an attempt to situate the film as an historical account rather than a commercial product designed merely for mass entertainment purposes. In the intense critical debate ignited by the film, elements of which are touched on above, the form of the film and its popular aesthetics are a major source of intellectual disquiet. Speilberg's radical act is to situate the Holocaust within a collective popular memory, yet most critics question his right to depict this particular story in a popular form even while they are aware that in our media-saturated times, collective memory resides not in scholarly works but in popular culture. Hansen points out that attacks on the aesthetics and form of the film reinscribe 'the debate on filmic representation within the old debate about modernism vs. mass culture, and thus with the binary oppositions of "high" vs. "low", "art" vs. "kitsch", "esoteric vs. "popular"'. But in a media-saturated world, 'high' and 'low' are both part of the same public sphere, 'part of the ongoing negotiation of how forms of social difference are both represented and produced in late capitalism' (Hansen 1997: 94). Similarly, Zelizer argues that much of the discourse about 'appropriate' and 'correct' forms of representation has to do with broader issues about history and film, historians and filmmakers, about the willingness to allow alternative voices to address the past. Even whilst Spielberg's film is celebrated, acceptance of the film is discursively framed in ways that make its popular form palatable – 'more like history and less like popular culture' (Zelizer 1997: 28). Within this context, Spielberg's complicity in resituating himself both as Jewish and as a serious filmmaker and artist is a significant (postmodern) irony.

Success and limitations

The question of how to represent the facts of injustice, exploitation and oppression in popular forms of narrative film remains a challenge to filmmakers seeking mass audiences. The three films examined above are all projects led by known filmmakers with track records in generating profits for investors, and are therefore able to finance films that enable contentious themes to be given epic treatment, ensuring high levels of public visibility. It is therefore no surprise that they chose to work in relatively conventional and safe dramatic frameworks rooted in the concept of the Hollywood 'prestige' picture. Following in a tradition established by the studio moguls in the classical era, who sought to gain cultural prestige and status by sponsoring films with political themes and high production values (the award-winning *The Grapes of Wrath* (John Ford 1940) is a case in point), the above filmmakers use their personal reputations (and, in Spielberg's case, his Jewish heritage) to promote their films and themselves as socially committed artists and serious commentators. Hence the ample use of European (modernist) techniques and quotations used in *JFK* and *Schindler's List* establishes their familiarity with the tropes of 'art' cinema and film history. Yet the very form they have chosen to work in, for all its prestigious associations, cannot shield either the films or themselves from public (particularly intellectual) censure because of their adherence to classical filmmaking conventions. When films contest dominant beliefs and attitudes, it seems that such a challenge can only effectively succeed at one level; events and characters are inevitably simplified for dramatic effect.

Thus, in *Cry Freedom*, the white regime can only be represented as evil by depicting all the aggressors as white. The complexities of the political situation, and, most significantly, the colonisation that created a situation where, for example, many foot soldiers on the front line of the security forces were black, is not depicted because, as Attenborough himself admitted, it would make matters far too complicated. In *JFK*, Stone defended his depiction of the conspirators as primarily a homosexual group on the basis that Clay Shaw was a known homosexual, while the Willie O'Keefe character was a composite of various witnesses – a composite that presents him not only as homosexual but as a Fascist psychotic. In *Schindler's List*, the Jewish survivors similarly become weak, effeminate individuals in need of a 'saviour' in the narrative economy of the film. In all three films female characters significantly lack narrative agency; they exist as cameo homemakers, upholders of family values or as spectacle, sexualised victims. The *Screen* solution to this problem, perhaps most effectively argued in the work of Stephen Heath and Laura Mulvey, is to condemn the form and seek other modes of expression. More recently, an interest in the reception of popular films and the discursive construction of interpretation has emphasised the determining agency of viewers as makers, rather than absorbers of meaning, but the legacy of emancipatory modernist critique, with its deep suspicion of popular culture as a negative ideological force, continues to permeate a range of critical perspectives.

Questions about the portrayal of political and historical events take on an increased urgency when assessing the effect of films that achieve the status of 'blockbuster' events because the films are seen by many millions of people, all of whom will, to varying degrees, engage with the issues presented on the screen through the characters and the situations they experience. This engagement, as we have suggested, is both intellectual and emotional; alignment is multi-layered and multi-perspectival; it can switch between characters as well as embrace more than one character at a time. We maintain, similarly to Ryan and Kellner, that 'progressive' political films are not determined by their use of formal devices and representational practices but are always shaped by historical and contextual constraints, by viewers, and prevailing social contexts (Ryan and Kellner 1988: 286). Thus *Cry Freedom*, whilst promoting a liberal multi-culturalist stance unacceptable to many on the left, punctured the British right's discourse of 'terrorism' as a way of denouncing the fight by black South Africans for the right to self-determine the future of their country. The banning of the film in South Africa further legitimised the film's claims that the regime was not only racially oppressive, but maintained power through exercising terror, murdering and exiling those who dared oppose its quasi-military rule. Attenborough's reputation as a maker of prestigious historical epics (*Young Winston*, 1972; *Gandhi*, 1982) and his position at the apex of the British film establishment undoubtedly added weight to the film's critical denunciation of the regime in Britain. The affront the film presented to establishment political sensibilities was amply demonstrated by the refusal to attend the film's premiere on behalf of some of its principal members: the royal family and the

Conservative government. The political points were scored not by those who attended the film and then offered politicised interpretations of its efficacy, but by public figures who refused to read the film in any way at all.

JFK articulates a similarly liberal concern with the public accountability of American governmental structures and the difficulty of sustaining an official 'master' (the word is used advisedly) narrative of the assassination events in the face of mounting evidence of competing conspiracy theories. Such a public denunciation of government integrity is only possible in the post-Watergate world; while it was possible to discredit Garrison as a 'crackpot' in the political climate of the mid-1970s, such accusations are more difficult to sustain in the early 1990s, not least because of growing doubts amongst the American public themselves of the government's ability to 'tell the truth' about the ways in which it exercises power. The 'facts' of the assassination are not the issue here, and neither, we suggest, is the evidential status of the photographic/moving image. Rather, the endless replay of the Zapruder footage of Kennedy's death used by Garrison in the courtroom sequence is used to emphasise the gap between the filmed evidence and its interpretation. This is less a crisis in the status of the image as a record of those events than a crisis in the authority of the state to legitimate an interpretation of the images, to control and present the official version of history. In this obsessive replaying of the Zapruder footage, it now seems impossible not to see subsequent events in the US courtroom writ large: the obsessive replaying and deconstruction of a video tape that depicts the assault and beating of Rodney King in a trial where a verdict of 'not guilty' was found in favour of four Los Angeles police officers charged with using excessive force to apprehend a suspect. The defence attorneys were able to provide a deconstructive reading of the video image using classic techniques of 'reading against the grain' (favoured by many film and media scholars as a counter-ideological tool) to provide not radical but conservative readings of King's behaviour that justified his treatment by the police officers. As Frank Tomasulo points out, the legal facts of the case were not in dispute; what was at stake was the interpretation and morality of those facts. Jurors were encouraged to read the video not as factual news footage, but rather as they would a classical Hollywood film (Tomasulo 1996: 77).[38]

Tomasulo cautions that the extreme scepticism towards history that accompanies much post-structuralist and postmodernist critique can undermine belief in even the most settled bodies of history, such as the existence of slavery and the Holocaust. If no meaningful distinction is drawn between the historical and the imaginary, if the fact of Rodney King's beating becomes little more than 'a fictive illusion of a media representation of that assault', then it is hard to argue for the use of the videotape as irrefutable evidence in support of a guilty verdict. For most spectators viewing the Rodney King tapes, the interpretation of what they see is already a pre-given attitude based on their pre-textual identities, just as for many viewers of *JFK* there was already a pre-textual climate of doubt surrounding the circumstances of Kennedy's murder. Disconnecting images from their ontological ground, while seemingly serving a radical cultural agenda that emphasises the constructed nature of representation in a media-saturated society, can equally serve conservative political agendas that deny the existence of injustice, exploitation and oppression. Just as form cannot, of itself, contain an innate 'progressive' meaning, nor can the tools of deconstruction necessarily deliver more enlightened interpretations. But a politically engaged popular cinema can place vast audiences in contact with contentious themes and topics by reinterpreting witnessed accounts, photographic and moving image records of injustice, exploitation and oppression, presenting them in entertaining forms in ways which can be, potentially, challenging and illuminating. The successes and limitations of these interventions can only be measured within the overall socio-historical context of a film's reception where the climate of interpretation is always and inevitably shaped by the pre-textual identities of individuals and groups and the currents of political and ideological thought that we, as individuals and members of groups, create and inhabit.

Notes

1 The key articles from *Screen* that debate the use of Brechtian techniques as part of a radical film practice are succinctly summarised and presented in Tony Bennett, Susan Boyd-Bowman, Colin Mercer and Janet Woollacott (eds) (1981).
2 For a discussion of Brecht's legacy, see Murray Smith (1995b).
3 See, for example, Jean-François Lyotard (1984).

4 See Chapter 5 for a more detailed account of how shifts in viewers' personal schemata can occur.

5 Robin Wood points out that Barthes in *Mythologies* uses the word 'exnomination' to signify bourgeois capitalism's principle of camouflaging its grossness by suppressing the terms that name it: if 'socialism' is a taboo word in Hollywood cinema, then so is 'capitalism'. In *Cineaction*, winter 1990/91, 63.

6 In the 1930s, Lukacs and Brecht debated how aesthetic form could be used to create a critical viewer who would support the progressive aims of communism. In contrast to Brechtian theories of distanciation and formal hybridity based on popular forms of entertainment such as music hall and variety, Lukacs favoured the 'critical' realism of the nineteenth-century novel, criticising modernist works for their ahistorical pessimism.

7 Ryan and Kellner point out that 'there are serious problems with a model of progressive cinema that excludes pleasure and defines ideology in terms of self-identity or the ego ... another, different Marxist theory would make the subjective potentials of the mass of the people ... into the basis of socialism. And it would promote a different sense of what a progressive cinema is' (1988: 86).

8 The success of this strategy is noted by Ryan and Kellner in their survey of audiences response to *Missing*, although the film appealed primarily to a liberal upper-class audience. Nevertheless, 'in interviews with people of various classes and races about the film, the most common words used to describe it were "upsetting", "frightening", "enlightening" and "realistic" ... Very few people reported disbelieving what they saw on the screen.' See Ryan and Kellner (1988: 280).

9 Some film- and drama-makers explicitly engage with the politics of the popular in order to achieve these aims. See, for example, Jonathan Demme and Ron Nyswater's comments on *Philadelphia* to Richard Corliss in *Time*, 7 February 1994, 62–4; and Jeanette Winterson's comments on adapting her novel *Oranges are Not the Only Fruit* for television, 'Adaptation', in P. Giles and V. Licorish (eds) (1992: 59–65).

10 For an account of the Movement see, for example, Robert Fatton Jr (1986).

11 Adam Mars Jones, *Independent*, 21 January 1988, 11.

12 J. Hoberman, *Village Voice*, 10 November 1987, 74.

13 Scarth Flett, *Sunday Express*, 22 November 1987, 19.

14 Victoria Mather, *Daily Telegraph*, 26 November 1987, 8.

15 'Although *Cry Freedom* has sweeping, scenic good looks and two fine performances to recommend it, not to mention the weight of moral decency on its side, what comes through most strongly is the ponderousness of the Attenborough style', Janet Maslin, *New York Times*, 6 November 1987.

16 David Robinson, 'Freedom has merely been delayed', *The Times*, 22 March 1990.
17 Gary Crowdus (1988), 'An Interview with Oliver Stone', *Cineaste* 16: 3, 21.
18 For a full discussion of Stone's recurring use of this trope, see Robin Wood (1990/91: 24, 60–9).
19 For a detailed analysis of the psycho-sexual implications of this 'slippage', see Michael Rogin (1993).
20 Jon Margolis, *Chicago Tribune*, 4 May 1991.
21 George Will, *Washington Post*, quoted by James Petras (1992) in 'The Discrediting of the Fifth Estate: the press attacks on *JFK*', *Cineaste* 19, 15.
22 Bernard Weinrab, *New York Times*, 24 December 1991. The practice of self-censorship by the studios has, of course, been common throughout Hollywood history with citizen pressure groups, such as the Catholic Legion of Decency in the 1930s and various organisations associated with the McCarthy witch hunts during the 1950s pressurising the studios to censor the work of producers, writers and directors who seek to make films with political and/or morally contentious content. See, for example, Gregory Black (1994) and Richard Maltby (1983).
23 See, for example, Pat Dowell, 'Last Year at Nuremberg: the cinematic strategies of *JFK*' in *Cineaste* 19, 8–11.
24 Grenier, 'Movie Madness', *Times Literary Supplement*, 24 January 1992, 16–17.
25 A Gallup poll conducted in May 1991 revealed that 56 per cent of the population believed this; by July 73 per cent of those polled suspected Oswald had not acted alone. See Janet Staiger (1996: 48).
26 Pat Dowell in *Cineaste* 19, 9–10.
27 Other notable films are documentaries rather than fiction: *Night and Fog* (Resnais 1955), *The Sorrow and the Pity* (Ophuls 1971) and *Shoah* (Lanzmann 1985).
28 Loshitzky references here a complex philosophical debate among Jewish scholars that links a moral argument in Jewish scriptures about the impossibility of representation to the issue of the Holocaust and 'its status as an event that is totally and irrevocably Other, an event that ruptures and is ultimately outside history'. See Miriam Hansen (1997: 84).
29 *Maclean's*, 3 January 1994, 58. Quoted by Barbie Zelizer (1997: 25).
30 Tom Shales, 'The Man at the Top of *Schindler's List*', *Washington Post*, 15 December 1993, 4. Quoted by Zelizer (1997: 25).
31 Richard Schicknel, 'Heart of Darkness', *Time*, 13 December 1993: 75. Quoted in Zelizer (1997: 28).
32 The tradition that the Holocaust defies representation emerges from Theodor Adorno's dictum that after Auschwitz poetry could no longer be written. See Loshitzky (1997: 108).

33 Von Sternberg was associated with the creation of Marlene Dietrich's American image in films such as *Blonde Venus* (1932) and *The Scarlet Empress* (1934).

34 The same contrast is apparent today in films such as *Open City*, which were of course regarded as highly 'realistic' in their day. See Chapters 1 and 6 for a more detailed account of Italian neorealism.

35 For a critical reading of this final sequence, see Judith E. Doneson (1997: 149–50).

36 Doneson singles out a Polish film *The Last Stop* (1948), a Czech film *The Distant Journey* (1949), the American film *The Diary of Anne Frank* (1959), the Italian film *Kapo* (1960), the French film *Black Thursday* (1974) and the American-British co-production *Voyage of the Damned* (1976) as particular instances of this tendency. See Doneson (1997: 140–52).

37 See Chapter 5.

38 The point he draws on is developed by Mike Mashon (1993).

Chapter 7

Space, place and identity: re-viewing social realism

When I left the theater, I was crying for all the dead black men in my family. (Wallace 1992: 123)

Form, theoretically, is always the fusion of specific methods of presentation, specifically selected experience, and specific relations between producer and audience. (Williams 1977b: 124)

Social realism is a discursive term used by film critics and reviewers to describe films that aim to show the effects of environmental factors on the development of character through depictions that emphasise the relationship between location and identity. Traditionally associated in Britain with a reformist or occasionally revolutionary politics that deemed adverse social circumstances could be changed by the introduction of more enlightened social policies or structural change in society, social realism tends to be associated with an observational style of camerawork that emphasises situations and events and an episodic narrative structure, creating 'kitchen sink' dramas and 'gritty' character studies of the underbelly of urban life. Contemporary forms of social realism are rather more eclectic, drawing on similar subject matter but using a range of stylistic features drawn from a spectrum of formal strategies. This chapter explores this new eclecticism, drawing on critical analyses of films that focus on a pervasive contemporary theme: the crisis in masculine identity wrought by changes in the industrial infrastructure of post-industrial, post-colonial global economies.

The 1990s have seen the emergence of numerous films on the international film festival circuit concerned with the displacement and alienation of masculine identities, to the extent that it is possible to speak of a cycle of films that share a collective concern with the effects of economic restructuring on their primarily male

characters. These films are characterised by a stylistic hybridity
that engages a spectrum of realist strategies from the expositional
methods and expressionistic elements formerly associated with
European art cinema to an embracing of popular generic forms.
What we want to suggest in this chapter is that these films address
a common theme in post-industrial, post-colonial societies – the
problem of disenfranchised, alienated males – by using a range of
strategies that aim to engage viewers with their plight. Economic
restructuring of the global economy during the 1980s and 1990s
has emphasised the problems and created new gaps in employment
opportunities and state welfare provision in the post-industrial,
post-colonial societies of the USA, Europe and New Zealand. The
films address issues of masculine identity within this context,
emphasising themes of entrapment and containment, frustrated
aspiration and lack of hope for the future. Using the socio-economic matrix of these localised situations as background, the films
play out dramas of 'universal' human significance: coming-of-age
stories, oedipal scenarios of growth, development and conflict
between the generations, domestic relationships and the traumas of
everyday family life.

The chapter examines five films that engage these themes from a
range of production contexts that vary widely in their uses of realism, all of which are claimed as varieties of 'social realism' by the discursive frameworks of popular criticism. This range of styles is
examined in relation to the films' themes, the range of formal
approaches employed to re-present 'the real' and their strategies of
engagement. For comparative purposes the films are broken down
into two thematic groups: the 'alienated youth' films and the 'dysfunctional family' films, although in practice there is considerable
overlap between the two.

The discussion is framed, first of all, by a broad consideration of
the 'spaces of identity' created by the restructuring of the global
economy, a transformation which is accompanied by new forms of
local and regional activity and a decline of traditional industries.
The people and places left on the margins by shifts in investment
capital and changed relations of production are the focus of attention in these films, the landscapes of inner city decline, suburban
poverty and isolation. Somewhat paradoxically the films circulate in
an increasingly internationalised market for all forms of audiovisual
products, feeding the voracious appetite of a global image market on

the cutting edge of new technological systems of delivery. Within the context of these transformations and changes, is it still possible to speak of 'social realism' as it was once thought of, as a potentially 'progressive' form of depiction that reveals social injustice and the exploitation of working peoples by capitalist production practices? How can socially concerned forms of filmmaking practice negotiate a place within the international image markets? What forms and styles are appropriate for consumption by local and global audiences?

Global markets, local products

Changes in the American film industry in the 1980s and 1990s have reorganised the relations of production, distribution and exhibition around new markets created by technological developments and economic trends towards globalisation. New distribution outlets, such as the home video market, have made viewing time more flexible, while cable and satellite provide a range of new programming possibilities and the opportunity to develop special interest channels that cater for the needs of particular audiences. The Hollywood majors have undoubtedly benefited from these technological changes; by taking advantage of new outlets for their products, risk is reduced on investment. Films that do well on theatrical release generate significant revenues in the video market, while less successful productions can recoup their costs through video and television sales. At the same time, some smaller companies have flourished by taking advantage of the opportunities offered by the new outlets such as the home video market and the increased demand from television for all forms of filmed drama.[1] Social realism has thrived in the context of these new production opportunities both on television and film.

The globalising tendencies of the Hollywood majors are linked to the distribution side of the business, which is owned by multinational communications conglomerates such as Paramount Communications, Time Warner, News Corporation and MCA. American films dominated the European box office during the 1980s, increasing their overall share from 64 per cent of the market in 1985 to 77.4 per cent of European revenues by 1990.[2] Additionally, it is estimated that 60 per cent of the European film distribution industry is controlled by US companies, who not only distribute American films but control the distribution of many European films as well as other media products.[3] A similar pattern of increasingly localised market penetration and expansion by American distribution companies is prevalent in more than eighty markets around the world, leading analysts to conclude that the developing international image markets are dominated by American interests, in spite of the challenge from other major players such as the Japanese.

The transformation of the markets in image production and distribution is one aspect of a growing trend across all areas of economic activity during the 1980s and 1990s which is increasingly associated with processes of cultural globalisation. At one level, this is about the manufacture and production of universal cultural products, of which blockbuster films and their associated tie-ins and merchandise are just one example. In the new cultural industries, there is a belief in 'world cultural convergence': a conviction that lifestyle, culture and consumer behaviour is consolidating amongst different consumer segments across the world. Kevin Robins argues that this faith in the emergence of a 'shared culture' and a common 'world awareness' appears to be vindicated by the success of products like *Dallas* or *Batman* and the spread of film-linked theme park attractions such as Disneyland. Global standardisation is about achieving economies of scale by targeting the shared habits and tastes of particular market segments at the global level, rather than by marketing on the basis of geographical proximity to different national audiences. Multinational industries and conglomerates are increasingly driven to recover their escalating costs from the maximum market base which is pan-regional and world wide. The media entertainment industries aspire to the creation of a borderless world without national frontiers: Sky beam their projects across the Northern hemisphere; satellite footprints spill over the former integrity of national territories. In the cultural industries the most dynamic actors are ensuring their control of a range of cultural products across world markets. Music, ethnic arts, fashion and cuisine, literature and cinema from all over the world are turned into commodities for the new 'cosmopolitan' market place. The local and 'ethnic' products of indigenous cultural traditions are taken out of their place and time to be repackaged for sale in the world bazaar: Balinese carvings, African music, Thai food, Aboriginal painting, Mexican jewellery. With the globalisation of culture, the link between culture and territory becomes significantly broken. What is being created is a new electronic cultural space, a 'placeless' geography of image and simulation, a world of instantaneous and depthless communication, a world in which time and space horizons have become compressed and collapsed (Robins and Morley 1995: 105–24).[4]

In contrast to the homogenising thesis sketched above, many commentators suggest that the new geographical territories created by globalisation are heralding a renaissance of locality and region. In spite of the homogenisation of cultural products, it is not possible to eradicate or transcend difference at the local/national level. The case for the local or regional economy as the key unit of production within the global network has been forcefully made by the 'flexible specialisation' thesis, which stresses the central and prefigurative importance of localised production complexes. Crucial to the success of local production initiatives are strong local institutions and infrastructures; relations of trust based on face-to-face contact; a 'productive' community historically rooted in a particular place; and a strong sense of local attachment and pride (Robins 1991: 28–31). But analysts such as Robins are wary of idealising the local, which, he maintains, is a relational and relative concept. If at one time the local and the regional had significance in relation to the national sphere, that meaning and significance is being recast in the context of globalisation. For the global corporation, the global-local nexus is of key strategic importance; the latest product must sell everywhere at once and that means producing products locally that have global (universal) appeal. Globalisation entails a corporate presence in, and an understanding of, the local arena. But the local in this sense does not correspond to any specific territorial configuration; the global–local nexus is about the relation between globalising and particularising dynamics in the strategy of the global corporation; the geographical terrain of locality is constituted only in and through its relation to the global. The 'flexible specialisation' thesis is not straightforwardly about the renaissance of local cultures; these are overshadowed by an emergent world culture – and by the resilience of national and nationalist cultures (Robins and Morley 1995: 117–18).

Within this context, the development of national/regional film cultures has become a renewed site of struggle in many European countries. In the UK, for example, devolution of political power to the national centres of Scotland, Northern Ireland and Wales has been augmented by arguments for cultural devolution of the broadcasting industries. The attempt to establish Glasgow, Belfast and

Cardiff as new national/regional centres of television and film production is linked to urban regeneration strategies which have turned
to the cultural industries as one possible source of new investment
and opportunity.[5] Films produced from these local centres are finding some success on the international market place; *Shallow Grave*
(1994), for example, was made and produced in Glasgow, where it
was part financed from local authority investment and European
structural funds as a strategic element of the city's urban regeneration programme. But, as Steve MacIntyre has pointed out, although
these local production schemes are often justified by cultural arguments about identity and representation, they are in fact driven by
commercial, rather than cultural incentives. Within the context of a
global media culture, there are no guarantees that groups formerly
denied access to the means of production will be able to find ways
to assert their cultural identities within the new commercial priori-
ties of regional/national and European funding policies.[6]

None the less, there have been significant developments in the
themes and content of some UK films that correspond with a shift in
film production away from its London base. The strand of prestige
heritage productions that characterised British films in the international marketplace in the 1980s is superseded in the 1990s by films
engaging with contemporary issues of male anomie, unemployment
and social exclusion. Films such as *The Full Monty* (1997),
Trainspotting (1995), *Twin Town* (1996), *Brassed Off* (1996), *Nil
By Mouth* (1997) and *Twenty Four Seven* (1997) are set in locations
where male members of the community traditionally worked in
heavy industries such as steel, shipbuilding, mining and industrial
manufacture. These films re-imagine the 'working-classness' of their
characters through their relations to consumption rather than production, purchasing power rather than labour power; working-class
identity becomes a site for exploring the personal stagnation, alienation and social marginalisation of their primarily white male characters. Some of these films, including the most successful British film
of all time, *The Full Monty*, are characterised by a formal hybridity
that is usefully illuminated by John Corner's distinction between
realism of form and realism of theme and content (Corner 1992:
100). The films engage with stories about everyday life, which characterises the substance of their content, but are less committed to an
aesthetics of verisimilitude. Contemporary filmmaking style in the
UK has become increasingly eclectic, drawing on a range of codes

and conventions associated with television drama, documentary practices, music video and art cinema. The rest of this chapter is devoted to examining the eclectic realism of contemporary social issue films and placing recent UK films in an international context; but before the films are discussed in detail, a few broad brushstrokes will sketch trends in contemporary social realism's stylistic modes.

Social realism

Social realism is generally understood as a mode of cinematic representation that focuses on the lives of characters in a particular milieu or environment that is at some remove from the images of people and places that populate most commercial generic production. Often termed 'slice of life' dramas, social realism is distinguished by the attention it pays to characters who usually figure as background presences in the generic mainstream, those marginalised by virtue of their social status and/or ethnic identity to perform in supporting, often servile roles. More recently, the term has become something of a catch-all in popular criticism, used to describe any moving image drama that engages relationships between everyday life, environment and character. In the UK social realism is commonly associated with 'kitchen sink' drama and soap opera, televisual forms that foreground family relationships and everyday life; controversial social issues such as incest, domestic violence, gay relationships, alcoholism, drug abuse and AIDS have all been explored within this context.[7] But not all social issue dramas are necessarily social realist in form. Social issue dramas often focus on individual characters and invariably have the dual narrative structure characteristic of mainstream films; social realism is associated with ensemble casts and multi-stranded narratives with narrative motivation dispersed across a range of diverse characters, events and situations. There is also a difference in their treatment of theme: in social issue films, the individual's problems present a problem *for* society (how to educate, to police, to contain, to treat), rather than being perceived as a problem created *by* society,[8] a perspective often attributed to social realism.

In the USA, similar themes are a common staple of the made-for-TV movie and those Hollywood films that deal with social issues, such as for example *The Accused* (1988) or *Philadelphia* (1993), which closely conform to the classical Hollywood model in terms of narrative structure and visual style. A common criticism of such social issue films is that their focus on an individual protagonist (usually played by a major star in films for theatrical exhibition) personalises what is a social/political issue, such as rape or AIDS, presenting the individual as either triumphant over tragedy or as an exemplary martyr to the cause. In *Philadelphia*, one of the few Hollywood films to deal with AIDS, Tom Hanks plays an ambitious and talented lawyer who is dismissed when his employers, a powerful Philadelphia law firm, discover his illness. The plot of the film concerns his fight for compensation for unjust dismissal. For all its attempts to deal with a contemporary social issue, the film remains a somewhat conventional Hollywood melodrama, with an heroic individual successfully fighting against the injustice perpetrated by corporate power and prejudice. As a white, middle-class male whose only 'tragic flaw' is his sexual orientation, Hanks provides a point of concern alignment that encourages empathy and moral allegiance with his situation. In a social climate where homophobia and prejudice against AIDS sufferers is widespread this in itself, of course, is deserving of significance. But the reformist aim is reinforced by the casting of Denzel Washington as a homophobic lawyer who is persuaded to take up his case, as a point of legal, not moral, principle, thus supplying a heterosexual and perhaps homophobic audience with a position of secure alignment from which to view the struggle and death of a gay AIDS victim. That Washington is a popular black actor, however, risks making an association between homophobia and the African-American community, and may also reinforce racial stereotypes of heterosexual black masculinity as essentially 'natural'. The filmic structure, like that of most social issue films, can only accommodate the positive representation of one minority group at a time because it hinges upon a liberal rhetorical strategy that unproblematically accepts that the only solution to social injustice is to stage an individual fight against it.[9]

One way of distinguishing the formal characteristics of social realism from social issue films is to examine the legacy of socially conscious filmmaking practice at particular moments. Chapter 2, 'Realist moments' explores how a particular combination of theme and style stimulated critical interest in the progressive potential of realism at a time when some European filmmakers and critical intellectuals sought to distance themselves both thematically and aesthetically from the 'vulgar, mass-produced films' of Hollywood and the commercial products of their own industries.[10] This legacy has informed contemporary filmmaking practice and continues to permeate contemporary discourses of social realism, emphasising the link between environment and character through the use of ensemble casts, character actors rather than stars and expositional narrative strategies. Often referred to in popular criticism as 'gritty' or 'raw' dramas, words that have close associations with 'the natural', and connotations of 'earthiness', social realism is associated with a lack of stylistic artifice and a transparent naturalism. The words 'gritty' and 'raw' tend to embrace both the thematic elements of the films – which often confront the troublesome relationship between deprived environmental conditions and human psychology – and the 'no frills' style in which they are made. Frequently low budget productions made on cheaper film formats that create grainy images unsaturated with colour, the camera style of social realism has traditionally favoured the use of a documentary 'look' achieved by coupling simple continuity editing strategies with observational camerawork. The plot contrivances associated with melodrama are absent; typically, the desires of characters are thwarted rather than achieved. Narrative structures are episodic and cyclical rather than driven by a logic of cause and effect, the time frame of the film governed by externally imposed structures that correspond to real time equivalence rather than internal (diegetic) deadlines of genre films, where superfluous detail is pared away to maintain narrative pace, tension and suspense. The hybrid forms of contemporary social realism continue to adhere to many of these basic properties but are far more eclectic in style, embracing a wide range of aesthetic strategies that often combine an episodic narrative structure with expressionistic techniques garnered from modernist 'art' cinema and popular melodramatic elements from generic fiction within their overall structure.

The films featured here foreground the relationship between place, character and identity that continues to be social realism's distinguishing feature; they are all set in economically marginalised communities, places where people are disenfranchised by poverty and lack of opportunity. In this sense, they continue to fulfil realism's traditional project of subjective incorporation, bringing to the centre of the screen those that traditionally inhabit the margins of other people's stories. All the films engage with the socio-economic and spatial confinement of contemporary urban life, whether lived in the inner cities of Los Angeles or London, the outer ring satellite housing estates of Paris or the suburban wasteland of Auckland. These are portraits of characters living on the margins of affluent societies, areas left increasingly isolated by the global movements of investment capital. This is the territory of what has become known as 'the underclass', those whose hopes of forging a better life for themselves have withered on the boughs of unemployment and a collapsing infrastructure of education, health and welfare provision. These are post-industrial, post-colonial spaces that international capitalism can no longer find a use for, places that society tries to contain because of the perceived threat their inhabitants pose to social stability. These are riotous places, both literally and in a Bahktinian sense, inhabited by gangs of marauding young men who fight territorial battles to retain control of their 'turf', insisting on their personal and collective identities.

These are the places where Others live – the dispossessed, the underclass, the homeless, the socially excluded, the migrants – all those Others who are not Us who can be found living in the gaps left by successive waves of industrialisation and economic redevelopment. The landscapes of contemporary social realism are abandoned inner city areas, satellite housing estates built to rehouse those displaced by earlier urban regeneration schemes, projects built to house migrant labour, industrial towns where the industries that once provided jobs and relative affluence have moved to new locations. Outsiders know these places from news bulletins and documentaries, which constantly represent them as dangerous places where internal tensions break out, erupting into violent confrontations with the police. Such images characterised the depiction of discontent in the inner cities of Britain in the 1980s – in Liverpool, Bristol, Brixton and Handsworth; and Los Angeles in the 1990s. Contemporary social realism speaks of life in these margins – the 'hood, the *banlieue*, the schemes and projects, the high-rise estates. The stories they tell have an explicit extratextual reference to the everyday world, which is both real – their locations are commonly known as materially existent places – and imagined: they are familiar to many through their mediated representations, not from lived experience. Only for some, of course, the places depicted in these films are home ground, the experiences they depict known and lived realities; they are stories about Us, about where we live, our lived realities, our experiences. Hence the fierce debates generated by these films circle around issues of representation and representativeness and the responsibility of the filmmakers, often writer/directors who claim 'insider' knowledge of the lives and places they depict, to provide positive images that are politically reaffirming and generative of community or group pride.[11]

Social realist films encourage identification not merely with characters but with the situations and events they experience. They offer a perspective from which it is possible to understand the broader social mechanisms that generate conflict between individual desire and what can be achieved within a given situation. The films considered here emphasise the containment of characters within tightly inscribed socio-economic and geographical boundaries. Social realism, in this context, is less a set of specific formal attributions than an attempt to re-view existing mediated associations between social-situatedness and personal identity through a focus on the lives of characters circumscribed by marginality. Characters are often victims of circumstance, unable to extricate themselves from situations that trap them in the poverty of unemployment and redundancy, the emotional prison of domestic violence and/or the socio-spatial-psychological confines of racism. The narrative structures of social realism vary in their difference from mainstream generic paradigms; the films focus on individuals or groups of people at particular crisis points in their lives, with a narrative trajectory that often works towards conventional patterns of resolution and a restoration of some kind of equilibrium.

But rather than a narrative momentum driven by character motivation and desire, the protagonists of social realism are often indecisive, immobilised by their situation and unable to act, or only able to respond to adverse circumstances and events that are outside their control. Even if dreams are realised, a price has to be paid, and the cost is far greater than envisaged. The struggles of central characters are often inter-generational (primarily between fathers and sons), but occasionally they engage confrontationally with figures who represent the institutional forces of authority and containment (police officers, social workers, teachers, employers and so forth). Social realism emphasises that characters are inextricably contained within a nexus of social/economic/geographical/historical factors that are far beyond the resources of any single individual to control or transcend. Characters face the violent and often tragic consequences of containment and exclusion: offering few solutions, the films express a profound ambivalence towards the existing social order. Although they rarely foreground the destructive weight of socio-economic forces that crush hope and aspiration for the future, such forces are a structuring absence that serves as a constant point of reference through recurring tropes of social surveillance and containment. In popular 1990s films such as *Boyz N the Hood*, *La Haine*, *Naked*, *Once Were Warriors*, *Trainspotting* and even *The Full Monty*, geographical and social containment create the frustrating conditions that may erupt in violence and death. There are no simple narrative resolutions in these films to the oppression that blights daily life, only an emphasis on how things are and the implied need for change.

Circulating within a global media market place, these very localised stories challenge traditional conceptions of national and nationalist film culture. They deconstruct the homogenising tendencies of commercial film culture by foregrounding locality through their use of local language idioms and indigenous actors, spatial specificity, detailed reference to local attitudes, beliefs, and points of cultural reference. They address local issues and concerns using dialogue peppered with specific references to an insider's knowledge of the locality and its culture. Their distribution on the international market is initially through the film festival circuit where they are sought by film audiences seeking a type of entertainment different from mainstream global products. Their difference from both the themes and conventions of commercial genre films is one of the primary mechanisms through which such films become labelled as realist; but as in the case of *Bicycle Thieves*, it is not only the shift in conventions which interests audiences. There is also a strong element here of what Urry (1990) has termed 'the tourist gaze' – a fascination with difference that enables the lives of unknown peoples and the places they inhabit to be represented as a commodity, a spectacle for consumption.

But the films also seek audiences willing to engage critically with the contradictions and difficulties of contemporary life as well as those who might be fascinated by images of 'low-life'. The style of such films is often a hybrid of aesthetic concerns that aims to reassert the cultural specificity of characters through the use of sharp, local dialect and culturally specific expressive forms such as music. Cultural products such as 'rap', commercially exploited for consumption by mainstream consumers, are recontextualised as the local sounds of the communities that have created them. In this sense, the films are Janus-faced: on the one hand, looking out towards the contemporary mediascape, they present spectacles of Other people and Other places as new fodder for the voracious appetites of the international media industries; but simultaneously the visual and aural iconographies of subcultural identities are reclaimed from the sea of global distribution and repackaged for local consumption. They also address a diasporic identity; those who have left the locality but continue to share similar cultural affiliations, as well as those who live in localities shaped by a similar nexus of socio-economic conditions of existence. For these groups, social realism can reaffirm cultural solidarities and subcultural identities across regional/national boundaries, projecting characters and situations that are not only a source of interest and concern alignment, but of potential moral and political allegiance.

Social realism in the late 1980s and early 1990s engages an eclectic range of narrational and visual styles that are more usefully understood as part of a realist continuum than isolated and discrete examples of particular filmic practice. By using a range of strategies, they seek to actively engage in the politics of representation, complicating MacCabe's thesis that 'reality equals what we can see, that perception equals cognition'.[12] Far from being closed textual systems, the hybridised forms of contemporary social realism engage with realism as a form of representation, sometimes commenting on the very conventionality of realism's mode of address. This is not a type of formal distanciation as envisaged by 1970s film theory that demands a radical revisioning of narrative form and visual style, nor a dogged insistence on the progressive political potential of contemporary realist forms. Nor is it a simple case of retelling the story from an oppositional viewpoint, although this is often part of their project. Aware of the changing, contingent nature of realism's codes and conventions and the dispersed identities of international film audiences, filmmakers who wish to engage realism's discursive potential use a range of methods in their attempts to mobilise the *social* dimension of social realism's project. The films discussed below attempt in different ways to tackle local issues within this challenging distribution environmentt, aiming to extend understandings of particular circumstances to the enlarged audiences they seek to address.

Angry young men of the 1990s

Boyz N the Hood, (Singleton, US 1991), *Once Were Warriors* (Tamohori, New Zealand 1994) and *La Haine* (Kassovitz, France 1995) are three films centred on confused and angry young men in the ghettos of South Central Los Angeles, Auckland and Paris. The most conventional forms of social realism, and, perhaps because of this, often the most popular at the box office, are those that use and adapt the stylistic traits of popular genres. *Boyz N the Hood* and *Once Were Warriors* are good examples of films that mix the stylistics of popular cinema with a social realist imperative. Both films were popular in their own countries – *Once Were Warriors* broke box-office records in New Zealand, becoming the highest grossing film of all time; *Boyz N the Hood* rose to No. 4 in the USA – and both have circulated in the international marketplace. Their production contexts are rather different. *Once Were Warriors* was funded by the New Zealand Film Commission and is the first Maori film to find international and popular acclaim. *Boyz N the Hood* was produced and distributed by Columbia Pictures, one of the nineteen films commissioned by Hollywood studios in 1991 from African-American filmmakers to tell black stories. It has emerged as one of the most important of these films because it was both a box office hit and a serious film about African-American life that addresses directly the issue of collective self-violence. *La Haine*, although it addresses a similar set of issues in contemporary French society, is made by an 'outsider', writer/director Mathieu Kassovitz and produced by European co-production funding. Upon its release in France, the film became a media event of such huge proportions that Kassovitz was forced to go into hiding due to the sensationalist press coverage and political storm fanned by the extreme-right Front National.[13] National interest was so intense that the film even received a special viewing from the prime minister. The thematic connections between the three films are not lost on the reviewers, who tend to use the African-American 'hood' films as a benchmark in their assessments of the other two.[14]

In Chapter 2, we suggest that independent black urban films belong within the realist tradition exemplified by Italian neorealism. Within the terms of this analysis, 'cross-over' films such as *Boyz N the Hood* are seen as compromised by their use of generic conventions and their circulation within the mainstream. Yet *Boyz N the*

Hood explicitly engages with the sub-cultural violence of inner city life, and its mixing of formal elements is undoubtedly the key to its success.[15] The film's relationship to anterior facts is formally signalled at the beginning of the film with captions that inform us, 'One out of every twenty-one black American males will be murdered in their lifetime' followed by 'Most will die at the hands of another black male'. The captions are accompanied by a soundtrack of indistinct voices, mumbling, police sirens, a car door opening, tyres squealing, shotgun fire and screaming as the titles fill the screen. At the end of the film, captions again inform us about the post-filmic fates of the two principal characters. These referents signify both the anterior socio-historical actualities of life in South Central LA, and establish the narrative fictionalisation of the characters in the film as inhabitants of a particular time and place, a process that the early part of the film goes to some lengths to establish. The opening sequence cuts to an image of a stop sign with a plane flying over it; the sign expands to fill the screen, then cuts again to a group of school children walking along the street. A further caption states: 'South Central Los Angeles 1984'. The children are discussing the sounds of a shooting they heard last night; one of them taunts the others, 'D'you wanna see something?' The direction of their journey is punctuated by the street signs that furnish the mise-en-scène: 'One Way', followed by 'Wrong Way'. They cross a police line that states 'Do not enter', pass a wall covered in election posters for Reagan and Bush that are riddled with bullet holes, picking their way through piles of rubbish to a wall covered in blood. A girl asks, 'Is that blood?' pointing to a pool of coagulating brown and yellow fluid full of flies; her young male companion responds, 'What do you think, someone got smoked, stupid.' The girl timidly responds, 'At least I can do my times tables.' The opening of the film aims to convince us that for some people the statistics quoted at the beginning of the film are a part of everyday reality, part of growing up as African-American citizens in South Central Los Angeles.

Not content with merely dramatising the facts, the film moves on to make a further series of points about this situation; the scene cuts to a series of children's drawings. A disembodied female voice narrates a history lesson on the survival of the first American 'settlers' while the camera pans a number of childish drawings – a person lying in a coffin, a police car, a helicopter in the night sky, its searchlight illuminating the neighbourhood – before moving across a classroom of bored African-American, Latino and Korean children. It settles on the source of the voice, a white teacher flanked by a map and pictures of white male historical figures. She finishes her story: 'And that's why we celebrate Thanksgiving, to commemorate unity between the Indians,' (slight pause), 'excuse me, the Native Americans and the settlers who were called, class?' 'Pilgrims,' chorus all the children obediently, apart from one dissenting voice. By such economical means we are rapidly introduced not only to the person who will become the focus of the narrative, the owner of this dissenting voice, Tre Styles, but to the contextual contradictions that structure the development of his life: childhood innocence confronted by violent death on the seemingly peaceful suburban streets, spatial confinement and constant surveillance of the neighbourhood by the Los Angeles Police Department and an educational system that makes no sense of his own family's history or his experience of growing up in South Central LA. The opening captions take on a significance beyond their denotative, factual reference, placing a question over this young man's future, a question that shapes the narrative trajectory of the film. Will Tre grow up to become yet another statistic or will he escape the tenacious pull that this destiny exerts on his future?

Tre is described on the video sleeve as 'a good boy growing up in a bad neighbourhood'. His 'goodness' is characterised by his determination to succeed educationally, securing a scholarship to college in Atlanta which will enable him to escape from the destructive violence of the ghetto. For the 'outsider' audience, alignment with a young black male may constitute a shift in personal schemata of empathic recognition, but little is demanded by way of a shift in values since Tre is broadly committed to the aims and values of mainstream society even though these values are couched in the terms of a nascent black nationalism. Alignment with Tre is complemented by that of his father, Furious Styles, and his friend Ricky. Furious is the moral centre of the film, instilling in his son the values of personal responsibility, self-discipline, self-respect and an ethic of leadership and care of others, described by Tre's friends as a 'Malcolm/Farrakhan' figure. Ricky and his half-brother Doughboy, brought up by their mother, are shown to lack the disciplined upbringing that will ultimately save them from death on the streets. Ricky, a talented footballer who, like Tre, hopes to win a college scholarship, is markedly different from Doughboy who falls foul of the police at an early age and spends much of his teenage life in and out of reform school.

Although structured in part as a conventional genre film, the style and pace of *Boyz'* narration lacks the paring away of superfluous detail characteristic of such films. Time is spent detailing small but significant episodes that build cumulatively to the cycle of events which ultimately leads to the deaths of Ricky and Doughboy. Gang culture is shown to be a pervasive part of everyday life; as children playing on the block, they are constantly harassed and bullied by older youths. As teenagers, they move about in a group threatened by shotgun-brandishing youths driving around in cars. Fear is pervasive – not only of other gangs, but also of the police who intimidate and bully without provocation. Once his friend Ricky is gunned down, Tre is faced with a stark choice: loyalty to his friends, or loyalty to his father's values. In choosing the latter, he secures a future for himself, but for Doughboy there is no choice; he has to avenge his brother's death, knowing that he places his own life at risk.

Doughboy forms a contrasting signifier of masculinity associated with the destructive power of guns, violence and the streets, an antithesis to Tre's promise of regenerative power realised through his heterosexual coupling with his girlfriend Brandi and their shared vision of a college future.[16] Played by South Central LA's well-known rap artist Ice Cube, it is Doughboy who forms the focus of identification for many in the African-American audience, not Tre.[17] Tre's apparent position of narrative centrality and moral alignment is less secure than it initially seems to 'outsider' viewers such as ourselves. The film's dual narrative structure offers two stories, a conventional heterosexual romance and an episodic tragedy, one of which fulfils the traditional function of 'happy ever after' closure, the other the inevitable trajectory of violence and death. If the heterosexual narrative offers a conventional message based on an individualist ethics of personal salvation through which Tre achieves his masculine identity, the tragic narrative offers an alternative ethos of responsibility for others and a principled gesture of revenge through which Doughboy achieves his self-esteem and maturity, an identity animated by Ice Cube's reputation and status within South Central LA. Glen Masato Mimura claims that as South Central LA's unofficial poet laureate forged in the context of rap music's alternative mode of production and expression outside the constraints and immediate influence of official culture, Ice Cube 'brings to *Boyz* a street-smart sensibility and cultural credibility rarely found in Hollywood cinema' (1996: 24). The presence of this local star and the use of his music throughout the film challenges conventional allegiance and moral alignment with Tre, offering an alternative focus for engagement based on the actor's reputation and his knowledge of local cultural idioms. Somewhat ironically, rap music, commercially exploited by the music industry for mainstream consumption, is recontextualised by the casting of Ice Cube in a Hollywood film as the authentic voice of the 'hood'.

Once Were Warriors shares similar themes within a very different cultural context, that of contemporary Aotearoa/New Zealand. New Zealand is a place that (unlike Los Angeles or Paris) tends to connote freedom and social opportunity to some in the United Kingdom, perhaps because of a legacy of post-war emigration policies, imports of agricultural produce, and more recently, tourist literature advertising the country as a 'natural' unspoilt paradise. Popular images of New Zealand tend not to include accounts of urban deprivation and racial conflict. And if the Maori people figure at all it is as exotic figures in the tourist landscape, a concept that was strongly challenged in 1994 when a visit by a member of Britain's royal family sparked a protest from Maori groups called upon to entertain the guests with an ethnic spectacle of traditional dances. The reports of the incident revealed the divisions between the Maori and white settlers, particularly in the politically charged arena of land rights.

Once Were Warriors arrived in the UK in the wake of this incident and hot on the heels of the internationally acclaimed *The Piano* (1994), a film that does nothing to challenge British myths about the peaceful colonisation of Aotearoa/New Zealand and the servile role of Maori people. A different historical memory informs *Once Were Warriors*, that of the Maori as fierce fighters who battled against the British colonisers, only to suffer severe population loss and eventual defeat. In its destruction of traditional ways of life, colonial subjugation and racism has led to unemployment or underemployment, welfare dependency and alcoholism among significant numbers of Maori people, who now constitute around 12 per cent of the population. *Once Were Warriors* concerns the blighted lives of a family struggling to rear their children in a suburban ghetto of Auckland, and shares a number of similarities with the work of African-American filmmakers such as Singleton. The filmscript was developed by Maori playwright Riwia Brown from a controversial best-selling

novel by Alan Duff, and directed by Lee Tamahori with a primarily
Maori cast and crew. In its home country, the film broke all box-
office records, and has sold in more than fifty countries world-
wide.[18] The first film to portray Maori life from the 'inside', the film
tells the story of an imploding, dysfunctional family trying to cope
with unemployment, alcoholism and male alienation. Jake loses his
job and takes to drinking heavily, beating up his wife Beth and ignoring the plight of his younger son Boogie, due to appear in court on
a minor charge. Boogie is sent to reform school, where a Maori
social worker teaches him traditional cultural values. The older son
Nig joins an urban gang that is similarly affiliated to Maori fighting
culture. During a night of heavy drinking, thirteen-year-old Grace is
raped by one of Jake's friends. Unable to cope with the humiliation
and her father's constant violence, Grace hangs herself from a tree
in the backyard. Beth arranges a traditional Maori funeral with her
high caste relatives who still live in the countryside. Jake, from a
lower caste group, resents his wife's reassertion of traditional identity and refuses to attend the funeral, embarking on yet another
drinking spree. Beth discovers the truth of the rape in Grace's diary;
in the bar, she confronts Jake and his friends with the truth and
walks out, taking the children with her.

   This 'slice of life' family drama has an expositional narrative
structure that is in some ways typical of social realism. From Jake's
losing his job and starting to drink heavily, which creates the initial
disruption to family life, the rapid spiral into chaos is motivated by
situation and events rather than deliberate actions undertaken by the
characters. Where the film departs from an aesthetics of social realism is in its apparent degree of artifice, particularly the stylised use
of costume and colour and its melodramatic closure. The film is
given a rich sepia look to emphasise the skin tones of its protagonists
and emphasises black, red and white, predominant colours in Maori
art.[19] All vestiges of green were removed from the urban scenes to
emphasise the barren, smog-laden urban environment. Women in
the film wear dresses printed with animal and snakeskin designs, the
men in Nig's gang flaunt plaited leather jackets, leather trousers,
dark sunglasses; their hair and faces are intricately patterned and
decorated. This attention to visual style is enhanced by the large,
muscle-bound bodies of the men and the beauty of the women,
creating an image of a resilient, proud people amidst the poverty of
the urban environment. The frequent fight scenes emphasise the

physical stature of the men, who appear large and powerfully erotic but increasingly self-destructive as their violence destroys not only their immediate environment but also those they love.

Urban confinement is contrasted in this film with the natural beauty of the New Zealand countryside. The film opens with a shot of the hills and mountains, typically reminiscent of tourist brochures, only for the camera to pull back and reveal an advertising billboard beside a drab urban highway where Beth walks with her shopping (see Figure 4). But there is vitality here; an urban market echoes with the sounds of rap music, children playing and the hustle and bustle of city life. The huge barn-like bars are full of people enjoying themselves, dancing and talking, until violent confrontation disturbs their pleasure. As the film progresses, these images of everyday life are increasingly fractured by the aggressive drunken behaviour of the men. In an attempt to bring the family together, Beth arranges a day out to the countryside; it is here that we learn of Jake's resentment of her upper caste (*ariki*) heritage. The film suggests that salvation for Beth and her family can only be found by returning to her family's roots in the *marae* – the ancestral place; Beth takes Grace to be buried here in a traditional ceremony that reunites the alienated sons Nig and Boogie with their cultural and spiritual roots. Jake, rejecting this heritage, is left alone in the city with Beth reminding him that he is still a slave – 'to your fists, the drink, yourself.'

Women tend to be a background presence or to feature as victims in many contemporary urban dramas, their aspirations and hopes for a better life doomed to unfulfilled resolution. *Once Were Warriors* repeats this trope through the rape and suicide of Grace, but it is Beth's ability to overcome her fear of Jake's violence and take the lives of herself and her children into her own hands that shifts the film from its stylised gang rhetoric. Although the key to Beth's empowerment – Grace's death – is something of a cliché, through her strength and resilience to the graphically depicted beatings and constant bullying she refuses to endorse Jake's nihilism and self-hatred or find solutions to her problems in the white world. From the beginning of the film, where she walks with her shopping next to the billboard image of the mountains, Beth is associated with nature and the traditional spiritual values of Maori culture. This cluster of feminine associations contrasts with the barren urban values of an exhausted modernity and the aggressive machismo that

4 Urban containment: Beth Heke (Rena Owen) in *Once Were Warriors*
(Tamahori, NZ 1994).

defines homosocial masculinity. These oppositions are present early
in the film, but become more apparent once Grace dies, shifting the
focus of narrative attention away from Jake towards Beth; with this
shift, the film becomes more melodramatic in structure so that what
begins as a stylised social realist 'boys movie' becomes a celebration
of female power, albeit couched in the rather conventional terms of
family melodrama.

Once Were Warriors has been criticised for its perpetuation of negative Maori stereotypes and for not contextualising its story within
an overall framework that depicts the oppressive effects of colonisation.[20] In New Zealand, debates about the social and political effectiveness of the film and its commercial entertainment value tend to
have pivoted around its portrayal of violence and modes of realism.[21]
On one level, there is little doubt about the film's capacity to raise
awareness about domestic violence as a personal and social issue:
reports of family violence increased by 80 per cent in the aftermath
of the film's screening and women's refuges were alleged to be full.
But the graphic depictions of wife-beating and the glamorisation of
street gangs have also been seen as gratuitous, providing vicarious

thrills for the audience (Simons 1996: 29–30). The film's portrayal of Maori culture is similarly ambiguous; Simons argues that Tamahori uses the pastoral idyll imagery associated with commercials and tourist brochures to present an image of desire and fulfilment usually associated with the lifestyles of the largely middle-class white world. 'But the locus has shifted; rather than a pastoral located in commercial capitalist commodities and urban landscapes, Tamahori's pastoral fulfilment lies in and with a revitalised Maori culture' (Simons 1996: 31). As in *Boyz N the Hood*, the film's strategies of representation recycle images used by mass-market commodification for a more localised, socio-political purpose that could be ambiguous to 'outsider' interpretations of the film. But the formal structures used by both these films present narrative resolutions to their underlying racial politics in rather stark terms; both advocate a separatist politics, one couched in the terms of black nationalism, the other through a return to traditional values.

La Haine provokes a similar set of arguments around questions of representation and representativeness, only this time the concern is less with the film's use of cultural and sub-cultural iconographies than an interrogation of the news media's depiction of urban disorder and the role of the police. The most critically acclaimed of the three films internationally, superficially the film has the appearance of an expensive documentary.[22] Shot in black and white, with fluid use of the camera and detailed attention to the construction of mise-en-scène, Kassovitz eschews generic narrative in favour of an episodic structure that focuses on twenty-four hours in the lives of three young men – one French-Jewish, one French-African and one French-Algerian – in the aftermath of a riot. The film opens with a blue satellite image of the earth with a voice-over that states, 'It's about a guy falling from a fifty-storey building and as he falls, he tries to reassure himself by repeating "So far, so good. So far, so good".' As the voice continues, 'It's the landing,' a flaming petrol bomb spirals towards the image, exploding into flames on impact. The film cuts to a black and white image of a burning car and what appears to be stock footage of a riot, shot in the style of a television news report, accompanied by the Bob Marley reggae track 'Burnin' and Lootin' '. The music changes to the voice of a TV announcer reporting on the previous night's rioting on a housing estate. The end of the newsflash focuses on a photograph of a youth 'allegedly' beaten by the police while in custody and now dangerously ill in hospital.

With a click, the image disappears, switched off by an unseen viewer. The time appears centrally on the screen, accompanied by a loud gunblast: it is 10.38. The image of the planet, the story of falling (so far, so good), TV news updates on the riots and the punctuated marking of time are recurring motifs throughout the rest of the film's episodic narration. The film monitors the time it takes to fall victim to circumstances, which in this case is less than a day.

The narrative is broken down into eleven episodes of roughly one to two hours, each marked by a time flash, and a final, fatal episode (the landing) signalled as one minute. Each episode marks the growing tensions between the youths and the police and between each other. Everyone is marking time, waiting for something to happen. Vince is woken by Saïd and they go to find Hubert. Hubert's boxing gym has been destroyed by the previous night's rioting; the youths wander the estate, gathering in groups on a rooftop, only to be dispersed by the police, who maintain a threatening presence. No-one has anything to do. Vince enthuses about his involvement in the riot; a newsflash on a domestic TV set announces a police gun was stolen during the night. Hubert suspects Vince was party to burning the gym; he sells hash to make money to pay his mother's gas bill. Abdul's brother arrives in a car, bearing a shotgun. Vince reveals he is in possession of the missing police gun. Hubert, Saïd and Vince try to visit Abdul in hospital, but argue with the security guards. Saïd is arrested; intervention from one of the local policemen secures his release. Vince and Hubert fight; Hubert goes home and talks to his mother. Abdul's brother tries to kill a policeman; riot police swarm over the estate. Chased by the police, Vince turns to shoot but Hubert pushes him out the way and knocks the policeman out with a punch. They go to Paris to collect money owed to Saïd; again, Saïd is hauled into the police station, this time with Hubert, for creating a disturbance outside the expensive flats where Saïd's debtor is staying. The two are physically and verbally abused. Vince escapes arrest and goes to the cinema, then to a boxing match where he meets friends from the estate. They try to go to a nightclub, but are denied entry; one of them pulls a gun on the doorman, a shooting match ensues; all are shot except Vince. Vince, Hubert and Saïd meet up again at the station and miss the last train home. They gatecrash an art exhibition, insult the girls they try to chat up, try to rob a car to get home but no one can drive. Running from the police again, they take refuge at the top of a high building looking out over Paris and

smoke some dope. In a large shopping complex, they watch a giant
TV screen that announces Abdul's death. Hubert and Vince argue
again and part company. Saïd and Hubert are attacked by skinheads,
but saved by Vince who again pulls out his gun and threatens to
shoot. Vince cannot bring himself to pull the trigger, and lets his cap-
tive escape. Returning home on the early train, Vince relinquishes
the gun to the more level-headed Hubert. The group part company
at the station, Vince and Saïd walking towards the street, Hubert in
the opposite direction. A car pulls up, the police jump out and hold
a gun to Vince's head. Hubert runs towards the car as a shot rings
out. Vince is dead; Hubert confronts the policeman, gun in hand.
With guns pointing at each other's heads, the camera cuts to a close-
up of Saïd's frightened face hiding behind the car. A shot is fired and
the screen goes blank.

The pivotal narrative points outlined above are juxtaposed with
long interludes, where the camera wanders around after the three
youths, cutting between their sometimes separate activities and
depicting their interaction with each other, their families and other
inhabitants of the estate. These sequences of *vérité*-style wandering
are intercut by the use of confrontational shot/reverse-shot
sequences at pivotal moments, which pay careful attention to the
details of framing. Typically, the camera depicts the back of the head
or the face of one of the youths (frequently Vince) in close-up,
flanked by the other two. We see what they see, but we also see how
they are seen and perceived by others. A good example occurs in the
second episode, just after the first confrontation of the day with the
police who have dispersed a gathering on one of the rooftops. It is
12.43; the three are sitting around on a children's playground talking about sex. A van stops in the street above and a female voice
shouts 'Excuse me, gentlemen, I'm from TV. Did you take part in the
riots?' Saïd walks towards the van, depicted as walking directly
towards the camera; as he replies, he is flanked in mid-shot by Vince
and Hubert. A reverse-shot, taken from behind the trio, shows them
advancing on the van while a man films them with a camcorder and
the woman talks. A medium close-up frames them from the front,
fists raised, then cuts to a medium close-up camcorder image of
Vince as he throws stones at the van. The reverse-shot shows the van
speeding off. Confrontational editing strategies are also used to
depict the growing tension that grips Vince, starting with an early
episode where he confronts his own image in the bathroom mirror,

adopting the persona of the vigilante character Travis Buckle in *Taxi Driver* (US 1976). Vince is frequently shown in extreme close-up, directly staring at and through the camera lens, sometimes pointing his gun, occasionally appearing vulnerable. If Vince is the object of the documentary gaze, it is a gaze that he responds angrily and aggressively to by confronting the audience with their own act of looking; he makes the point to the TV news crew, 'Stirring up shite for a scoop? ... This isn't a zoo' (see Figure 5).

The documentary look is frequently undercut by juxtaposition within the mise-en-scène itself. The youths are sitting in front of boarded-up shops; a younger kid is telling Vince a story. The camera slowly pans in and cuts. It is 14.12. A reverse-shot now looks out from the shops towards a road, where a car pulls up. The camera cuts to a close up of a foot, playing with an abandoned syringe, then pulls back to depict Hubert against a wall of graffiti claiming 'We're the future'. On the train to Paris, Hubert is framed against a poster of the planet featured in the opening sequence which claims 'The world is yours', echoing a similar scene in *Scarface* (1982). Later, Vince changes the '*vous*' to '*nous*' so that the poster now reads 'The world is ours'. The youths are framed against murals of great French leaders, sculptures on the streets of Paris, against a bus shelter poster with graphics that claim 'This kills', the bottom of the poster obscured by their bodies. This attention to the detail of framing and shooting places the film in a rich tradition of filmmaking practice. Like the French 'New Wave' of the late 1950s and early 1960s (and Godard's films in particular), it combines a heritage of self-conscious political filmmaking with that of American genre cinema. The film creates a social realism for the 1990s that continues to foreground the relationship between character and environment, emphasising the role of surveillance and containment by the police and the media through its confrontational editing structure. Vince's tension and mental instability are accentuated by the use of extreme close-ups of his face. Hubert's sense of futility, his loss of hope for the future is brought to the fore through juxtaposition within the mise-en-scène. A conversation with his mother sums up the situation succinctly; in response to his comment, 'I must get out,' she replies, 'Bring me back a lettuce.' There is nowhere else to go. The conclusion is similar to that reached by *Boyz N the Hood* and *Once Were Warriors*, but here there is no exhortatory solution, no wish-fulfilment or fantasy of escape.

5 Looking back in anger: Vinz (Vincent Cassel), Saïd (Saïd Taghmaoui) and Hubert (Hubert Kounde) confront the viewer in *La Haine* (Kassovitz, France 1995).

Dysfunctional family films

The containment, surveillance and uncontrollable violence that permeates the 'hood' films as the visible face of socio-economic depression and poverty crosses the domestic threshold and enters the home in the dysfunctional family films. *Once Were Warriors* straddles this threshold, dividing its narrational space between the street activities of the men and their behaviour in the home. *Straight Out of Brooklyn*, discussed in Chapter 2, emphasises how the violence of the street and the racism that is its underlying cause has distorted family relationships, leading to domestic violence and death. In the final section of this chapter, we focus on two films that focus on the domestic environment and female characters in relation to themes of personal alienation and despair, both of them made in the UK. One, *Nil By Mouth* (1997), places female characters more centrally, somewhat redressing the tendency of these films to treat women as passive presences. The other, *Ladybird, Ladybird* (1994), is the only film completely devoted to a female perspective on the situation.

Ladybird, Ladybird, directed by the British director Ken Loach from a screenplay by Rhona Munroe, is a dramatised true story of a single mother's attempts to retain the care of her four children in the face of accusations from social workers that they are 'at risk' in her care. In some ways, Loach is revisiting familiar territory here; the contentious filmed drama made for BBC television in the 1960s, *Cathy Come Home* (1966), examined the plight of a homeless family[23] and later domestic dramas such as *Family Life* (1971) and *Raining Stones* (1993) explored themes of mental illness and unemployment. Throughout his long career, Loach has consistently returned to examining the effects of social and economic policies and institutional practices on the lives of those who are most vulnerable to the enactment of social policy directives – the homeless, the mentally ill and the unemployed. Often based on the documented experiences of individuals, Loach's family dramas are dramatised case studies that claim 'true story' status. Maggie's story in *Ladybird, Ladybird* is based on her experience of conflict with a welfare bureaucracy that cannot find a place of safety for her and her children which will allow her to escape the abuse and beating she suffers at the hands of her partner. The official solution to the vicious circle that Maggie finds herself in is to remove the children to a place of safety.

In Britain, Loach's film style has become synonymous with what is commonly understood as social realism. Typically, he eschews generic narratives, formal virtuosity and postmodern eclecticism in favour of a plain visual style that emphasises performance, the development of character and the pre-filmic referentiality of situations and events. The narratives of these films are characteristically open-ended; because the characters cannot determine or control their desires and the direction of their lives, there is no simple resolution at the level of plot closure. The plot structures are inevitably and inexorably deterministic, the movement and patterning proceeding from a bad situation to a worsening one, carrying through the consequences that are built into the initial conditions of the narrative situation; hopes and desires are unrealised, or only realised at considerable cost to the characters involved. Deborah Knight argues that this style situates Loach within a tradition of naturalism that can be traced to nineteenth-century naturalist novelists and their emphasis on the effects of environment on character. According to this argument, 'naturalist' characters cannot bring about changes for the better in their own circumstances or those around them because their circumstances are profoundly circumscribed (Knight 1997: 60–81).

Rather than selecting characters because we might like or admire them, films described as 'naturalist' choose characters that are often difficult to like; Maggie in *Ladybird, Ladybird* is a case in point. A working-class Liverpudlian with four children fathered by different men, Maggie is a volatile, angry woman whose aggressive language and violent temper reinforce the social workers' and the court's opinion of her as an unfit mother. The product of an abused childhood, she predictably chooses to have relationships with men who continue to ill-treat her until she meets Jorge, a gentle, empathetic Paraguayan political refugee who offers her compassionate understanding, love and support. In spite of Maggie's obvious character flaws, she loves and is deeply committed to her four children. Removing them from the violent domestic environment, she takes refuge in a hostel for battered women. One night, she leaves them locked in their room alone while she sings at the local pub; a fire breaks out and her oldest son is badly burned. In consequence, the welfare authorities decide to place him in a foster home and then pursue the removal of the other three children. Maggie's character makes it difficult to like her, even though she is the central figure of narrative action; alignment with her narratively does not necessarily lead to allegiance with her morally. Although one might feel sympathy for her situation, it is also possible to feel that many of her problems are caused by her aggressive, volatile nature and even her own lapses in care for her children. Yet if Maggie is an unsympathetic character, Chrissie Rock's performance brings to the role a vivacity and tenacity which questions the simple alternatives that Maggie is either a victim of circumstances beyond her control or that she is wholly responsible for her own fate. Because of this it is possible by the end of the film to empathise with her plight – the loss of all her children – even while judging her a less than ideal parent (see Figure 6). It is the faceless bureaucracy she has to deal with, in the form of social workers who are not ogres but working in accordance with inflexible policies that make little allowance for the particulars of any given situation, that aggravate and intensify the tragedy of her situation. One scene in particular conveys the difficulties of talking to the authorities; Maggie and Jorge host three different social workers, offering tea and biscuits while trying to

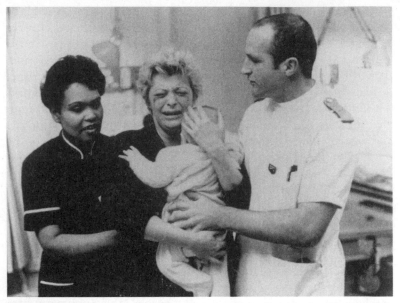

6 Chrissie Rock's intense performance creates alignment with Maggie's situation in *Ladybird, Ladybird* (*Loach*, GB 1994).

convince them that they are capable of being supportive, loving parents. Finally, Maggie can no longer contain her anger and frustration; her quick temper and acerbic tongue once again let her down. Her anger, by this stage, as Jorge tries to patiently explain, is the result of pain and anguish; as the film progresses, it becomes a sign of her strength and love. We may not like her, or agree with the way she deals with her own situation, but we cannot doubt her love for her children, or the sense of helplessness that engulfs her. Finally, her anger and aggression become for us, as for Jorge, a sign of inner strength, a refusal to give up her right to lead a normal life with the man she loves and to have a family.

Knight argues that the narration of what she defines as naturalist films is frequently 'behaviourist': third-person, observational, non-interventionalist and descriptive, which 'is no guarantee that things are as they appear to be, or that there is a narrator who knows everything about the characters and their circumstances' (Knight 1997: 72). It is objective in the sense of restricting itself to how characters act; it does not try to get 'into' the characters' minds, and cannot communicate 'subjective' states of characters. Unlike omniscient narration, which claims a position of knowledge greater than the sum of the characters in a text, behavourist narration shows the audience less than some of the characters know, think or feel because what can be shown is restricted to 'reporting' or 'presenting' what characters say and do. Knight argues that in his films Loach uses subject matter and style 'to establish a moral perspective for the examination of his characters; what his films do not do is *tell* us what to think' (Knight 1997: 72). This is a controversial position in relation to *Ladybird, Ladybird,* not least because there are inconsistencies in the story Maggie tells Jorge. It is unclear why only her eldest child is taken into care after the fire. The barman in the pub where she is singing when the accident occurs seems to know her well. Is it possible to believe this was a 'one-off' event, which is what she tells Jorge? The authorities believe her ex-partner abused her children. She denies this, but we do not know if she is telling the truth. These inconsistencies led some critics to accuse Loach (and the film) of manipulating facts to present a biased account of Maggie's experiences.[24] But this is to ignore the point of the film, which emphasises the constraining and regulatory function of social institutions on the lives of those they are designed to help. Maggie is trapped and constrained not only by her poverty, but by official institutions that do little to alleviate her situation even though that is their ostensible purpose. The refuge that is her only source of support is a voluntary organisation, underfunded and struggling to provide a service. Staying in the refuge exacerbates her situation rather than solving it because it is, through no fault of those who run it, an unsafe environment.

By showing the social and economic inequities which shape the lives of those who lack the economic power or the personal resources to overcome them, Loach reworks conventional melodramatic structures to show that the coincidence of events over which individuals have no control cannot be solved by a trite narrative resolution. What makes Loach unique as a contemporary filmmaker is his continuing adherence to the depiction of situation without offering any obvious solutions. At the end of *Ladybird, Ladybird,* Maggie has lost two of her children fathered by Jorge and the four children she has had to different fathers. Although we are told that Maggie and Jorge remain together and have three more children who they are allowed to keep, the fact remains that she has borne six children who are lost to her. There is an equilibrium restored at the end of the film through the announcement of these facts, but it is not an equilibrium that recovers Maggie from her loss, or a solution to the problems that created the cycle of events in which she becomes trapped. Loach's family dramas suggest that there is little point in those who are marginalised from mainstream society attempting to achieve the 'normal' goals and values of society within the current social and political climate. As George McKnight points out, these values create and *are* the problems (1997: 82–98). There are no simple resolutions to these dilemmas in life, and it is the refusal of the film to depict a fictitious resolution that is the source of its claim on reality.

Nil By Mouth (1997) covers similar domestic terrain, but this time the emphasis is on a masculine point of view and the moral and spiritual bankruptcy of contemporary working-class life. Unlike Loach's films, which have an outsider's eye for the social forces that destroy ambition and curb desires, Gary Oldman's self-avowedly confessional film concentrates on actorly performances to create an intense portrayal of masculine degradation. Rather like Matty Rich's *Straight Out of Brooklyn*, *Nil By Mouth* is strongly influenced by writer/director Oldman's own upbringing in the place where the film was shot, a housing estate in an area of South London left behind by the property and financial boom that swept London in the 1980s. Within the confines of this decaying modernist vision of concrete corridors and boxed interiors, the film depicts a distorted cycle of family dependence and abuse. The main protagonist, Ray (Ray Winstone) is, like Maggie, a product of family malfunction; an alcoholic and a drug abuser like his father before him, he perpetuates the cycle by taking out his frustration and anger on those closest to him. His wife Val (Kathy Burke) is part of an extended family network that includes her younger brother Billy, her mother and her grandmother. Billy is a heroin addict with a £60-a-day habit that their mother Janet can no longer afford to fund. It is the women who bear the brunt of male aggression, despair and alienation, their resilience constantly undermined by the physical and mental anguish created by the men. There is little by way of a conventional narrative structure to the film: it cuts between Ray and Val's council flat and Billy's activities hanging around on the streets and scrounging from his relatives. From its opening sequence in the local pub, the screen filled with a tight close-up of Ray's sweating, engorged face, the air redolent with foul language and South

London expletives, there is more than a hint of the grim determinism that shapes the downward spiral of events. Ray and his friend Mark enlist the help of Billy in a scam, spending the proceeds on a night on the town in the pubs and strip clubs, drinking and taking cocaine. The following day, Ray savagely beats Billy for stealing his drugs, biting him viciously on the nose. Billy hassles his mother for money for heroin, but she is broke. He breaks into Ray and Val's council flat and steals a painting. Val is out with Janet and a group of friends in the local pub, playing pool with one of the men. Ray arrives and orders Val to go home; he accuses her of being unfaithful and beats her up so badly that she miscarries and decides to leave him. Ray drinks himself into a stupor, smashing up the home in a self-pitying rage. Billy meanwhile, has been arrested for robbery and is in prison. Val returns to Ray, who has repaired the flat and curbed his drinking; they leave to visit Billy in prison.

This episodic narrative of domestic hell is filmed with an 'in your face' style that creates an intense claustrophobia. Extreme close-ups of faces fill the screen, revealing not their beauty, but their haggard, imperfect sweaty and porous appearance. Conversations rarely happen in group or two-shots, but through confrontational sequences of individual close-ups that accentuate the characters' feelings of isolation and alienation. This is social realism with a distinctly psychological edge to it, filmed with a view to cinema rather than television. A telephoto lens was used on a highly mobile camera to create a 'fly on the wall' effect with characters partially obscured by objects such as glass panels and doors. Long takes and an emphasis on the use of extreme close-up creates a claustrophobic intensity that is matched by the performance of the actors, who bring to their roles an emotional integrity and power. The film's designer was given the brief of creating 'realism with a lot of detail so that the camera felt like it was in the room with the people'.[25] The artistic direction of the film has similarities to *Once Were Warriors*: an emphasis on soft, yellow light, few bright colours in the set design, and the exclusion of any greenery such as trees or grass from the film frame. If it was sunny, filming had to stop.

Critically acclaimed as a new development in British social realism, Oldman's film fuses the homegrown realist tradition with the work of American filmmakers such as Scorsese or Cassavetes, both known for depicting long, intense dialogues between characters trapped by their surroundings and circumstances.[26] Several critics

have noted the voyeuristic quality of the work and questioned
where it would find an audience, outside of a middle-class professional group 'who might like to discuss it over dinner as a piquant
slice of anthroplogy',[27] on the assumption that it is difficult to imagine that anyone living in similar circumstances would chose to
watch this film or wish to recognise themselves in it; it is too unrelenting, too grim. This is an insider's film for outsiders, a film that
aims to show Them (the middle-class professionals?) that there are
people who can retain a glimmer of humanity even while surviving
the depths of degradation. Perhaps Richard Williams is right in suggesting that 'by offering not nihilism but the nearest thing to realism that cinema can achieve',[28] *Nil By Mouth* is finally not merely
sensational but also honourable.

End note

The British tradition of social realism tends to have equated an
'objective' distancing from what characters think and feel (what
Knight terms 'naturalism') with a political project that suggests that
the circumstances that shape characters' lives can be remedied by
structural change in society or by the application of improved (social
democratic) policies. Social realism in the 1990s is less optimistic
about the possibilities for change, but arguably far more confrontational in its presentation of characters who in different ways refuse
or negate the possibility of solutions through changes in social
policy. The debates generated by the films in this chapter show that
contemporary social realism comes in a range of stylistic variations,
incorporating hybridised elements garnered from traditions of
European art cinema to advertising, remaining committed to a
humanist politics of individual self-worth but offering little by way
of political solutions to environmental and social factors. There are
clear correspondences here with Italian neorealism, which, as recent
reassessments have pointed out, tends to focus on the psychological
depiction of characters governed by the chaotic forces of everyday
life, rather than proffering political solutions to their problems. But
unlike the neorealist films, the specific locations of characters in
environments that are crowded, claustrophobic, inescapable and
fraught with internecine disputes, both familial and territorial, gives
additional emphasis to the psychological relationship between environment and character. Doughboy, an overweight child, has to find

a way to negotiate his masculinity or be bullied by others in an environment where escape, for him, is not even a remote possibility.
Likewise, Nig attempts to find self-respect by drawing on his warrior
heritage, denying any possibility of a solution within the confines of
dominant white culture. In contrast, Hubert is torn by conflicting
loyalties: to his family, his friends and the welfare of other young
people on the estate, a conflict which cannot be resolved and which
results in his death. For many of the critics, mise-en-scène in these
films is not merely a spectacle of poverty and urban decay; it also
reinforces the contradictions in which lives are lived by emphasising
surveillance, entrapment and claustrophobia.

Characters' situations are premised on their relations to the environment, which is integral to their psychological state. Rather than
suggesting reformist or revolutionary solutions to social conditions
the signs are, at the end of the millennium, that filmmakers will continue to explore themes of identity and alienation through forms of
realism that increasingly emphasise the psychological consequences
of poverty and exclusion, bringing to the centre of the screen individuals who are no longer the object of a detached, observational
gaze, but who look back angrily and aggressively, refusing to become
the victims of 'outsider' perceptions of their identity. Whether this
discomforting form of cinema will continue to find audiences and
survive in the increasingly commercialised global marketplace has
yet to be seen, but the success of films such as *Boyz N the Hood,*
Once Were Warriors and *La Haine* on both the local and international film circuits is a sign that such a cinema can still speak in innovatory ways to the realities of social and economic deprivation,
injustice and inequity.

Notes

1 For a detailed account of these developments, see Janet Wasko (1994).
  Wasko uses the example of Republic Pictures which was able to profit
  from these developments in the 1980s: 242–3.
2 Taken from Wasko (1994: 222), who uses figures from Hancock and
  Lange, *IDATE Industrial Analyses*, vol. 1: The World Film and Television Market, Institut de l'audiovisuel et des telecommunications en
  Europe, Montpelier, France: 135–7.
3 Wasko (1994: 222), quoting Henry Sutton, 'The $64,000 Question in
  Cannes', *European*, 11 May 1990.
4 Kevin Robins and David Morley (1995) provide an in-depth explo-

ration of the globalisation thesis. Of particular interest to the current context is their essay 'Tradition and Translation: National Culture in its Global context', 105–24.

5 A succinct overview of these developments is provided by Sylvia Harvey and Kevin Robins (1993).

6 For an overview of developments in cultural policy and their relationship to local production in the British context, see Steve MacIntyre (1996).

7 All of these issues have featured across the spectrum of British urban soaps in recent years – *Eastenders* (BBC 1), *Brookside* (C4) and *Coronation Street* (Granada).

8 John Hill (1986) provides an overall assessment of the formal aspects of the British social problem film.

9 For a fuller discussion of rhetorical realism's strategies, see Chapter 4.

10 For an excellent account of the development of this critical discourse in the British context, see John Ellis (1996).

11 See, for example, the criticisms levelled at *My Beautiful Laundrette* (1985) by the Muslim community in Britain in *Black Film, British Cinema*, ICA documents (1988). Other culturally disenfranchised groups make similar claims; for example, some commentators argue that only those who have experienced living with HIV and AIDS should make films about it. See Glyn Davis (1998).

12 The quote is taken from Gledhill's summary of MacCabe's thesis, quoted in Hill (1986: 60).

13 Chris Darke (1995).

14 See, for example, on *La Haine:* Allister Harry 'Hiding Out in the Hood Again, *Village Voice*, 10 October 1995, 25–6 and Keith Reader (1995). On *Once Were Warriors*, see Onyeachi Wambu (1995).

15 Elizabeth Mermin (1996: 10) comments that the 1990s ghetto films 'leapt into Hollywood as hybrids between pseudo-documentaries and gangster films, constructing a lucrative new nineties realism'.

16 Glen Masato Mimura (1996) discusses this point in detail.

17 'When I left the theater, I was crying for all the dead black men in my family': Michelle Wallace (1992: 123).

18 *New Zealand Film* (1995) 53:5, 10–11.

19 The design of the film's colour scheme is discussed at some length by the director; see Robert Sklar (1995).

20 See, for example, Leonie Pihama (1996).

21 For a summary of this debate, see Rochelle Simons (1996).

22 See, for example, Alex Duval Smith's comments on the 'strong documentary quality' of the film: *Guardian Arts*, 23 June 1995, 20–4.

23 For a more detailed discussion of this film, see Chapter 8.

24 See, for example, Carol Sarler, 'Nothing But The Truth', *Sunday Times Magazine*, 18 April 1994, 43–44, 46 and 49.

25 Nick James (1997), interview with designer Hugo Luczyc-Wyhowski.

26 See Nick James (1997) and Phillip French, *Observer*, 12 October 1997, 10.

27 Anne Billson, *Sunday Telegraph Review*, 12 October 1997. The *Empire* review commented, 'as awful yet as compelling as a motorway pile-up ... [it] makes an audience feel like voyeurs' (1997: 47, 103–4).

28 Richard Williams, 'Cinema doesn't get any more real than this', *Guardian*, 'Arts', 10 October 1997, 6.

Chapter 8

Violent appropriations: realising death

'Violence is part of this world and I am drawn to the outrageousness of real-life violence ... Real life violence is, you're in a restaurant and a man and his wife are having a argument and all of a sudden the guy gets mad at her, he picks up the fork and stabs her in the face ... I am interested in the act, in the explosion, and in the entire aftermath of that.' (Quentin Tarantino, quoted by Michael Wood 1995: 9)

As it is made, art can press up so close against its subject that it seems nearly impossible to tell the flesh from its reflection. Time pulls the two away from each other. If I see Seven in five or ten years' time, it will no longer feel too close for comfort ... that won't be because something more shocking and violent will have pushed back the frontiers of violence but because what is real will have taken on a different form, will have a different fashion. (Gerrard 1996: 89)

During the mid-1990s in Britain questions of the effect of violent films on those who consume them returned with a vengeance to the policy agenda in the wake of a series of violent crimes which generated wide media coverage. The mass murders committed by Rosemary and Fredrick West in Gloucestershire, the killing of two-year-old James Bulger by two ten-year-old boys in Liverpool, and the Dunblane massacre have kept issues related to acts of violent crime in the foreground of public consciousness. In the USA, a similar pattern of violent killings (the Oklahoma bombing, the murder of several schoolchildren by two of their classmates, for example) has had similar effects. Demands for tougher law and order policies followed in the wake of two contentious court cases, the Rodney King and O. J. Simpson trials. The mass media are often blamed for creating a more violent society, with films (particularly on video) bearing much of the brunt of public concern. In the USA, for example, Michael Medved has argued stridently that films are increasingly responsible for acts of copycat violence that bear an uncanny resemblance to scenes of filmic violence (Medved 1993). In a more recent article he makes a direct association between a pointless and sadistic act of violence committed against a New York subway employee and scenes from a film released only days prior to the event. The victim was squirted with highly flammable liquid and then ignited; his burns were so extensive that he died in hospital two weeks later. In the film *Money Train* (1995) Wesley Snipes and Woody Harrelson play New York City cops on the trail of a vicious pyromaniac who executes two assaults identical in almost every detail to the killing of the subway employee (Medved 1996: 20).

Similar claims of feature film influence have been put forward in Britain. At the trial of the two ten-year-old boys accused of murdering James Bulger, the judge claimed that the boys had probably been unduly influenced by exposure to violent videos. The only evidence to support this claim was a copy of *Child's Play 3* (1991), found in the home of one of the boys, although there was no indication that either boy had actually watched the film. Reporting on the trial, *The Times* claimed that '[t]he role which one particularly notorious film *Child's Play 3* played in the Bulger trial brought urgency in what had been an academic debate about the effects of screened brutality'.[1] The *Independent*'s leader took a similar view: 'young minds are in need of protecting'.[2] Yet far more provoking to a public imagination accustomed to equating image iconicity with actuality and evidence were the images retrieved from a security camera in the shopping mall where Bulger was abducted. These depicted a small figure being led away by two older children, who could not be identified because of the blurred camera imagery. This picture, reproduced in still form across the front pages of the nation's newspapers, became a symbol of moral fear and national panic.

The debate grew in the British parliament during the ensuing months as politicians eagerly took up the beating of the moral drum, forcing the Conservative government to honour their election pledges and amend the Criminal Justice Act and Public Order Bill. During the Bill's stormy progress through parliament, only one amendment proved uncontroversial with the opposition; a private member's bill that sought to ban the video sale or rental of all '18' certificate films on the basis that they were not suitable for home consumption. The proposal claimed that these films could damage children whose negligent parents allowed them to watch. The incident recalls an earlier, mid-1980s moral panic provoked by the circulation of so-called video nasties. Underlying these panics and their simplistic claims of media cause-and-effect are deeply entrenched beliefs about the power of the mass media to deprave and corrupt our sensibilities, a belief rooted in nineteenth-century attitudes to the damaging effects of popular cultural forms and a paternalistic attitude towards those 'others' who consume them. Barker points out that similar accusations were brought against 'penny dreadfuls' (in Britain) and 'dime novels' (in America), followed by music hall (Britain), vaudeville (America) and then cinema. Later, radio, comic books, television, video games, computers and, most recently, the Internet have all been subject to accusations that they corrupt the young and are damaging to social and cultural life (Barker and Petley 1997: 26).

Whether or not such fears are grounded in evidence or based on speculation, it is exactly this argument that was used by the Movement for Christian Democracy in their bid to increase the powers of the British Board of Film Classification to censor videos in the wake of the Bulger case. Supported by Liverpool MP David Alton, the Movement successfully lobbied parliament for an amendment to the Criminal Justice Bill based on persuasive arguments that British children need to be protected from gratuitously violent films and videos. To support their case, they commissioned a report from Elizabeth Newson, a psychologist who believes that media violence amounts to nothing short of electronic child abuse which has to be regulated against in order to protect our children (Newson 1994). The report was co-signed by twenty-four of her colleagues, other professionals with an interest in the protection of children. In essence, Newson imputes effects to films based on what she claims is a consistent and overwhelming body of evidence, that media violence causes violent and aggressive behaviour in both children and susceptible adults. Her claim is not without some substance; American 'effects' researchers have conducted endless experiments on the topic over the years, many of which have the sole objective of establishing a connection between an increase in screen violence and escalating social violence. But as Guy Cumberbatch and Dennis Howitt (1989) point out after an extensive analysis of effects studies and their evidence, the results often contradict each other. The publications present a range of opinions, speculations and arguments on the

probability of a causal relationship between screen violence and violent behaviour, but it is impossible to isolate any causal factors which
are consistently scientifically verifiable. Furthermore, in spite of the
apparent success of the behaviourist wing of the effects lobby in US
congressional debates on media policy, it has been singularly unsuc-
cessful in achieving what it set out to do, which is to curb the depiction of violent images on the largely unregulated, commercial
American networks (Rowland Jr 1997). This failure is a clear indication to many researchers of how effects research is used by politicians to manipulate media policy and public opinion but contains
little of real substance. As Barker has unwaveringly argued over the
years, part of the reason for this is because the concept of media violence is itself so slippery (encompassing everything from news bulletins to horror films, from cartoons to hardcore pornography and
action adventure films) that it easily dissolves into a useless confla-
tion of quite different things (1997: 27). But Barker's position is
open to criticism on a number of fronts, not least because it is generally assumed that the media influence many aspects of everyday
life, such as our consumer activities and our social behaviour. If the
media now constitute part of our lived experience of everyday reality, as Silverstone (1994) and others suggest, it is inconceivable that
mediated violence does not play some part in shaping our relations
to the material realities of violence in society. Current conceptions
of the active audience have virtually pushed questions of media
influence to the margins of the academic research agenda, but, as
Miller and Philo point out, 'anti-effects arguments can look very
dubious when applied to other areas of social life' (Miller and Philo
1996: 18–20). The question posed by these researchers is not
whether mediated violence has a direct effect on behaviour, but how
violence becomes part of a human vocabulary of potential behaviours, and whether the media play a role in this process.

Definitions of realism have proved to be a crucially determining
factor in more recent academic analyses of media violence, but most
of these pertain to television drama rather than to fiction films, no
doubt because of the different institutional contexts in which film
and television are studied in the academy.[3] For example, a British
analysis of TV violence commissioned by the Broadcasting Standards Council differentiates between depictions of violence as shallow play in cartoons and generic fictions such as horror, gangster
and westerns, and deep play, when the violence depicted is closely

associated to the kinds of aggressive behaviour that viewers are familiar with or assume to be an indictment of their own society. Corner points out that the problem with this formulation is that it places too heavy an emphasis on the more serious, social realist forms of drama somewhat at the expense of considering what is at stake, socially and psychologically, in the watching of violent fictions for entertainment purposes. For Corner, the function of realist depictions draws on the system of ethics the audience might be expected to use in assessing actual situations and events, whereas entertaining violence appeals to 'interpretative criteria other than those provided by ethical norms' (1995: 146), such as pleasure. But this formulation too has its problems, since most generic fiction, which is often highly real-ised for spectacular, entertainment purposes by the use of special effects and stunt choreography, is contained within narrative frameworks that justify their use. As a rule, generic fiction supports a Manichean ethics of good versus evil, where the hero continues to be a repository of moral and ethical values. Within this context, death is often depicted as a functional disposal of 'villains' who die simply, cleanly and (because there is no audience alignment with them) apparently painlessly as part of their role in the plot. Violence is justified in the service of these values, allowing the pleasure of violent entertainment within a moral and ethical framework that sits securely in the realms of fiction, but corresponds to the socially sanctioned uses of violence in society serving the interests of a justifiable personal revenge, perhaps, or perpetrated on behalf of public institutions such as the police force or the military, or by a hero demonstrating the superiority of the individual over these institutions in securing the safety of society.

The cycle of films now termed 'the new brutalism' are central to debates about realism in the 1990s because of the outraged moral judgements they provoked from critics of their use of realist codes and conventions to represent violence.[4] Deeply rooted fears about the power of realist forms to corrupt viewer sensibilities were revealed when *Reservoir Dogs* (1992), *Man Bites Dog* (1992) and *Bad Lieutenant* (1992) opened within weeks of one another on London's independent cinema screens in 1993. Termed 'the new brutalism' in the popular press, the films are characterised by graphic depictions of violence that many journalists and critics consider more 'realistic' than that of their Hollywood action thriller counterparts;[5] the violence tends to be perpetrated by individuals against individuals and is filmed using camera and audio techniques frequently employed by documentary filmmakers. This method of shooting is often accompanied by a loose narrative structure: rather than being driven by narrative causality, as in conventional Hollywood thrillers and action films, the characters in these films seem to lack narratively adequate motivations for the violent acts they commit. Rather, events just happen: the style of narration is expositional rather than classical, the camera offering a viewpoint of detached specularity. Unlike conventional Hollywood action films, where the omniscient camera can align viewer empathy with a Manichean hero who commits violent acts in the name of a 'greater good', the use of expositional strategies creates an ethical vacuum which can only be filled by the viewer's own assessment of the moral issues. Arguably, these representations raise questions about the nature of violence in the individual and in society that are suppressed in more conventional uses of it in fictional narratives. This more neutral moral coding proved to be part of the attraction for audiences bored with Hollywood's predictable action movies, their larger-than-life hero figures and crude moral pieties.[6]

The three films selected for discussion in this chapter are chosen for the range of techniques they employ in pursuit of disrupting conventional images of violence in Hollywood action films. A key film in the development of the new brutalism is *Henry, Portrait of a Serial Killer* (1986), a film that Tarantino (the most prominent of the 'new brutalism' directors) claims as an important influence on *Reservoir Dogs*. Also considered a part of the 'new brutalism' cycle, but less well known and therefore less controversial, is the self-reflexive Belgian production *Man Bites Dog*, a film that became cult viewing on the art house circuit. Finally, the most controversial serial killer film to date, and the most popular of the trio, Oliver Stone's *Natural Born Killers* (1994) is non-realist in its generic intertextuality and use of parody and pastiche, but graphically depicts violent rape and murder. All three films, in different ways, attempt to blur the boundaries between different generic forms of realist representational practice by using codes and conventions associated with televisual forms such as documentary and the new hybrid formats of Reality TV, which combine documentary techniques of observation and reportage with elements of narrative and spectacle to create 'infotainment'. The rest of this chapter is devoted to an examination of these forms and their

codes and conventions, starting with a brief résumé of documentary's relations with the real, and its relation to the less well-known
fictional genres of snuff and mondo. Short sections then follow on
each of the three films chosen for discussion, emphasising their
formal structures and the filmmaking traditions they draw on.
Finally, we return to questions of viewer alignment and moral allegiance in order to pose questions about the role of these films as
active agents of intervention in debates about screen violence.

Constructing reality: fictional realism and documentary films

'Documentary' is the loose and often highly contested label given,
internationally, to certain kinds of film and television (and sometimes radio programmes) which, according to John Corner, reflect
and report on the 'real' through the use of the recorded images and
sounds of actuality (1996: 2). In recent years, the relationship of
documentary film to the 'real' has become a hotly contested area of
theoretical debate. Documentary film practitioners, from the time of
John Grierson's first recorded use of the word to designate a mode
of film practice in the 1920s, have predicated their social role on a
special relationship to the 'real' which, according to Brian Winston,
has its roots in the political legacy of nineteenth-century realist
painting – that of incorporating the labourer as a fit subject for art.
By 'claiming the real' (Winston's term) as their preferred terrain of
activity, based on the scientific legitimisation of the evidential nature
of their work afforded by the technology of the camera, documentary filmmakers created a body of work characterised by its status as
'fact'. In his detailed and illuminating study of the development of
documentary film practice in Britain, France and America, Winston
points out how the impetus to claim the evidential character of documentary film practice has relied on the camera as an objective scientific recording mechanism which, like other scientific instruments,
enables an inscription to be made. Watching actuality on the screen
is analogous to watching the needle dance on a physiograph: the
apparatus that produces the image becomes transparent; the film
becomes an inscription which is accepted as evidence (1995: 137).
But Winston, like many film theorists, in his determination to prove
the constructed nature of the photographic image, plays down the
iconic relationship of the image to that which it records, constructing realism solely as indexical reference and ignoring the perceptual

capacity of the viewer to real-ise images that correspond to their real-world visualisation and auditory experiences.[7] Winston overemphasises 'scientific' conventions at the expense of considering the cultural conventions that attend all viewing situations, and the degree of scepticism that often accompanies the reception of documentary films.

Documentary film's social status as a factual or reality genre circulates around questions of inconicity and evidence, revelation and argument – all of which, to varying degrees, are used in realist fiction films to enhance their claims to 'true story' status by depicting ostensibly accurate recreations, not only of events and circumstances, but also of the feelings and emotions of characters caught up in them. The differential relationship between fiction and documentary, however, hinges upon the degree to which their depictive strategies play on audience knowledge of their respective conventions. In fiction films, as in documentary films, the closer certain aspects of a film's depictive elements correspond to actuality recording practices, the greater their capacity to appear to mediate actuality directly, rather than perform a representative or symbolic function.

This creates an apparent blurring between fictional and factual modes of expression which, in films such as *JFK*, are a cause of considerable debate and concern in contemporary academic media circles, as we pointed out in Chapter 6. But such a use is not without historical precedents: from its earliest inception as a medium, both filmmakers and film theorists have been aware of the capacity of the filmic image to not only mediate but also manipulate the recording of actuality. One of the earliest examples of such a use is a British newsreel which recreates the coronation of King Edward VII; the filmmakers, unable to obtain permission to film inside the cathedral where the investiture was taking place, created a full-scale reconstruction which circulated as a 'live' account of the event. We have already pointed out how Eisenstein's fictional account of the 1905 uprising in Odessa, *Battleship Potemkin* (1925), created considerable disagreement amongst filmmakers in revolutionary Russia because it blurred the boundaries between fiction and reality by using filmmaking techniques associated with factual genres to reconstruct a fictional account of historical events. Dramatic reconstruction in the service of actuality is commonly associated with televisual forms such as drama documentary, where reconstruction is an

accepted part of the form. In the UK, this blending of factual and fictional modes has often been used by filmmakers wanting to make
controversial statements about social and political issues.

A notable use of the technique in the mid-1960s, which proved
to some critics the political efficacy of using actuality techniques in
the service of socially responsible fiction, was the BBC's 'Play for
Today' production *Cathy Come Home* (1966). Written by Jeremy
Sandford from his extensive research on the problem of homeless-
ness in the apparently affluent society of 'swinging London', the
play was produced on 16mm film using techniques associated at
the time with the realist aesthetics of British cinema. Produced by
Tony Garnett and directed by Ken Loach, the film created a widespread public response, including, it has been claimed, the establishment of the housing charity Shelter, a direct response to the
drama's intervention in a contemporary public issue. Watching
Cathy Come Home today, what is striking about the piece is how
the use of actuality shooting conventions (hand-held camera,
follow-on action shooting and found sound), particularly in the
construction of contextual, public space, still creates a sense of
immediacy in spite of the obvious 'datedness' of setting and costumes. The continuing use of shooting and recording strategies culturally associated with the formal codes and conventions of
documentary filmmaking in campaigning drama documentaries
such as *Hillsborough* (1997) suggests, somewhat in contradiction
to prevailing orthodoxies, that the use of actuality conventions to
convey realism of setting and action remains relatively stable. It is
the ways in which these techniques inflect the fictional realism of
films whose primary objective is to entertain rather than enlighten
viewers that provokes comment from critics and journalists,
demonstrating their concern with the ethical implications of using
such techniques in an entertainment context.

Although the codes and conventions of actuality filmmaking have
changed somewhat since *Cathy Come Home* was produced (the
most notable addition to the repertoire perhaps is the hidden camera
footage made available by the miniaturised palmcorder), the criteria
for judging fiction films as 'realist' seem to remain remarkably consistent. Documentary films stake their claim on reality through the
use of a wide range of conventions, including narrativisation, witness accounts, reportage and recorded evidence. Corner points to
three broad innovatory shifts in documentary practice in the UK in

the 1990s that include the use of dramatic reconstruction and *vérité* in programmes about the emergency services such as 999 (BBC 1992) and *Blues and Twos* (ITV 1994), the emergence of 'do-it-yourself' camcorder-shot programmes such as the BBC's *Video Diaries* and *Video Nation* and the use of hidden cameras in programmes such as *Undercover Britain* (Channel 4 1994). There is also a tendency towards an increasingly self-conscious use of aesthetic hybridisation drawing on narrative fiction, music video and forms used in advertising (Corner 1996: 182). In contrast, contemporary feature films are invariably judged as realist by the reviewing establishment if they conform to one of two criteria. Either they broadly correspond to what we have termed expositional films, with formal conventions that continue to have close associations with Italian neorealism, as we suggested in Chapter 4, or they are judged to accurately represent the psychological landscape of a character or characters. Traditionally, these realist techniques have been critically valorised because of their association with humanistic values and a 'progressive' political impulse, with the incorporation of excluded or marginalised groups (primarily the working class) as fully realised subjects rather than as outmoded stereotypes. More recently, as we discussed in Chapter 7, the use of realist strategies has extended to the portrayal of a range of 'outsiders', in particular alienated black male youth (*Straight Out of Brooklyn, La Haine*) and 'dysfunctional' families and individuals (*Once Were Warriors, Nil By Mouth*). Within this context, psychological realism continues to be broadly equated with humanistic values and a 'progressive' social morality, if not explicitly with a 'progressive' politics. But the use of realist strategies to depict the lives of those conventionally considered to be outside the framework of moral values on which such a liberal humanist project of incorporation is predicated can raise uncomfortable questions about realism's 'progressiveness'. This is particularly acute when they are fictional re-creations of those whose alieniation is enacted through violence.

The characterisation of Henry Lee Lucas in *Henry, Portrait of a Serial Killer* is a good example of such a use of realist strategies. The film, ostensibly based on revealing the everyday life of a convicted rapist and murderer, includes graphic sequences of the rape and killing of women. These victims, re-constructions of people who were actually assaulted and killed, are treated as superfluous objects within the narrative economy of the film. Can depicting a serial killer as a focus of narrative alignment, in any context, be deemed progressive? Does the film present Henry as a glamorised spectacle, an object to be looked at? Are the graphic scenes of rape and murder gratuitous and exploitative, included primarily to attract an audience? Or does the film, by refusing to offer a secure position of ethical judgement, create an awareness of viewer complicity that is deeply unsettling in its depiction of casual violence? An analysis of the reviews of the film in Britain sheds some light on these issues, but first, one further use of documentary strategies in feature films needs to be considered.

Real death: snuff and mondo

Henry's production history situates the film on the fringes of the mainstream, in the independent production sector associated with exploitation films and pornography. Elements of this tradition of filmmaking practice are rarely touched on in academic film analyses; we consider them here because both are associated with controversial elements of realist film practice. Henry Lee Lucas, the source of inspiration for John McNaughton's film, claimed on several occasions after his arrest that he had been introduced to a satanic cult called 'The Hands of Death' by his partner Otis Toole and that many of his crimes had been committed according to their commands. This confession was later retracted due to Lucas's stated belief that the cult would kill him for revealing their secrets, but no law enforcement agency has been able to establish the existence of the cult. The stories of secret cults, satanism and human sacrifice have led some reporters and commentators to believe that Lucas, Toole and their associates were involved in snuff filmmaking (Kerekes and Slater, 1993: 299). Although this has never been proved, the rumour lends force to the suspicions of some British journalists that *Henry*'s roots lie in the underground film industry of porn and exploitation, where snuff became a byword for the ultimate blurring of violent fiction and actuality, the portrayal of real murder in front of the camera, enacted for the sole purpose of entertainment and sexual excitement. Rumours of the circulation of snuff movies, which lay at the heart of the 'video nasties' scare in Britain in the mid-1980s, were again the cause of a national moral panic in 1992 when trading standards investigators seized over 3,000 videos depicting, according to the *Guardian*, 'scenes including torture, mutilation and cannibalism ... It is claimed that some videos depict real-life footage from autopsies and medical surgery'.[8]

Kerekes and Slater, in their extensive investigation of the snuff movie phenomenon, trace its development to the production of a film called *Snuff*, made by an American exploitation producer in the mid-1970s, which purported to show the actual sexual assault, murder and dismemberment of a woman. The release of the film was accompanied by a lurid advertising campaign stage managed by Allan Shackleton, owner of the distribution company Monarch Releasing Corporation. The publicity material claimed that the film was made in South America where 'life is cheap' (Kerekes and Slater 1993: 19). Shackleton's marketing tactics ensured that the film was greeted controversially. Feminist groups in particular protested against the film's screening, leading to further TV and press coverage. The resulting increase in public interest ensured a healthy profit for what was a cheap pornographic production. Although the film's actuality claims have since been discredited as simulation, since the mid-1970s claims about the existence of snuff movies have flourished in the fertile territory of the tabloid press and exploitation magazine market. The sensationalist blend of fact, fiction and rumour which circulates around the snuff phenomenon has ensured that the myth continues to reverberate, reinforcing public anxieties about the depiction of actual sexual violence and death on the screen.

If the snuff movie is the end point of depicting 'reality' in fiction films, then the mondo film is the predecessor of Reality TV and exploitative infotainment formats parodied, for example, in the depiction of Wayne Gale as the host of the 'American Maniacs' tabloid TV show in *Natural Born Killers*. Mondo has become the generic name for actuality representations of cannibalism, torture and various forms of mutilation and sensational atrocities strung together and given spurious coherence by a voice-over narration that purports to be informative but is rarely educational (Kerekes and Slater 1993: 104). Accompanied by pompous orchestral scores and catchy theme tunes, the mondo films present, in documentary fashion, raw footage of outrageous and incredible events. *Mondo Cane* (1962) – literally translated as 'Dog World' – is now regarded as the founding film of the genre, a compilation of customs and rituals from around the world, mostly drawn from actuality footage but with some staged sequences, that illustrates the proposition that 'it's a dog's life'.[9] By contrast with today's depictions, the content of the original film seems relatively tame: most of its content focuses on the juxtaposing of bizarre cultural customs such as the force-feeding of geese in France to provide pâté de foie gras and the excessive eating habits of women on a Pacific island who are considered ineligible for marriage if they weigh less than three hundred pounds. The world-wide success of this film at the box office ensured the continuation of the genre throughout the 1960s and 1970s, exploiting the market for explicit sexual material and hardcore pornography. In spite of the genre's 'claim on the real', contrivance and simulation are common. Often masquerading as educationally instructive, mondo films depict the slaughtering and ill-treatment of animals with sickening regularity, exploiting the ritual practices of disappearing tribal cultures in what has become a cinematic tradition of animal slaughter and racism.

The 1980s saw a marked shift in the genre away from these images towards an emphasis on scenes of human butchery and carnage. New video technology and broadcast television's increased appetite for images of disaster created an excessive volume of footage of human death, disaster and despair, rejected by broadcasters, that depicted not only the effects of natural disasters such as famine and the man-made carnage of war but mass killing sprees, suicides and accidental death. In the 1990s, video technicians and editors have replaced the globetrotting filmmakers looking for sensational footage that characterised the mondo enterprise; instead, compilations culled from TV news reports, medical documentaries and home-shot camcorder footage have found their way onto American domestic TV screens via cable and satellite, where Reality TV provides an outlet for independently produced shock footage.

On the terrestrial TV channels in the UK, Reality TV is associated with the new blend of infotainment programming that uses documentary observational techniques to record the day-to-day lives of ordinary people in everyday situations. Recent popular successes include programmes such as *Hotel* and *Cruise* where a month or so in the day-to-day running of an institution is presented through a focus on a few key personnel and a small number of clients. All the participants are aware of the presence of the camera and often address it, presenting their own work practices and those of their organisation as both entertainment and spectacle for the TV audience. Other forms combine documentary footage with reconstruction, such as the emergency services drama 999. In the USA, Reality TV encompasses a broad spectrum of programmes from controversial recreations of rapes, shootings and stabbings in *America's Most Wanted* and camcorder footage of personal tragedy, suicide and death featured on NBC's *I Witness Video*, to the afternoon chat show confessionals familiar to viewers in the UK in the form of the *Oprah Winfrey Show*, *Ricky Lake* and the notorious *Jerry Springer Show*, among others. With one in every six Americans now owning a camcorder, providing sensational footage for television is fast becoming something of a national pastime.[10] Critics claim that Reality TV blurs the conventional boundaries between fact and fantasy, with news becoming the raw material from which entertainment is crafted. Some academics claim that the 'blur effect' is desensitising people to reality and distancing them from 'real' life.[11] This anxiety seems to underlie much of the press commentary on the violence in contemporary film, as the following analysis will suggest.

Henry, Portrait of a Serial Killer

The writer/director of *Henry* claims to have based his film on the life of Henry Lee Lucas, who confessed to killing 360 people in the US, including his mother when he was 23 years of age (although he later recanted his confession and was finally convicted of only eleven murders).[12] A maker of documentaries by trade, John McNaughton was commissioned in 1985 by MPI Home Video to make a sex film: *Henry* was the result. Shot on 16mm on a miniscule budget of around $120,000, the story presents an unspecified period of time in Henry's life when, just out of prison for murdering his mother, he is living with an ex-convict friend and his sister and engaging in his favourite pastime, the unmotivated killing of nameless individuals. The film is disturbing because Henry is not diegetically punished for these murderous acts; the lack of narrative closure suggests a realistic possibility, not only of unsolved murders, but of unrecorded killings. As indicated by its title, the film stakes a generic claim on a 'true life' story, depicting a stark and gloomy slice of life cut from the underbelly of American society through what are commonly referred to as the 'gritty' realist strategies of social realism. The focus of these films, as we discussed in detail in Chapter 7, is invariably a character(s) whom we may not actively like even though we are narratively aligned with them, but this does not prevent a 'concern alignment' with their situation; examples included Hubert, Vince and Abdul in *La Haine* and Maggie in *Ladybird, Ladybird*. *Henry* focuses on the serial killer as an ordinary citizen, a free man who walks around and kills other people as a regular part of his everyday life. Henry is the kind of character that we normally meet and 'know' in fiction films through his representation as the villain, the bad guy, in the detective and slasher genres. As a symbolic representation in a paradigmatic film the serial killer's character, whether he is an updated conception of Dracula, such as Hannibal Lecter in *Silence of the Lambs* (1991), or a stereotypical religious maniac, as in *Se7en* (1995), maintains a credibility gap between what we perceive as a fictional representation and what we perceive as factual mediation. *Henry* creates an uncomfortable jarring because the fictional treatment of the theme is not usually associated with the communicative strategies in use. By turning the killer/villain of popular detective fiction into the 'hero' of the film through his position of narrative centrality, the viewer is inevitably aligned with Henry's view of the world (see Figure 7). It is a cold, blank stare, barely alleviated by his brief romantic entanglement with the sexually abused and battered sister of his friend Otis.

Sparse, uncluttered, poorly lit location settings shot on cheap film stock with low levels of colour saturation accentuate the poverty, boredom and claustrophobia of Henry's life. Scenes in the bare, shabby flat where Henry, Otis and Becky live are cut against Henry and Otis foraging in the backstreets of the city for people to satisfy their appetite for excitement and sexual pleasure. With a minimum of dialogue, the film is motivated by a shooting style that apparently seeks to enhance its claim to 'true story' status true by posing as 'fly on the wall' *vérité*. But although *Henry* is critically perceived as effecting a raw, actuality style through its use of mise-en-scène and static camerawork, documentarists would probably find the film's representational codes closer to those of drama documentary than *vérité*. There is sufficient use in the film of shot/reverse-shot and point-of-view editing techniques to keep the film firmly within the conventions of fictional realism, in spite of the raw, cheap quality of the image, sparse dialogue and static camerawork. The film opens with Henry paying his bill in a diner and complimenting the waitress on her smile; he is stitched together piece by piece – a hand stubs out a cigarette, an image of the diner waitress is taken from the

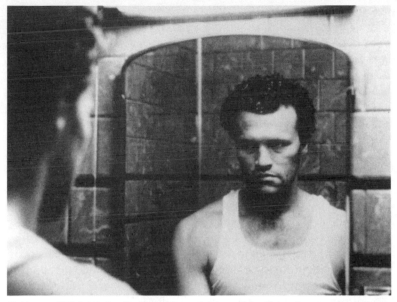

7 Henry (Michael Rooker) looking at himself in the mirror: reflexivity in
Henry, Portrait of a Serial Killer (McNaughton, US 1986).

back of his head. These images are cross-cut with pictures of dead
women staring blankly out of the frame, their mutilated bodies reminiscent of the forensic photographs of mutilated bodies that pepper
office walls in television detective stories. A causal relationship is
established between Henry and images of the dead women; the rest
of the film shows Henry (later Henry and Otis) murdering people
for his/their own amusement. Part of this amusement involves
recording on camcorder the rape and murder of a family, which they
later play back and watch on TV at home. The murders are performed almost perfunctorily, with little attention paid to camera
positioning or revealing detail through editing and close-ups, apart
from the protracted sequence where Henry murders Otis for committing incest with Becky: he then dismembers the body before disposing of it.

First seen on a British cinema, the London Scala, in 1990, the
film was screened without a certificate. The British art house dis-
tributor Electric Eye pursued the case for certification with the
censor, who released the film some eighteen months later after con-
sultation with forensic psychiatrists and psychologists. Thirteen

seconds were cut from the notorious camcorder 'snuff scene' and a shot of a half-naked dead woman staring directly at the camera was excised from the opening sequence. Following these cuts, the film was granted an '18' certificate and released through the independent and art house cinema circuits. A version of the film is now available on video.

An analysis of the reviews of the film when it first opened to the general public on the London screens provides an interesting snapshot of how the discourse of realism was used to both praise and condemn the film. What the analysis reveals is the differing status of realism among journalists writing for their implied reader communities. The form of the film is not at issue, but the use of the form in relation to the subject matter deeply disturbs a number of commentators. Adam Mars Jones, writing in the *Independent*, is one of the few reviewers to dismiss the film, which he finds 'lurid and unedifying' and 'proof that even low budget films can be cheap'.[13] His main objection is that the psychology of the film is unconvincing and that its semi-documentary realist form cheats the audience, presenting no explanation for why Henry acts as he does. The prevailing climate of criticism tended to disagree, claiming that *Henry* was shorn of artifice and pretension, its documentary style a refreshing contrast to the glamorised psycho-killers presented in films like *Silence of the Lambs*. (Many reviewers use *Silence of the Lambs* as an obvious point of comparison because of the close release dates of the two films.) Michael Odell in *The Voice*, for example, sees the film as a 'sober and realistic view of a sad twisted young man, neither glamorous nor appealing in this grim, harrowing film'.[14] Sue Heal writing in *Today* claimed that 'the grainy, low-budget neorealistic approach' created a 'fascinating and challenging piece that straddles a perilous tightrope between the presentation of horror devoid of flashy frills and gratuitous carnage'. She finds the film 'alarmingly hypnotic and unglamorous' and that it 'left a very nasty taste in the mouth'.[15] Tom Hutchison in the *Mail on Sunday* commented that the real horror of Henry is that he could live next door: it 'makes *Silence of the Lambs* seem like a fairy tale'.[16] Alexander Walker in the *Evening Standard* takes this view to the extreme: 'Many films feature violent death but they dramatise it – all *Henry* does is record it'.[17] Claiming that the film is more disturbing than titillating, Walker uses the opinions of forensic scientists to support his view that the film is a 'document of contemporary life and death'. He sees the film as a necessary corrective to films such as *Silence of the Lambs* that present murder and killing as abnormal exotica.

These reviewers find difference from generic detective thrillers such as *Silence of the Lambs* the principal ground on which to place *Henry* as a realist film. Some invoke traditional concepts of filmic realism as articulated in Bazinian concepts of the ontology of the photographic image, others a classical theory of artistic unity where synthesis between content and form is taken as a measure of whether a fictional film work can achieve the status of work of art. Nick James in *City Limits*, for example, found the film 'beautifully constructed', with its deadpan unexploitative treatment of its subject matter 'leavened by a sly grain of mordant humour'.[18] Nigel Andrews in the *Financial Times* commented that it 'is hard to think of a film that, while gloating so little over the evil it portrays, holds back so firmly from offering spurious morals or cures ... [this is] a film about an affectless killer that has the nerve to adopt a matching affectlessness of style'.[19]

What may be seen at work here is a contemporary reworking of a nineteenth-century schism in realism's discursive construction: that of realism's claim to scientific objectivity and verisimilitude based on the iconicity of the photographic image as evidence (most pronounced in Walker's comments 'that all *Henry* does is record'), and realism's claim to present an image of authentic experience through a cosy marriage of content and form (most pronounced in Andrews's comments on the 'affectless' killer and the 'matching affectlessness' of the film's style). These differing uses of realist discourse, and the varying claims on knowledge of both an external reality and human nature that they represent, have their roots in the ability of the camera and the microphone to record raw actuality and the paradoxical ability of these recordings to be used in the pursuit of both scientific (objective) and artistic (subjective) practices that construct mediated accounts of the 'real'. This seems to indicate that the ethical and moral concern of 'blurring the boundaries' between fiction and fact is a discursive property of different academic practices rather than a property of texts *per se*, which are invariably framed by viewing and interpretative contexts. Our own position accepts the play of signification in the text and locates the search for meaning within the epistemes or regimes of knowledge that shape interpretative discourse, rather than within aesthetic forms themselves. Two further examples will serve to underline the point.

One of these has its roots in what is now known as 1970s *Screen* theory, a concern with the underlying ideologies of the text; the other displays knowledge of the blurred boundaries between art and popular culture which is a familiar feature of theories of postmodernism. The commentaries in *Spare Rib* and the *Morning Star* can be read as an indication of the former position. Both condemn the film as a simulated snuff movie, an exploitation picture made to make easy money that is by now cashing in on the wave of public interest in serial killers following *Silence of the Lambs*.[20] The *New Yorker* was also deeply suspicious, unconvinced that the 'gore movie carnage and Jarmusch-style aimless minimalism' amounted to anything more than 'a stark, relentless quality that is sometimes taken for art', but whose substance is 'hip and deeply conservative tabloid chic'.[21] For these reviewers, the message of the movie is that mothers are to blame for producing maladjusted murderers; and the real horror of the movie is that Henry could be the beer-drinking lower-class man next door or down the road. This meaning can be extrapolated from the film because of the lack of any social context within the film's diegesis that explains why Henry is the way he is. These reviewers claim that the film is deeply conservative; by situating a lower-class male as the focus of narrative alignment and offering no explanation of his motivations, the cultural prejudices of the primarily middle-class art house audiences are reinforced rather than challenged. They would prefer to see a text that offers some explanation of the character's behaviour through recourse to personal or social conditions; the type of text that offers a point of moral alignment for the viewer because of its evaluation of character.

But it is precisely the exclusion of a moral perspective on Henry and his actions that other reviewers found intellectually refreshing and provocative. In an article entitled 'Serial Killer's Brute Reality', Tim Pulleine in the *Guardian* sees the film's visual style emerging from the 'underground' cinema of the 1960s, where *vérité* style realism is used to 'blur the line between the "brute reality" of the film's subject matter and our ability to comprehend it'.[22] In this interpretation of the film, the snuff movie sequence, by positioning the viewer as a voyeur who is aligned not only with Henry's acts of killing but with Henry's own voyeuristic gaze, reveals the viewer's own complicity with the murderer and his voyeuristic activity. For Pulleine, voyeurism is redefined as an active, complicit act that privileges aesthetic alignment with a character's motivations and actions, rather than identification as that character. The film's status as art in this case turns upon the neatness of the conceit; we think we are watching the actions of someone engaged in the act of killing, until we realise that we are watching the killer watch a video of himself enacting the killings. This conceit captures the essence of the film in microcosm. Andrew Anthony, writing in the *Sunday Times*, claims that the camcorder was a tactic employed by McNaughton to confront a cinema going public reared on Freddy Kreuger films, inured to horror on celluloid and therefore complacent about violence in society:

> The immediacy of the video image, with its connotations of 'happening now' is much more terrifying than the filmed image. You think you're seeing it [the video murder] as it happens. But the camera pulls back and you realise you're watching it with them, on the couch. Later you're forced to ask 'What am I doing here'?[23]

It is possible to see in the latter approach a theoretical position that claims that by foregrounding the means of production – the technology and conventions used in the construction of the image – an aware and conscious viewer is created, one who is distanced from the narrational pull of the fiction, who can intellectually engage with the issues rather than indulge in the fantasy. But as Colin Donald points out in *Scotsman Weekend*, there is a suspicion that the irony perceived in the film on which such a reading depends is unintended, that the numbers of dead naked women scattered on the screen, together with the amateur production values, 'would not be allowed within 100 miles of art house cinema without a prevailing critical wind and the justification of the film being based on a true story'.[24] The sensationalism of *Henry* is less a blurring of boundaries between fact and fiction, more a blurring of distinctions between art and popular culture typical of recent trends in fine art such as the highly successful 'Sensations' exhibition shown at the Royal Academy of Arts in London in 1998. Somewhat surprisingly, and unlike the public furore created by this exhibition displaying a portrait of convicted killer Myra Hindley, none of these reviewers questions the ethics of depicting the activities of a convicted murderer when relatives of those affected by the case may still be living.[25]

The reviewers are divided; does the film align the viewer uncritically with the psychopath because there is no aesthetic distancing from him as the central character of narrative agency? Can such an alignment offer a moral critique of Henry's character or concern with his situation? Or does the film seek to persuade viewers to consider the morality of their own position as a voyeur, to question the nature of voyeuristic pleasure? Is it a deeply conservative film that confirms stereotypical attitudes about the underprivileged and the disadvantaged? Or does the disinterested moral stance challenge the prevailing didactic orthodoxy of the classical Hollywood text? An analysis of the reviewers' responses to two other controversially violent films will serve to illuminate some of these questions in greater depth.

Man Bites Dog

The year 1993 saw the release of three films all of which fell foul of the British censor because of their violence; these were the two independent low-budget American films *Bad Lieutenant* and *Reservoir Dogs* and a Belgian film, *C'est arrivé près de chez vous*, released in Britain as *Man Bites Dog*. Although a popular success in Belgium, where it ousted *Batman Returns* at the box office, *Man Bites Dog* belongs securely in the art house in Britain, if only because the grainy texture, the use of black and white *vérité* filming techniques and English subtitles effectively situates the film outside the mainstream. The film is a mock documentary shot initially in true *vérité* style. The camera is not a static 'fly on the wall' observational tool, but follows the actions of the principal character, catching events as they happen, displaying a faithful adherence to the use of *vérité* techniques. The overall effect, with its straight-to-camera soliloquies, has some similarities to the video journalism of contemporary television news. Only in this case the 'news' so eagerly sought after is that of a serial killer caught in the act of committing his atrocious crimes, who then recounts, straight to camera, a catalogue of his murderous techniques. It is this disjunction between form and theme that is the source of the film's black humour. Ben, the object of documentary study, cold-bloodedly murders his victims, then directly addresses the camera with detailed information on how to dispose of the bodies. The camera follows the exploits of this character as he robs, rapes and kills his victims. Murder, he claims, is his job; it is how he makes a living, whether it is from killing the postman and raiding the mailbag, murdering the elderly and stealing their life savings or assaulting and killing whole families and robbing their houses.

Throughout the opening sequences of the film, the camera is firmly fixed on Ben as the object of study. When he is not engaged in murderous activities, it follows him visiting his family in a small provincial town, discussing art at a gallery opening with his middle-class girlfriend, and recording his views in a direct address to the camera while proclaiming on art, architecture and urban design. Unlike Henry, this man is educated, cultured and charming; but, as the film's French title *It Happened Near You* suggests, he too is an 'ordinary' person who, like Henry, could be your next-door neighbour.

In recent years, theoretical analyses of documentary such as those of Winston (briefly outlined above) and Nichols (1994) have advocated a more self-conscious form of documentary practice that favours baring the device and revealing the transparency of the constructed image. This school of thought advocates formal display as a way of creating the distanced or critical observer in the interests of generating a media-literate viewer. It is to this audience that the film is designed to appeal, its use of realist conventions a product of film school training and the close reading and deconstruction of media texts. The visible separation between filmmaker and subject is generally sustained in mainstream documentary formats, even within the more contemporary forms of *vérité* such as hidden camera reportage – although some documentary makers, such as Nick Broomfield, regularly make their presence visible by taking on the role of investigative reporter and inserting themselves as part of the *vérité* project.[26] In *Man Bites Dog*, a similar shift occurs about halfway through the film: the presence of the filmmakers gradually becomes overt as they begin to record their dialogue with their subject. It is but a short step from this disembodied aural intrusion to a full depiction of an increasingly intense relationship between the filmmakers and their subject. The camera records the filmmakers discussing the problems of financing the film with Ben over drinks in the pub; as he agrees to part fund the production, the complicity between filmmakers and film subject becomes ever more apparent. Ben takes control of editorial decisions, while the filmmakers' participation in drunken sessions with Ben leads to their participation in a debauched party that ends in rape and finally murder. The death of the sound recordist, shot by accident during an affray with a rival gang, seems to parody the deaths of TV news journalists killed in the line of duty in war zones. The filmmakers piously mourn his demise, but continue on what is now an orgy of destruction, murdering a family in their own home, including a child. Throughout all their participatory activities, the filmmakers continue to film. Finally, the complicity of the filmmakers with their subject is complete; intent on earning money by selling the record of their murderous activities, they are gunned down with Ben by an unknown rival gang. The abandoned camera continues to record the bleak emptiness of the environment until it runs out of film, emphasising the rawness of the depiction and the evidential status of the image, but at the same time creating a self-conscious awareness of the camera as a recording instrument.

Man Bites Dog is made by Remy Belvaux, André Bonzel and Benoit Poelvoorde – a trio of Belgian film school graduates who wrote, produced, directed and shot the film as well as playing the star roles. Whereas *Henry* fictionalises a known character and his actions, this mock documentary is entirely fictitious. The film school roots of the piece are somewhat obvious in its low budget, grainy format and the pretension of its conceit, which draws its effectiveness from a combination of formal critique and choice of theme. This strategy created unease amongst the critics; many saw it as a seriously intended criticism of a growing 1990s preoccupation with violent entertainment, driven by public criticism of the media as not only the recorder of violence in society but increasingly as the generating source of that violence. Geoff Andrew of *Time Out* saw it as a witty, uncompromising acknowledgement of filmmakers' and audiences' often unhealthy fascination with the spectacle of violence.[27] Others considered it a filmmaker's film, a moral warning to filmmakers themselves. In a satirical comment on current trends in Reality TV, Anne Billson remarks that the film epitomises 'Camcorder Man on the March'. The implication here is that the film highlights the fall from critical grace of the documentary ideal (epitomised in the high-minded morality of Vertov's *Man with a Movie Camera*) and the public service aims of the newsreel. Billson hails the film as the ultimate 1990s movie, combining two of society's current obsessions – murder and media ethics – in a reflexive and self-referential fashion that is typical of contemporary popular culture.[28] Jonathon Romney in the *New Statesman and Society* describes the fictional documentarists as spineless hippie wets, cowed by an awful Ben into following him around, hanging onto his every word and gunshot. For Romney, these fictional filmmakers are as monstrous as their subject.[29] Hugo Davenport in the *Daily Telegraph* claims that the film successfully dissolves the increasingly blurred line between reality and fiction – and is a critical comment on the film industry's increasing tendency to make films (such as *Henry*) based on horrific real events. Phillip French agrees, seeing in the film a grim allegory of contemporary movie making where ethical considerations disappear in the quest for generating exciting footage.[30]

Not all reviewers were quite so comfortable with the film's apparently critical stance; some, such as Sheila Johnstone in the *Independent*, found the diegetic filmmakers' lack of institutional context (their lack of funding positions them as 'independents') too similar to the position of the actual filmmakers themselves, making the film 'the kind of cynical attention-grabbing exercise it pretends to deplore'.[31] Others found the film too ironic and detached, the crimes lacking emotional weight, reduced to trivial and boring performance spectacles devoid of contextual substance. The apparent lack of contrivance with which the violence is shot, combined with the characterisation of Ben as an attractive, almost charismatic figure, invites us to admire the cleverness of its formal conceit, but according to Alexander Walker this creates a deadening effect. Lacking 'pity, remorse or any of the other purgatives that art applies when it seeks its subject matter in the psychopathology of everday life', its effect is analogous to pornography.[32] But it is Manhola Dargis of the *Village Voice* who is the most critical of the film's artistic pretensions, accusing the filmmakers of behaving 'like a gaggle of adolescent boys desperately trying to gross someone out who will pay attention' so that, finally, the film is more tedious than outrageous.[33]

Man Bites Dog remains securely within the discourse and distribution of the art cinema market, its formal attributes and its positioning outside mainstream film culture ostensibly alleviating the propensity for creating the kind of voyeuristic viewing activity that moral guardians suspect will lead to the kind of copycat behaviour that Medved finds associated with popular action films such as *Money Train*. Due to the restricted nature of its distribution, the film censor in Britain passed *Man Bites Dog* for public distribution with an '18' certificate. As a subtitled foreign language film aimed primarily at a fellow community of filmmakers and film aficionados, its impact on the general public was not a major consideration, yet the film is widely available in video rental outlets and has something of a cult following. By comparison, *Henry* was denied a rating for some time in the USA and only granted release in the UK after substantial cuts were agreed. An analytical comparison between the rape sequences as they are now portrayed in the video released versions of *Henry* and *Man Bites Dog* reveals little difference in their formal attributes other than that of colour: both rapes are shot on a grainy textured film stock that gives them the quality of low budget home movie or camcorder immediacy; both use shooting styles associated with certain forms of documentary practice; both are graphic depictions of inhumane, savage behaviour. The principal difference between the two films is that *Man Bites Dog* still contains graphic images of killing. The British censor's reasoning behind the decision to cut sections from *Henry* but not *Man Bites Dog* seems to be based on considerations of character identification and point of view and *Henry*'s potential appeal to a lower-class male audience. In an interview in the *Daily Telegraph*, film censor James Ferman claims that it is the degree of audience complicity with Henry and Otis that is the problem: 'We had to remove the bits that could give pleasure through repeated viewing – masturbatory fantasies build to climaxes, so we have taken out all the climaxes. All the killings now take place off screen'.[34]

The implication behind this decision is that the censors thought it possible to determine which forms of address are more likely to engage the (lower class) male audience at an emotive, psychological level and are therefore more capable of eliciting masturbatory fantasy. The underlying theory of identification which supports the censor's views is based on a psychoanalytic model, where identification leads to loss of ego and, potentially, over-identification with the leading character, in this instance the murderous Henry. Identification with Ben in *Man Bites Dog* is considered less of a problem, although it is, of course, theoretically feasible that viewers, like the film's filmmakers, might be seduced by his charm or attracted to his lifestyle. The text's evaluation of Ben is, however, morally condemnatory of his activities; although he is not conventionally captured and tried for his crimes, he meets, with the filmmakers, a violent death. Henry, on the other hand, after disposing of Becky's dismembered body in a suitcase left by the side of the road, drives off, his murderous activities unchecked either by narrative retribution or any visible signs of remorse. This equation of film form with audience identification and moral alignment is precisely the issue confronted head-on by *Natural Born Killers*, a film which crystallises the ethical issues into a full-scale confrontation

between poststructuralist theories of deconstruction and distanciation and cine-psychoanalytic theories of spectator identification
and ego loss.

Natural Born Killers

Natural Born Killers tells the story of Mickey and Mallory, the type
of male and female white 'trash' killers whose story has been the
source of many an acclaimed Hollywood movie from *Bonnie and
Clyde* (1967) to *Badlands* (1973); only this is less an attempt to
depict character psychology and motivation through conventional
narrative forms, than an exercise (or visual extravaganza, depending
on your view) in showing how a range of audio-visual strategies can
be brought to bear on the representation of violent behaviour.
Eschewing the expositional realism of *Henry* or the self-reflexivity
of *Man Bites Dog*, *Natural Born Killers* is a compound of formal
methods honed for screen through avant-garde film practice and
music video. The film moves with intricate precision through a
range of formal strategies, starting with a virtuoso montage
sequence of murder in a roadside cafe that (perhaps deliberately)
makes the diner killers of *Pulp Fiction* (1994) look like the naïve
amateurs that they are. Aping the camera style of many an MTV
video, this juxtaposition of camera angles, colour changes and a
combination of stylised advertising images intercut with simulated
home movie footage is edited to the sound of a mesmerising soundtrack. Unlike the observational camerawork used to depict the
actions of Henry or Ben, here the act of killing is given visceral sen-
sation through the use of fast cut sequences and pounding music.
Excitement is generated by the jittery pace of fast cut, nervous visu-
als which move at the breakneck speed of an action movie, but the
strange angles, jump cuts and constant shifts in visual style, combined with the dislocation of the verbal soundtrack from its visual
anchor, create a chaotic sense of jarring and confusion, or furious
excitement and variation. Like the films discussed above, it is not a
movie for the squeamish. Numerous murders are depicted during
the course of the film, many of them in considerable graphic detail.[35]

But arguably, the actual content of the film is less violent than its
formal structure. As well as ranging across a range of Reality TV and
documentary formats, it satirises sensationalist journalism and comfortable family entertainment genres such as sitcom and soap. This

parody of popular forms is generated through a somewhat simplistic iconography of character which some reviewers found deeply
cynical. Both the investigating detective and the prison warden are
characterised as embodiments of corrupt, self-seeking officialdom;
the policeman is himself both a rapist and murderer, the warden a
slick seeker of publicity and fame. Mallory's parents are a parody of
the dysfunctional family, their home life depicted as a sick sitcom of
sexual abuse and sadistic violence perpetrated by evil incarnate in
the shape of a monstrous father, whose swearing and violence is
accompanied throughout by the canned laughter of a mock studio
audience. Throughout the first part of the film, the action is often
accompanied by footage of filmed violence apparently projected
against the landscape or the windows of shabby motel rooms: documentaries of twentieth-century horrors such as the First World
War, the Holocaust and Vietnam; violent sequences from films such
as *Midnight Express*, *Scarface* and *The Wild Bunch*; clips from
famous contemporary criminal trials such as Lorena Bobbitt, who
cut off her husband's penis, and the Menendez brothers, accused of
murdering their wealthy parents.[36] Images from Japanese animation
flicker amongst representations of Navaho Indian philosophy, creating a phantasmagoria of anarchic imagery. Mickey and Mallory
commit their murderous acts sandwiched between faction and fiction, products of a twentieth-century media sensibility that turns
psychotic killers into social celebrities. The subject matter of the film
and the dazzling array of formal devices brought to bear on its depiction, combined with its banning in Britain due to a fear of copycat
crimes, created a climate of high expectation amongst reviewers and
audiences when it was eventually released for public exhibition –
some three months after it was first shown in America.

In an article in *Sight and Sound*, Gavin Smith calls this mélange of
formal strategies 'schizophrenic realism', a reclaiming of the experimental techniques developed by avant-garde experimental filmmaking appropriated by MTV and fed back as a critique of
contemporary representation (1994: 10). In the face of intense criticism, Stone claims vociferously that his film is a critique of popular
culture's obsession with the cult of media celebrity, a critique most
apparent in the character of Wayne Gayle, host of the 'American
Maniacs' tabloid TV show.[37] Wayne is a man who will do anything
for a scoop, including assisting the killers in their escape from
prison so that he can capture it for live TV. Like many such critiques,

however, the film exploits and celebrates that which it claims to criticise. Initially, the use of experimental formal strategies disrupts the character-centred narration of the film, dispersing it across the range of different formal strategies, denying the possibility of any normative 'reality' from which a clear moral judgement on the film can be made. As the film progresses, however, alignment with the principal characters is inevitable at some level: Mickey and Mallory are the central characters of narrative action; they maintain a constant presence on the screen. The only motivation for their pathological behaviour is heavily satirised in the incestuous abuse of the sitcom sequence, which positions Mallory as a victim of violence, and flashbacks to Mickey's childhood, which position him as a spectator of violence:[38] otherwise, their killing is depicted as aimless and random, a form of entertainment that relieves boredom and satisfies frustration and aggression. The hectic fusion of sound and image seems aimlessly chaotic, an allegory of a state of mind that perceives the world through the recycled products of mass-mediated culture. Once they are in prison, the tenor of the film changes: the screened media images disappear and the film slips into the generic shape of the prison movie. Narrative causality asserts itself, generated by character motivation – their desire to escape. As they eliminate their adversaries and reunite, Mickey and Mallory are again the central focus of the action, and narrative alignment with them is complete. They shoot Wayne Gale as he cringingly bargains for his life, promising them continuing celebrity status, and then disappear into the proverbial Hollywood sunset, an absolution for their crimes underlined in a brief coda set some years later with Mickey and Mallory on the road again, but now in a motor home with a number of children. This narrative closure effectively grants them redemption, positioning Mickey and Mallory as superhero killers for our time, simultaneously rewarded and redeemed by family life.

The film enjoyed considerable box office success in America. In Britain, release was delayed whilst the censor investigated reports that the film had induced copycat killings in America and Paris. The controversy was fuelled by the battle between Quentin Tarantino and Oliver Stone over the scriptwriting credits amidst the growing cult status of Tarantino's *Reservoir Dogs*. When the film finally opened in cinemas nation-wide, people flocked to see it. On the Internet, it has the largest cult following of any of the films discussed above, appealing primarily to its targeted audience of young

adults raised on MTV. Critical opinions of the film are harshly
divided: is the film a 'masterpiece' of contemporary popular
cinema or an exploitation movie masquerading as art? Undeniably,
the film ventures further into the hermeneutic circle of violent representation than either of the two films discussed above, while at
the same time achieving both blockbuster and cult movie status.
The film's use of graphic screened violence seems to support a Bau-
drillian concept of an excess of simulcra detached from any point
of reference to 'the real' that foregrounds the kinaesthetics of violence in its rollercoaster aesthetics, combining the visceral sensations of action cinema and music video. But such a conception does
not rule out viewer engagement on a number of levels; the furious
excitement in itself generates the possibility of aesthetic alignment
with the narrative, and with the energy of the principal characters.
And while the text's moral evaluation of the characters positions
them as 'bad, bad, bad', it does not situate them in relation to
anyone who is 'good'. Again, there is something of an ethical
vacuum that can only be filled through recourse to Stone's much
publicised avowed intentions: 'the cosmos of this century is linked
most horrendously to violence, *genocidal* violence. In a sense,
Mickey and Mallory are just the rotten fruit at the end of this century'.[39] Mickey and Mallory are 'media monsters', the product of an
age obsessed with generating not only violent images, but mass
human slaughter on a previously unimaginable scale. Yet if they are,
indeed, finally redeemed, the seeds of this can be located throughout the film in their love for each other and their almost joyous
acceptance of the vulnerability which comes from transgressing all
moral codes and attaining 'outsider' status.

Violence and viewers

Our interest in serial killers seems to be based on a fascination with
their monstrousness, an allure exploited by the mythologising of
actual serial killers such as Henry Lee Lucas and Myra Hindley. Cynthia Freeland (1995) claims that this fascination with 'ordinary'
people who commit monstrous acts feeds the popularity of 'realist
horror' in the cinema which began in the early 1960s with the
release of *Peeping Tom* (1959) and *Psycho* (1960). Studies by Tudor
and Twitchell point to this sub-generic tendency becoming increasingly prevalent in horror movies during the 1980s.[40] Unlike the

supernatural monster in classical definitions of horror, in 'realist horror' the monster is a fictional recreation of a real murderer, neither supernatural nor merely fictional. Henry in *Henry, Portrait of a Serial Killer* shares certain features with his wholly fictional counterparts: he does seem all-powerful, unpredictable and the source of hideous violence; but unlike conventional monsters in horror movies, Henry is a real possibility, the reconstruction of a living individual who has confessed to similar acts of brutality. The source of his power seems rooted in his 'ordinariness', the lack of motivation or a fixed pattern of killing. He makes murder look easy, and easy to get away with. But Henry is also glamourised: played by a handsome unknown young actor (Michael Rooker), wearing jeans and a tight white T-shirt that is reminiscent perhaps of an earlier filmic generation of rebellious, disturbed young men (and Marlon Brando in particular), this glamorisation of the male serial killer reveals, according to Freeland, the converse of the traditional all-American rebel. A macho loner, unable to communicate except through his violent deeds, Henry murders for his own pleasure, with no apparent motivation or explanation provided by the narrative. Although it is suggested that Henry was abused as a child, three different versions of his early life are presented; this confusing explanation undermines its authenticity and increases our 'basic fascination with the sheer fact of [his] monstrousness' (Freeland 1995: 131).

Freeland claims that a further feature of 'realist horror' is a dependence on spectacle where, as in hardcore pornography or the musical, the plot serves 'to bridge together the "real thing" that the film promises to deliver', which in this case is the spectacle of rape and death (Freeland 1995: 132). But most mainstream generic fictions, whether categorised as horrors, thrillers, crime films or action movies, use plot to stitch together their spectacular sequences, as we discussed in Chapter 3. Freeland's formulation collapses the stylistic difference of independent low budget expositional films such as *Henry* into the star-laden generic spectacle of mainstream films such as *Silence of the Lambs*, where virtuoso performances by known actors and a plot heavily dependent on character motivations can create a different kind of engagement in the 'make-believe' of the fictional world.

Freeland's analysis is couched in terms of Baudrillard's concept of the simulacrum; for Baudrillard, the contemporary media landscape is saturated with an excess of signification that makes the secure anchorage of images as referents to events and information in actuality an impossibility; they can only exist in chains of perpetual simulation (Baudrillard 1983). Within this context, 'realist horror must be understood as a particularly post-modern phenomenon' (Freeland 1995: 134). News stories quickly become integrated into feature film plots, while fictitious characters become the means of attributing personality traits to actual people. As news and actuality interweave, plot becomes diminished in favour of spectacle; realist horror is, on the one hand, familiar, formulaic and predictable, but, on the other, emotionally disturbing because of its immediacy and gruesomeness. Baudrillard's theory, while providing an encompassing analysis of the contemporary mediascape, avoids all manner of cultural and social difference that can potentially influence processes of reading and interpretation; rather like Adorno and Horkheimer in the 1930s, Baudrillard conceives contemporary viewers as controlled by the entertainment conglomerates, to the extent that they are unable to discriminate between fiction and reality. Freeland tries to rescue viewers of realist horror from this morass of insignificance, claiming that the films offer self-reflexive viewing positions that can place viewers in an ironic relationship to their conservative value systems, but in the society of media spectacle rational response to horrific violence has become an impossibility. We can only enjoy it as hyperbolic charade or reject it in revulsion. This is the world envisioned by Stone in *Natural Born Killers*, a world where differentiation between fiction and reality has become meaningless; Mickey, however, does find a rational voice which enables him, unlike Henry, to provide an explanation of his murderous activities. During the interview with Wayne Gale, Mickey claims that he is 'a natural born killer', blaming his genetic inheritance for his behaviour. Fascinated, the TV crew and the prison officers drop their guard and Mickey is able to grab a gun. This is a turning point in the film: Mickey and Mallory break out of jail and the media spectacle that frames his and Mallory's life. Self-identification as a rational, thinking subject reinserts Mickey into causal narration: the glamorised but alienated male hero/monster, armed with pseudo-scientific psychological justification for his behaviour, proceeds to the end of the film fully in control of narrative motivation. Alignment with the reunited lovers can open up on a number of levels, but the text's moral judgement of the characters remains ambivalent.

In one of the few studies to engage with the pleasures of viewing violent movies from an audience studies perspective, Annette Hill (1997) provides some insight into why viewers find pleasure in the 'the new brutalism', using audience studies research methods that emanate from the qualitative methodologies of sociology, anthropology and media studies, rather than the behavioural psychology approaches common to 'effects' studies.[41] Hill's study reveals that the question of what kind of violence is entertaining is closely linked to conscious awareness of actual violence; stylistic presentation creates a distance from actual violence which makes violent films more entertaining than movies that use strategies to make them appear similar to viewing mediated images of actual violence. *Man Bites Dog*, for example, was criticised by viewers for its lack of narrative drive, its lack of Hollywood style and its use of actuality filmmaking techniques. Participants in Hill's study claim that they abhor actual violence; they chose to watch violent movies because by watching these films they can understand their own response to violence without necessarily experiencing it directly as part of their everyday lives. Fiction films provide a safe environment in which to test responses to violence, but only when the films use aesthetic strategies that distance them from a conscious awareness of actual violence. Aesthetic devices such as character portrayal, witty dialogue and stylised techniques of framing and editing, combined with the use of colour and music, create a generic distance from mediated depictions of actuality such as news or documentary footage that allows participants to feel safe in the imaginary world of the fiction. This feeling of safety is central to the enjoyment of viewing violence (1997: 84–5), perhaps suggesting why *Natural Born Killers* was a far more popular film than *Henry* or *Man Bites Dog*. Hill's analysis of viewer response constructs the pleasure of viewing violence as a psychological game that filmmakers play with their audiences and viewers play with the films. In *Mimesis as Make Believe*, Kendall Walton similarly describes the construction of fictionality as a game between a maker who prescribes a number of opportunities to engage in a fictional world and an appreciator who, while perfectly aware that the specified world is fictional, none the less psychologically engages in the game as if it were real in certain respects (Walton 1990: 185). Viewers are aware that in these films their tolerance levels to violence are being tested: anticipation of forthcoming scenes of violence allows them to prepare themselves in complex ways for a range of individual responses, including self-censorship. A key element of interpretation is the building of character relationships; if characters are too disturbing, viewers choose not to engage with them as an act of self-preservation. Relationships with characters are built on the basis of individual experience and imaginative hypothesising: many of Hill's participants found the phrase 'identification' inadequate to describe their engagement and response to characters, qualifying their reactions with terms such as 'sympathy', 'empathy', 'relate', 'feel for', and 'understand' (Hill 1997: 40). This would suggest that, rather than assuming simple models of 'identification', Murray Smith's distinctions may be a more accurate account of viewer response. Some aspects of the actions and emotions of a character might elicit an engaged response, but this did not necessarily mean participants aligned themselves with the character emotionally, or that only one character might be a source of such alignment for a viewer.

Hill's study is open to a number of criticisms, not least of which is the social situatedness of her sample, which corresponds to the target audience for the 'new brutalism' films identified by the Cinema Advertising Association. Thus, white British males educated to GCSE/A level standard and above in the 20–24 age group predominate, a group with considerable cultural capital. The choice of films is congruent with the taste of a middle-class, educated audience looking for forms of entertainment that offer something a little different from the normal Hollywood fare. What is striking to us about the 'new brutalism' is the wide variety of stylistic approaches used to graphically depict violence acts. The most popular films (*Pulp Fiction* and *Reservoir Dogs*) combine witty humorous scripts and complex engaging soundtracks with violent actions that often conceal more than they reveal. The notorious ear amputation scene in *Reservoir Dogs*, for example, builds anticipation of violence by using a catchy popular song which Mr Blonde (the perpetrator) dances to while the cop, his mouth taped, can only utter muffled cries, blood running from his nose. The sense of anticipation that Mr Blonde will further torture his victim leads many viewers to believe that they witness the ear being sliced off when they see the film at the cinema, and that the sequence is edited in the video version. The expectation of seeing the visual depiction is so strong that viewers construct the scene in their imaginations, and it is this that makes the violence realistic (Hill 1997: 87–101). Other films in the cycle use different techniques in their depictions of violence, some of which we have touched on above, yet all are deemed 'realist' (including *Natural Born Killers*) because, according to Hill's viewers, they significantly depart from the generic violence of Hollywood action films.

As we suggested at the beginning of the chapter, this is a recurring theme in popular definitions of what constitutes realism in film: stylistic difference from mainstream genre fictions continues to be a benchmark of defining realism, somewhat irrespective of the film's formal conventions. Films such as *Natural Born Killers* are read as psychologically realist depictions of disturbed mental states ('schizophrenic realism' in Gavin Smith's terms), suggesting that the attribution of an aesthetics of 'realism' is, as Raymond Williams claims, less to do with the formal codes and conventions of the films themselves than with changing 'attitudes toward reality itself, toward man and society and toward the character of all relationships' (Williams 1977b: 121). Changes in attitude are illuminated by comparing contemporary attributions of realism with their earlier counterparts; recent definitions dislocate realist films from a humanist politics of 'progressiveness' in favour of a more ambivalent, less didactic treatment of themes. This lends weight to our proposition that, at the end of the 1990s, realism's political project of progressive humanism is waning, but the impetus to create films which address contentious issues in contemporary life, whether couched in terms of the tawdry exploitation of *Henry*, the vicious clarity of *Man Bites Dog* or the furious excitement of *Natural Born Killers*, continues unabated.

Notes

1 *The Times*, 22 January 1994.
2 *Independent*, 20 March 1994.
3 A good overview of the literature can be found in D. Docherty (1990).
4 The films include: *Reservoir Dogs* (1992), *Pulp Fiction* (1994) and *Natural Born Killers* (1994) as well as *Man Bites Dog* (1992), *Henry, Portrait of a Serial Killer* (1986, released in 1990), *True Romance* (1993), *Bad Lieutenant* (1992) and *Killing Zoë* (1994). 'What these movies share, in terms of content, is a preoccupation with violence towards the individual as opposed to the state, and, in terms of style, the use of realism when representing violence' (Hill 1997: 11–12).
5 Jim Shelley uses the term in two articles written at the beginning of 1993: *Guardian*, 7 January, 7 and *The Times*, 'Saturday Review', 20 February, 12.

6 For a detailed account of viewer response to the 'new brutalism', see Annette Hill (1997).

7 Cognitive theory emphasises the latter, stressing the iconic properties of audio-visual texts: see Chapter 5.

8 *Guardian*, 8 May 1992.

9 *Variety* greeted the film as a 'hard-hitting documentary feature ... while nearly all bits are patently real, there are two sequences ... which, despite assurances to the contrary, smack of staging. Yet the overall effect is grimly stimulating from the visual standpoint, depressing in the conclusions drawn' (*Variety* review 1962, reprinted in D. Elley (ed.) (1996: 621).

10 Laura Grindstaff (1997) provides a useful summary of current Reality TV trends.

11 See, for example, N. Postman (1985).

12 *Focus*, April 1997, 11–12.

13 *Independent*, 12 July 1991.

14 *The Voice*, 11 June 1991.

15 *Today*, 12 July 1991.

16 *Mail on Sunday*, 14 July 1991.

17 *Evening Standard*, 11 July 1991.

18 *City Limits*, 11 July 1991.

19 *Financial Times*, 11 July 1991.

20 *Spare Rib*, August 1991 and the *Morning Star*, 12 July 1991.

21 *New Yorker*, 25 April 1990.

22 *Guardian*, 11 July 1991.

23 *Sunday Times*, supplement, 14 July 1991. But see Jeffrey Sconce (1993) for an alternative argument; he suggests that the critical acclaim invested in *Henry* is less a consequence of its aesthetics than the cultural context of its release and distribution on the art house circuit.

24 *Scotsman Weekend*, 14 July 1991.

25 The ethics of using true stories based on the lives of convicted killers as suitable subjects for art were brought to the fore in this instance. Myra Hindley and Ian Brady were convicted for murdering numerous children in the 1960s; recently, Hindley has made several appeals to have her life sentence commuted on the basis that she is now a reformed character. The conventional 'mug shot' of Hindley, taken at the time of her arrest and often reprinted in the tabloids, was reconstructed by the artist on a giant scale using children's handprints to create a deliberately provocative and highly controversial 'identikit' image of the convicted killer. Relatives of the murdered children protested against what they perceived as exploitation of their children's deaths, publicly airing their distress and voicing their disgust with artists and promoters prepared to take advantage of the murders

in the interests of achieving artistic recognition and personal financial gain.

26 Nick Broomfield's work also includes a preoccupation with serial killers, in this instance the only woman convicted in the US of serial murder: *Aileen Wuornos: Selling of a Serial Killer*, US 1993.

27 *Time Out*, 13 January 1993.

28 *Sunday Telegraph*, 17 January 1993.

29 *New Statesman and Society*, 8 January 1993.

30 *Observer*, 17 January 1993.

31 *Independent*, 15 January 1993.

32 *Evening Standard*, 14 January 1993.

33 *Village Voice*, 16 July 1993.

34 James Ferman interviewed by Peter Guttridge, *Daily Telegraph*, 22 January 1993.

35 Karen Boyle points out that Mickey and Mallory are charged with a total of 52 murders, not all of which take place on screen; numerous violent killings are depicted in the riot and prison-break (correspondence 1998).

36 In her detailed analysis of the gendering of contemporary cinematic violence, Boyle (1998) points out that this footage functions to position *men* as killers.

37 See, for example, the interview with Stone in *Empire*, December 1994, 70–6.

38 Boyle (1998) points out that the flashbacks suggest that violence is Mickey's *genetic* inheritance, whereas Mallory, like other fictional female killers, is only violent because she is the victim of a violent, abusive childhood.

39 Stone, in *Empire*, December 1994, 73.

40 See James B. Twitchell (1985), and Andrew Tudor (1989).

41 For an overview of this approach, see, for example, Sean Moores (1993).

Bibliography

Abercrombie, N., Lash, S., and Longhurst, B. (1992), 'Popular Representation: Recasting Realism' in S. Lash and J. Friedman (eds), *Modernity and Identity*, Oxford and Cambridge Mass., Blackwell.

Acker, A. (1991), *Reel Women*, London, B. T. Batsford Ltd.

Adorno, T. and Horkheimer, M. (1972), *Dialectics of Enlightenment*, New York, Seabury Press.

Altman, R. (1989), *The American Film Musical*, London, British Film Institute.

Andrews, D. A. (1976), *The Major Film Theorists*, Oxford, Oxford University Press.

Andrews, D. A. (1990), *Andre Bazin*, New York, Columbia University Press.

Ang, I. (1985), *Watching 'Dallas': Soap Opera and the Melodramatic Imagination*, London and New York, Methuen.

Armes, R. (1975), 'Vertov and Soviet Cinema' in *Film and Reality*, Harmondsworth, Penguin Books, 38–43.

Armes, R. (1978), *A Critical History of British Cinema*, London, Secker and Warburg.

Armes, R. (1986), *Patterns of Realism*, New York and London, Garland Publishing.

Aspinall, S. (1983), 'Women, Realism and Reality in British Films' in J. Curran and V. Porter (eds), *British Cinema History*, London, Weidenfeld and Nicolson.

Bach, S. (1986), *Final Cut: Dreams and Disaster in the Making of 'Heaven's Gate'*, London, Faber.

Balio, T. (ed.) (1990), *Hollywood in the Age of Television*, Boston, Unwin Hyman.

Barker, M. and Brooks, K. (1998), 'Bleak Futures by Proxy', paper presented at Commonwealth Fund Conference in American History, 'Hollywood and Its Spectators: The Reception of American Films 1895–1995', University College, London.

Barker, M. and Petley, J. (eds) (1997), *Ill Effects: The Media Violence Debate*, London and New York, Routledge.

Barthes, R. (1968), 'L'Effect de réel', *Communications II*, 84–8, trans. Gerald Mead (1978), 'The Realistic Effect', *Film Reader 3*, 131–5.

Bartov, O. (1997), 'Spielberg's Oskar: Hollywood Tries Evil' in Loshitzky Y. (ed.), *Spielberg's Holocaust: Critical Perspectives on* Schindler's List, Bloomington and Indianapolis, Indiana University Press.

Baudrillard, J. (1983), *Simulations*, trans. P. Foss and P. Patton, New York, Semiotext(e).

Baudry, J. L. (1974), 'Ideological Effects of the Basic Cinematographic Apparatus' in G. Mast, M. Cohen and L. Baudry (eds) (1992), *Film Theory and Criticism*, 4th edn, New York and Oxford, Oxford University Press.

Baudry, L. (1976), 'Genre: the conventions of connection' in G. Mast, M. Cohen and L. Baudry (eds) (1992), *Film Theory and Criticism: Introductory Readings*, 4th edn, New York and Oxford, Oxford University Press.

Baudry, L., Mast, G. and Cohen, M. (eds) (1992), *Film Theory and Criticism*, 4th edn, New York, Oxford, Oxford University Press.

Bazin, A. (1948), 'An Aesthetic of Reality: Cinematic Realism and the Italian School of the Liberation' in H. Gray (ed. and trans.) (1967), *What Is Cinema?*, vol. 2., Berkeley, University of California Press.

Bennett, T., Boyd-Bowman, S., Mercer, C. and Woollacott, J. (eds) (1981), *Popular Television and Film*, London, British Film Institute /Open University Press.

Bentley, E. (1947), *Bernard Shaw: a reconsideration*, Connecticut, New Directions Books.

Black, G. (1994), *Hollywood Censored*, Cambridge, Cambridge University Press.

Bogle, D. (1973), *Toms, Coons, Mulattoes, Mammies and Bucks: An Interpretative History of Blacks in American Films*, New York, Viking Press.

Bordwell, D. (1972), 'Dziga Vertov: An Introduction', *Film Comment* 3:1, 38–45.

Bordwell, D. (1985), 'The Classical Hollywood Style' in D. Bordwell, J. Staiger and K. Thompson (eds), *The Classical Hollywood Cinema: Film Style and Mode of Production to 1960*, London, Routledge.

Bordwell, D. (1988), *Narration in the Fiction Film*, New York and London, Routledge.

Bordwell, D. (1993), *The Cinema of Eisenstein*, Cambridge, Massachusetts, Harvard University Press.

Bordwell, D. and Carroll, N. (eds) (1996), *Post-Theory: Reconstructing Film Studies*, Wisconsin, Madison, University of Wisconsin Press.

Bordwell, D., Staiger, J. and Thompson, K. (1985), *The Classical Hollywood Cinema: Film Style and Mode of Production to 1960*, London, Routledge.

Boyle, K. (1998), *Violence and Gender in Contemporary Cinema*, unpublished Ph.D. thesis, University of Bradford.

Bratton, J., Cook, J. and Gledhill, C. (eds) (1994), *Melodrama: Stage, Picture, Screen*, London, British Film Institute.

Brooks, P. (1976), *The Melodramatic Imagination: Balzac, Henry James, Melodrama and the Mode of Excess*, New Haven, Yale University Press.

Brownlow, K. (1990), *Behind the Mask of Innocence. Sex, Violence, Prejudice, Crime: Films of Social Conscience in the Silent Era*, Berkeley and Los Angeles, University of California Press.

Burnett, R. (ed.) (1991), *Explorations in Film Theory: Selected Essays from Cine-Tracts*, Bloomington and Indianapolis, Indiana University Press.

Butler, C. (1984), *Interpretation, Deconstruction and Ideology: An Introduction to Some Current Issues in Literary Theory*, Oxford, Clarendon Press.

Byars, J. (1991), *All That Hollywood Allows: Re-reading Gender in 1950s Melodramas*, London and New York, Routledge.

Carroll, N. (1996), *Theorising the Moving Image*, Cambridge, Cambridge University Press.

Cartmell, D., Hunter, I. Q., Kaye, H. and Whelehan, I. (eds) (1998), *Sisterhoods Across the Literature/Media Divide*, London and Sterling Virginia, Pluto Press.

Christie, I. and Taylor, R. (1993), *Eisenstein Rediscovered*, London and New York, Routledge.

Clover, C. (1993), *Men, Women and Chainsaws*, London, British Film Institute.

Cohan, S. (1992) 'Boys Who'd Like to be Men', paper presented at 'Melodrama: Stage, Picture, Screen', British Film Institute conference, London.

Collins, J. (1993), 'Genericity in the Nineties: Eclectic Irony and the New Sincerity' in J. Collins, A. Preacher-Collins and H. Radner (eds), *Film Theory goes to the Movies*, AFI readers, London, Routledge.

Collins, J., Preacher-Collins, A. and Radner, H. (eds) (1993), *Film Theory goes to the Movies*, AFI readers, London, Routledge.

Conrich, I. and Davy, S. (1997), *Views From the Edge of the World: New Zealand Film*, Studies in New Zealand Culture No. 1, London, Kakapo Books.

Corner, J. (1992), 'Presumption as Theory: "Realism" in Television Studies', *Screen* 33:1, 97–102.

Corner, J. (1995), *Television Form and Public Address*, London, Edward Arnold.

Corner, J. (1996), *The Art of Record*, Manchester, Manchester University Press.

Corner, J. and Harvey, S. (eds) (1991), *Enterprise and Heritage: Crosscurrents of National Culture*, London, Routledge.

Crafton, D. (1995), 'Pie and Chase: Gag, Spectacle and Narrative in Slapstick Comedy' in H. Jenkins and K. Brunovska Karnick (eds), *Classical Hollywood Comedy*, New York and London, Routledge.

Cripps, T. (1977), *Slow Fade to Black: The Negro in American Film 1900–1942*, New York, Oxford University Press.

Croft, S. and Rose, O. (1977), 'An Essay Towards *Man with the Movie Camera*', *Screen* 1:1–19.

Cumberbatch, G. and Howitt, D. (1989), *A Measure of Uncertainty: the Effects of the Media*, London, John Libbey.

Currie, G. (1995), *Image and Mind: Film, Philosophy and Cognitive Science*, Cambridge and New York, Cambridge University Press.

Darke, C. (1995) '*La Haine* review', *Sight and Sound* 5:11, 43.

Davis, G. (1998), 'Loving the Abject: the Confluence (and Effluence) of Melodrama and Horror in Mainstream AIDS Cinema' in N. Moody and J. Hallam (eds), *Medical Fictions*, Liverpool, Association for Research in Popular Fictions/Liverpool John Moores University Press.

Dayan, D. (1974), 'The Tutor Code of Classical Cinema' in G. Mast, M. Cohen and L. Baudry (eds) (1992), *Film Theory and Criticism*, 4th edn, New York, Oxford University Press.

Dent, G. (ed.) (1992), *Black Popular Culture*, Seattle, Bay Press.

Diawara, M. (1993), 'Black American Cinema: The New Realism' in M. Diawara (ed.), *Black American Cinema*, New York and London, Routledge.

Diawara, M. (ed.) (1993), *Black American Cinema*, New York and London, Routledge.

Docherty, D. (1990), *Violence in Television Fiction*, Broadcasting Standards Council Annual Review, London, John Libbey.

Docherty, D., Morrison, D. and Tracey, M. (1987), *The Last Picture Show? Britain's Changing Film Audience*, London, British Film Institute.

Donald, J. (ed.) (1989), *Fantasy and the Cinema*, London, British Film Institute.

Doneson, J. E. (1997), 'The Image Lingers: The Feminisation of the Jew in *Schindler's List*' in Y. Loshitzky (ed.), *Spielberg's Holocaust: Critical Perspectives on* Schindler's List, Bloomington and Indianapolis, Indiana University Press.

Duff, A. (1990), *Once Were Warriors*, Auckland, Tandem.

Duval Smith, A. (1995), *Guardian*, 'Arts', June 23, 20–4.

Eisenstein, S. (1925), 'Toward the Question of a Materialist Approach to Form' in P. Adam Sitney (1978), *The Avant-Garde Film*, New York, New York University Press.

Elley, D. (ed.) (1996), *Variety Movie Guide 1997*, London, Hamlyn.

Ellis, J. (1996), 'The Quality Film Adventure: British Cinema Critics and the Cinema, 1942–1948' in A. Higson (ed.), *Dissolving Views: Key Writings on British Cinema*, London and New York, Cassell.

Elsaesser, T. (ed.) (1990), *Early Cinema: Space, Frame, Narrative*, London, British Film Institute.

Fatton Jr, R. (1986), *Black Consciousness in South Africa: the Dialectics of Ideological Resistance to White Supremacy*, New York, Suny Press.

Fell, J. L. (1974), *Film and the Narrative Tradition*, Berkeley and Los Angeles, University of California Press.

Freeland, C. A. (1995), 'Realist Horror', in C.A. Freeland and N. Wartenburg (eds), *Philosophy and Film*, London, Routledge.

Freeland, C. A. and Wartenburg, N. (eds) (1995), *Philosophy and Film*, London, Routledge.

French, K. (1996), *Screen Violence*, London, Bloomsbury.

Furst, L. (1992), *Realism*, London and New York, Longman.

Gabo, N. and Pevsner, A. (1922), 'A Realist Manifesto', trans. Naum Gabo, in Teresa Newman (1967), *Naum Gabo*, London, Tate Gallery.

Gaines, J. (ed.) (1992), *Classical Hollywood Narrative: The Paradigm Wars*, Durham and London, Duke University Press.

Garber, M., Matlock, J. and Walkowitz, R. L. (eds) (1993), *Media Spectacles*, New York and London, Routledge.

Gasiorek, A. (1995), *Post-War British Fiction: Realism and After*, London, Edward Arnold.

Gaskel, R. (1972), *Realism and Drama*, London, Routledge and Kegan Paul.

Gauntlett, D. (1995), *Moving Experiences: Understanding Television's Influences and Effects*, London: John Libbey.

Gerhardie, W. (1979), 'The Emergence of Realism in European Theatre' in *Realism in European Theatre and Drama 1870–1920: A Bibliography*, Connecticut, Greenwood Press.

Gerrard, N. (1996), 'Suffer the Little Children' in K. French (ed.), *Screen Violence*, London, Bloomsbury.

Giles, P. and Lorisch, V. (eds) (1992), *Debut on Two*, London, BBC Publications.

Gledhill, C. (1992), 'Between Melodrama and Realism: Anthony Asquith's *Underground* and King Vidor's *The Crowd*' in J. Gaines (ed.), *Classical Hollywood Narrative: The Paradigm Wars*, Durham and London, Duke University Press.

Gledhill, C. and Swanson, G. (eds) (1996), *Nationalising Femininity*, Manchester, Manchester University Press.

Goodwin, J. (1993), *Eisenstein, Cinema and History*, Urbana, University of Illinois Press.

Gorbman, C. (1987), *Unheard Melodies: Narrative Film Music*, London, British Film Institute.

Grindstaff, L. (1997), 'Trashy or Transgressive? "Reality TV" and the Politics of Social Control', *Plugged In*, T:VC/V09 at:

www.arts.ucsb.edu/~tvc/v09/section3/v09s3.grind.html, visited July 1998.

Grodal, T. (1997), *Moving Pictures: A New Theory of Film Genres, Feelings and Cognition*, Oxford, Clarendon Press.

Gunning, T. (1990a), 'Weaving a Narrative: Style and Economic Background in Griffith's Biograph Films' in T. Elsaesser (ed.), *Early Cinema: Space, Frame, Narrative*, London, British Film Institute.

Gunning, T. (1990b), 'The Cinema of Attractions: Early Film, its Spectator and the Avant-Garde' in T. Elsaesser (ed.), *Early Cinema: Space, Frame Narrative*, London, British Film Institute.

Guttridge, P. (1993), 'Are These Films Too Violent?', *Daily Telegraph*, 22 January, 18.

Hallam, J. and Marshment, M. (1995), 'Framing Experience: Case Studies in Reception of *Oranges are Not the Only Fruit*', *Screen* 36:1, 1–15.

Hansen, M. (1997), '*Schindler's List* is not *Shoah*: Second Commandment, Popular Modernism and Public Memory' in Y. Loshitzky (ed.), *Spielberg's Holocaust: Critical Perspectives on* Schindler's List, Bloomington and Indianapolis, Indiana University Press.

Harry, A. (1995), 'Hiding Out in the Hood Again', *Village Voice*, 10 October, 25–6.

Harvey, S. and Robins, K. (1993), *The Regions, the Nation and the BBC*, BBC Charter Review Series, London, British Film Institute.

Hayward, P. and Wollen, T. (1993), 'Surpassing the Real' in P. Hayward and Wollen, T. (eds), *Future Visions: New Technologies of the Screen*, London, British Film Institute.

Hayward, P. and Wollen, T. (eds) (1993), *Future Visions: New Technologies of the Screen*, London, British Film Institute.

Hibbin, S. (1998), 'Pinewood not Hollywood', *New Statesman*, 27 March, 40–1.

Higson, A. (1984), 'Space, Place and Spectacle', *Screen* 25:4/5, 2–21.

Higson, A. (1995), *Waving the Flag: Constructing a National Cinema in Britain*, Oxford, Clarendon Press.

Higson, A. (ed.) (1996), *Dissolving Views: Key Writings on British Cinema*, London, Cassell.

Hill, A. (1997), *Shocking Entertainment: Viewer Response to Violent Movies*, Bedfordshire, John Libbey/University of Luton Press.

Hill, J. (1986), *Sex, Class and Realism: British Cinema 1956–1963*, London, British Film Institute.

Hillier, J. (1992), *The New Hollywood*, London, Studio Vista.

Hoggart, R. (1958), *The Uses of Literacy,* Harmondsworth, Penguin.

hooks, bell (1992), *Black Looks: Race and Representation*, Boston, Southend Press.

Horowitz, S. R. (1997), 'But Is It Good for the Jews? Spielberg's Schindler and the Aesthetics of Atrocity' in Y. Loshitzky (ed.), *Spielberg's Holo-*

caust: Critical Perspectives on Schindler's List, Bloomington and Indianapolis, Indiana University Press.

Huston, P. (1992), *Went the Day Well?*, London, British Film Institute.

Independent (1996), 'Dustin Hoffman Blames Hollywood Over Dunblane', 11 May, 6.

James, N. (1997), 'Being There', *Sight and Sound* 7:10, 6–9.

Jancovich, M. (1996), *Rational Fears: American Horror in the 1950s*, Manchester, Manchester University Press.

Jenkins, H. and Brunovska Karnick, K. (1995) (eds), *Classical Hollywood Comedy*, New York and London, Routledge.

Kerekes, D. and Slater, D. (1993), *Killing For Culture: An Illustrated History of Death Film from Mondo to Snuff*, London, Creation Books.

Knight, D. (1997), 'Naturalism, Narration and Critical Perspective: Ken Loach and the Experimental Method' in G. McKnight (ed.), *Agent of Challenge and Defiance: The Films of Ken Loach*, Wiltshire, Flick Books.

Krutnik, F. (1995), 'Genre, Narrative and the Hollywood Comedian' in H. Jenkins, and K. B. Karnick (eds), *Classical Hollywood Comedy*, London, Routledge.

Kuhn, A. (1988), *Cinema, Censorship and Sexuality 1909–1925*, London, Routledge.

Kuhn, A. (ed.) (1990), *Alien Zone: Cultural Theory and Contemporary Science Fiction*, London, Verso.

Laing, S. (1986), *Representations of Working-Class Life 1957–64*, London, Macmillan.

Lang, R. (1989), *American Film Melodrama: Griffith, Vidor, Minnelli*, Princeton, New Jersey, Princeton University Press.

Lapsley, R. and Westlake, M. (1988), *Film Theory: An Introduction*, Manchester, Manchester University Press.

Lash, S. and Friedman, J. (eds) (1992), *Modernity and Identity*, Oxford and Cambridge Mass., Blackwell.

Liehm, M. (1984), *Passion and Defiance: Film in Italy from 1942 to the Present*, California, University of California Press.

Loshitzky, Y. (1997), 'Holocaust Others: Spielberg's *Schindler's List* versus Lanzmann's *Shoah*' in Y. Loshitzky (ed.), *Spielberg's Holocaust: Critical Perspectives on* Schindler's List, Bloomington and Indianapolis, Indiana University Press.

Loshitzky, Y. (ed.) (1997), *Spielberg's Holocaust: Critical Perspectives on* Schindler's List, Bloomington and Indianapolis, Indiana University Press.

Lovell, A. (1972), 'Free Cinema' in *Studies in Documentary*, London, Secker and Warburg.

Lovell, T. (1990), 'Landscapes and Stories in 1960s British Realism', *Screen* 31:4, 357–76.

Lyotard, J. F. (1990), 'The Postmodern Condition' in J. Alexander (ed.),

Culture and Society: Contemporary Debates, Cambridge, Cambridge University Press.

MacCabe, C. (1974), 'Realism and the Cinema: Notes on some Brechtian Theses', *Screen* 15:2, 7–27.

MacCabe, C. (1976), 'Theory and Film: Principles of Realism and Pleasure' in L. Baudry, G. Mast and M. Cohen (eds) (1992), *Film Theory and Criticism*, 4th edn, New York, Oxford, Oxford University Press.

MacIntyre, S. (1996), 'Art and Industry: Regional Film and Video Policy in the UK' in A. Moran (ed.), *Film Policy: International, National and Regional Perspectives*, Routledge, London, 215–34.

McKnight, G. (1997), 'Ken Loach's Domestic Morality Tales' in G. McKnight (ed.), *Agent of Challenge and Defiance: The Films of Ken Loach*, Wiltshire, Flick Books.

McKnight, G. (ed.) (1997), *Agent of Challenge and Defiance: The Films of Ken Loach*, Wiltshire, Flick Books.

Malcolm, D. (1993), 'Dogs of Gore', *Guardian*, 7 January, 6.

Maltby, R. (1983), *Harmless Entertainment: Hollywood and the Ideology of Consensus*, Metchuen NJ, Scarecrow Press.

Maltby, R. (1994), 'The Social Evil, the Moral Order and the Melodramatic Imagination 1890–1915' in J. Bratton, J. Cook and C. Gledhill (eds), *Melodrama: Stage, Picture, Screen*, London, British Film Institute.

Maltby, R. and Craven, I. (1995), *Hollywood Cinema*, Oxford, Blackwell.

Masilela, N. (1993), 'The Los Angeles School of Black Filmmakers' in M. Diawara (ed.), *Black American Cinema*, New York and London, Routledge.

Masham, M. (1993), 'Losing Control: Popular Perception(s) of the Rodney King Video', *Wide Angle*, 15:2, 16.

Masood, P. J. (1996), 'Mapping the Hood: The Genealogy of City Space in *Boyz N the Hood* and *Menace II Society*', *Cinema Journal* 35: 2.

Medved, M. (1993), *Hollywood vs. America: Popular Culture and the War on Traditional Values,* London, Harper Collins.

Medved, M. (1996), 'Hollywood's Four Big Lies' in K. French (ed.), *Screen Violence*, London, Bloomsbury.

Mercer, K. (1994), 'Black Art and the Burden of Representation' in K. Mercer (ed.), *Welcome to the Jungle: New Positions in Black Cultural Studies*, London and New York, Routledge.

Mercer, K. (ed.) (1988), *Black Film, British Cinema*, ICA Documents 7, London, Institute of Contemporary Arts.

Mercer, K. (ed.) (1994), *Welcome to the Jungle: New Positions in Black Cultural Studies*, London and New York, Routledge.

Mermin, E. (1996), '"Searing portraits": The Persistence of Realism in Black Urban Cinema', *Third Text*, Spring, 3–14.

Messaris, P. (1994), *Visual Literacy: Image, Mind and Reality*, Bolder Colorado, Westview Press.

Miller, D. and Philo, G. (1996), 'Against Orthodoxy', *Sight and Sound* 6:12, 18–20.

Mimura, G. M. (1996), 'On Fathers and Sons, Sex and Death: John Singleton's *Boyz N the Hood*', *The Velvet Light Trap*, 38, 14–27.

Moody, N. and Hallam, J. (eds) (1998), *Medical Fictions*, Liverpool, Association for Research in Popular Fictions/Liverpool John Moores University Press.

Moores, S. (1993), *Interpreting Audiences: The Ethnography of Media Consumption*, London, Sage.

Moran, A. (ed.) (1996), *Film Policy: International, National and Regional Perspectives*, Routledge, London.

Morrison, R. (1996), 'Who Supports Violent Films Now?', *The Times*, 16 March, 17.

Mulvey, L. (1975), 'Visual Pleasure and Narrative Cinema', *Screen* 16:3, 6–18.

Murphy, B. (1987), *American Realism and American Drama 1880–1940*, Cambridge, Cambridge University Press.

Murphy, R. (1989), *Realism and Tinsel: Cinema and Society in Britain 1939–1949*, London and New York, Routledge.

Murphy, R. (1992), *Sixties British Cinema*, London, British Film Institute.

Neale, S. (1980), *Genre*, London, British Film Institute.

Neale, S. (1990), 'Questions of Genre', *Screen* 31:1, 45–67.

New Zealand Film (1995) (unattributed) '*Warriors* Opens in New York, then throughout USA', 53, 10–11.

Newson, E. (1994), *Video Violence and the Protection of Children*, Report of the Home Affairs Committee, London, Her Majesty's Stationery Office.

Nichols, B. (1994), 'Eisenstein's *Strike* and the Genealogy of Documentary' in *Blurred Boundaries: Questions of Meaning in Contemporary Culture*, Bloomington and Indiana, Indiana University Press.

Nochlin, L. (1971), *Realism*, Harmondsworth, Penguin.

Pearson, R. E. (1992), *Eloquent Gestures: The Transformation of Performance Style in the Griffith Biograph Films*, Berkeley, University of California Press.

Perlez, J. (1993), 'Spielberg Grapples With the Horror of the Holocaust', *New York Times*, 13 June, 15–17.

Petras, J. (1992), 'The Discrediting of the Fifth Estate: the Press Attacks on *JFK*', *Cineaste* 19.

Petric, V. (1993), *Constructivism in Film*, Cambridge, Cambridge University Press.

Pihama, L. (1996), 'Some Thoughts', *Midwest* 6, 21.

Postman, N. (1985), *Amusing Ourselves to Death: Public Discourse in the*

Age of Showbusiness, New York, Penguin Books.

Prince, S. (1996), 'True Lies: Perceptual Realism, Digital Images and Film Theory', *Film Quarterly* 49:3, 27–37.

Quart, B. K. (1989), *Women Directors: The Emergence of a New Cinema*, New York, London, Praeger.

Reader, K. (1995), 'After the Riot', *Sight and Sound* 5:11, 12–14.

Reid, M. (1993), *Redefining Black Film*, Berkeley, Los Angeles, London, University of California Press.

Rich, B. R. (1992), 'Art House Killers', *Sight and Sound* 2:8, 5–6.

Robins, K. (1991), 'Tradition and Translation: National Culture in its Global Context' in J. Corner and S. Harvey (eds), *Enterprise and Heritage: Crosscurrents of National Culture*, London, Routledge.

Robins, K. and Morley, D. (1995), 'Tradition and Translation: National Culture in its Global Context' in *Spaces of Identity: Global Media, Electronic Landscapes and Cultural Boundaries*, London, Routledge.

Robins, K. and Morley, D. (1995), *Spaces of Identity: Global Media, Electronic Landscapes and Cultural Boundaries*, London, Routledge.

Rogin, M. (1993), 'Body and Soul Murder: *JFK*', in M. Garber, J. Matlock and R. L. Walkowitz (eds), *Media Spectacles*, New York and London, Routledge.

Rogin, M. (1998), *Independence Day*, London, British Film Institute.

Romney, J. (1993), 'One Way Ticket to Hell', *New Statesman and Society*, 19 February, 34–35.

Rowland Jr, W. D. (1997), 'Television Violence Redux' in M. Barker and Petley, J. (eds), *Ill Effects*, London and New York, Routledge.

Ryan, M. and Kellner, D. (1988), *Camera Politica: The Politics and Ideology of Contemporary Hollywood Film*, Bloomington and Indianapolis, Indiana University Press.

Schaz, T. (1993), 'The New Hollywood' in J. Collins, H. Radner and A. Preacher Collins (eds), *Film Theory Goes to the Movies*, London, Routledge.

Sconce, J. (1993), 'Spectacles of Death: Identification, Reflexivity and Contemporary Horror', in J. Collins, H. Radner and A. Preacher Collins (eds), *Film Theory Goes to the Movies*, London, Routledge.

Silverstone, R. (1994), *Television and Everyday Life*, London, Routledge.

Simons, R. (1996), 'Driving Force: Narrative in Lee Tamahori's Television Advertisements and *Once Were Warriors*', *Media International Australia* 80, 27–31.

Sklar, R. (1995), 'Social Realism with Style: An Interview with Lee Tamahori', *Cineaste* 21:3, 25–7.

Smith, G. (1994), 'Why do I Have to Provoke', *Sight and Sound* 4, 12, 8–14.

Smith, M. (1995a), *Engaging Characters: Fiction, Emotion and the Cinema*, Oxford, Clarendon Press.

Smith, M. (1995b), 'The Logic and Legacy of Brechtianism', in D. Bordwell and N. Carroll (eds), *Post-Theory: Reconstructing Film Studies*, Wisconsin, University of Wisconsin Press.

Smith, V. (1992), 'The Documentary Impulse in Contemporary US African-American Film' in G. Dent (ed.), *Black Popular Culture*, Seattle, Bay Press.

Sobchack, V. (ed.) (1996), *The Persistence of History*, New York and London, Routledge.

Sorlin, P. (1996), *Italian National Cinema 1896–1996*, London and New York, Routledge.

Staiger, J. (1985), 'The Package-Unit System: Unit Management after 1955' in D. Bordwell, J. Staiger and K. Thompson, *The Classical Hollywood Cinema: Film Style and Mode of Production to 1960*, London, Routledge.

Staiger, J. (1996), 'Cinematic Shots: the Narration of Violence', in V. Sobchack (ed.), *The Persistence of History*, New York and London, Routledge.

Steedman, C. (1986), *Landscape for a Good Woman: A Story of Two Lives*, London, Virago.

Stone, O. (1992), 'Who Defines History?', *Cineaste* 19, 23–4.

Tasker, Y. (1993), *Spectacular Bodies: Gender, Genre and the Action Cinema*, London, Routledge.

Taubin, A. (1993), 'Girl N the Hood', *Sight and Sound* 3:8, 17.

Tullock, J. and Tulloch, M. (1992), 'Discourses About Violence: Critical Theory and the "TV Violence" Debate', *Text* 12:2, 183–231.

Thompson, A. (1994), 'Making History', *Entertainment Weekly*, 21 January, 14–20.

Thompson, K. (1985), 'The Formulation of the Classical Narrative' in D. Bordwell, J. Staiger, and K. Thompson, *The Classical Hollywood Cinema: Film Style and Mode of Production to 1960*, London, Routledge.

Thompson, K. (1988), *Breaking the Glass Armour: Neoformalist Film Analysis*, Princeton, New Jersey, Princeton University Press.

Thompson, K. and Bordwell, D. (1994), *Film History: An Introduction*, London, New York, Sydney and Tokyo, McGraw Hill Inc.

Tomasulo, F. P. (1996), 'I'll See It when I Believe It: Rodney King and the Prison House of Video' in V. Sobchack (ed.), *The Persistence of History*, New York and London, Routledge.

Tudor, A. (1989), *Monsters and Mad Scientists: A Cultural History of the Horror Movie*, London, Basil Blackwell.

Twitchell, J. B. (1985), *Dreadful Pleasures: An Anatomy of Modern Horror*, New York and Oxford, Oxford University Press.

Urry, J. (1990), *The Tourist Gaze: Leisure and Travel in Contemporary Societies*, London, Sage.

Vardac, N. A. (1949), *Stage to Screen. Theatrical Origins of Early Film: David Garrick to D. W. Griffith*, Harvard, Harvard University Press. This edition 1987, New York, Da Capo Press.

Vincendeau, G. (ed.) (1995), *Encyclopedia of European Cinema*, London, British Film Institute, Cassell.

Walker, A. (1974), *Hollywood, England: the British Film Industry in the 60s*, London, Michael Joseph.

Walker, A. (1992), 'Shooting the Dogs of Gore', *Evening Standard*, 5 November, 43–4.

Walker, J. (1993), *Couching Resistance: Women, Film and Psychoanalytic Psychiatry*, Minneapolis, University of Minnesota Press.

Wallace, M. (1992), '*Boyz N the Hood* and *Jungle Fever*' in G. Dent (ed.), *Black Popular Culture*, Seattle, Bay Press.

Walton, K. (1990), *Mimesis as Make Believe: On the Foundations of the Representational Arts*, Cambridge, Mass., Harvard University Press.

Wambu, O. (1995), 'Boyz in the hood down under', *The Voice*, 9 May.

Wasko, J. (1994), *Hollywood in the Information Age*, Cambridge, Polity Press.

Watt, I. (1957), *The Rise of the Novel: Studies in Defoe, Richardson and Fielding*, Harmondsworth, Penguin.

Weissman, G. (1995), 'The Fantasy of Witnessing', *Media, Culture and Society* 17, 293–307.

Whatling, C. (1997), *Screen Dreams: Fantasising Lesbians in Film*, Manchester, Manchester University Press.

White, H. (1996), 'The Modernist Event' in V. Sobchack (ed.), *The Persistence of History*, New York and London, Routledge.

Williams, C. (1973/4), 'Bazin on Neo-realism', *Screen* 14:4, 61–8.

Williams, C. (1980), *Realism in the Cinema: A Reader*, London, Routledge and Kegan Paul and the British Film Institute.

Williams, C. (1994), 'After the Classic, the Classical and Ideology: the Differences of Realism', *Screen* 35:3, 275–92.

Williams, R. (1977a), 'A Lecture on Realism', *Screen* 18:1, 61–74.

Williams, R. (1977b), 'Realism, Naturalism and their Alternatives' in R. Burnett (ed.) (1991), *Explorations in Film Theory: Selected Essays from Cine-Tracts*, Bloomington and Indianapolis, Indiana University Press.

Willmott, P. and Young, M. (1957), *Family and Kinship in East London*, London, Routledge and Kegan Paul.

Winston, B. (1995), *Claiming the Real*, London, British Film Institute.

Winston, B. (1996), *Technologies of Seeing: Photography, Cinematography and Television*, London, British Film Institute.

Wood, M. (1995), 'My Kind of Psychopath', *London Review of Books*, 20 July, 9.

Wood, R. (1990/1), 'Radicalism and Popular Cinema: The Films of Oliver

Stone', *Cineaction* 23/24, 60–9.

Wyatt, J. (1994), *High Concept: Movies and Marketing in Hollywood*, Austin, University of Texas Press.

Yearwood, G. L. (1982), 'Toward a Theory of a Black Cinema Aesthetics' in G. L. Yearwood (ed.), *Black Cinema Aesthetics*, Ohio, Ohio University Centre for Afro-American Studies.

Yearwood, G. L. (ed.) (1982), *Black Cinema Aesthetics*, Ohio, Ohio University Centre for Afro-American Studies.

Zelizer, B. (1997), 'Every Once in a While: *Schindler's List* and the Shaping of History' in Y. Loshitzky (ed.), *Spielberg's Holocaust: Critical Perspectives on* Schindler's List, Bloomington and Indianapolis, Indiana University Press.

Index

Note: 'n.' after a page reference indicates a note number on that page.

Accused, The 111, 112, 113, 114, 190
Ackerman, Chantal 107
acting style: in expositional realism 109; histrionic code 21; Method acting 84–6; typage 31, 109; versimilar code 20–2
actors: physical verisimilitude 102; unknown or non–professional 16, 31, 40, 109, 170
actuality 226, 227–8, 231, 237, 250
aesthetic alignment 136
aesthetic hybridisation 229
African-American cinema 52–60, 98–9, 197–201
AIP (American International Pictures) 79
alien invasion narratives 77, 78, 79
Alien Resurrection 64–5, 67–8
alignment 56, 133, 134–7; in 'new brutalism' films 234, 238–9, 247, 248; in political films 152, 153–4, 155–7, 172–3, 178; situations and 137–41; in social realist films 199, 211; and suspense 137–9
allegiance 131–2, 133, 134
Altman, Robert 69, 73

American narrative films 13, 186–7
Anderson, Lindsay 49
Andrews, Dudley 15–16
Ang, I. 124
angry young men 45–7, 197–208
animation 81
antecedent realities 90, 95, 100–1, 102, 103, 119–20
Aotearoa/New Zealand 201, 203
apartheid 158–9, 161
art: and popular culture 176, 238, 239; realism in 4
art cinema 17, 45, 81, 105, 240, 243
artistic motivation 15, 63, 74–5, 92
artistic production 27, 28
Attenborough, Richard, *Cry Freedom* 158, 160, 161
authenticity 19, 30, 75, 77, 102, 115; in political films 147; Soviet filmmakers and 130–1
automised practices 129–30

Baby Boom 86
Bad Lieutenant 106, 224
Balcon, Michael 40
Barker, Martin 78–9, 222, 223
Barthes, Roland 123
Battleship Potemkin 31, 227
Baudrillard, Jean 249–50

Bazin, André 14–15, 41–2, 43
Beatty, Warren 153
beauty 136
Beauty and the Beast 81
behaviourist narration 212–13
Bernstein, Sidney 39
Bicycle Thieves 16–17, 42
Biko, Steve 158, 159, 160
biographical sources 102, 110,
    112, 116
biographies of historical and
    political figures 150–1, 155
Black, G. 87–8
black and white images 47, 55, 91,
    108, 170, 205
black consciousness 159
black urban cinema 52–60, 197–8
Blade Runner 65
Bodyguard, The 70
Bordwell, David xiv, 24, 31, 41,
    124; and cognitive theory
    125–7, 128; and filmic
    narration 12–13, 62–3, 106;
    and objective realism 104
Born on the Fourth of July 117,
    162
bourgeois ideology 10–11
Boyz N the Hood 52, 57, 127, 197,
    198–201
Brando, Marlon 85, 107
Brassed Off 189
Brecht, Bertolt 145, 149–50,
    181n.6
British cinema 33–4, 189–90; New
    Wave 45–51; war–time
    34–40
Broadcasting Standards Council
    223
Brooks, K. 78–9
Brooks, Peter 18
Broomfield, Nick 241
Brown, Riwia 201
Brownlow, Kevin 88

Bulger, James, murder of 221
Burnett, Charles 54, 55
Busby Berkeley films 72–3
Butler, Christopher 128
byplay 21

Cagney, James 90
camcorders 102, 108, 229, 233,
    239
camerawork 13, 28, 55–6; African-
    American 47; handheld 103,
    118, 170; hidden 228, 229;
    neorealist 42; in 'new
    brutalist' films 234–5, 240–1,
    245; observational 104, 106,
    107, 184; in social realist films
    192, 207–8, 213
capitalism 7–8
captions, use of 198
Carroll, Noel xi, 131–2, 137
cartoons 81
Casino 117
Cassavetes, John 215
Cathy Come Home 228
Caughie, John 45
causality 15, 16, 17; *see also*
    narrative causality
Cavalcanti, Alberto 39
censorship 46, 222, 243–4
Chaplin 150
character/s 16, 42, 63, 102–3,
    108–9; alignment with *see*
    alignment; confrontational
    presentation 194, 207, 216;
    environment and 192,
    216–17; in genre 63, 67–8; in
    high concept films 70; in
    musicals 73–4; social realism
    and 190, 192, 194–5, 210
character motivation 63, 94, 100,
    105–6, 111, 247
characterisation 10, 20, 51, 84, 85,
    107–8, 109; in 'new brutalism'

films 246; in political films
154–5
Child's Play 3 221
children, protection of 221–2
Christie, Ian 32–3
Cimino, Michael 176
cinema *vérité* 106, 108, 125, 165,
234, 238, 240, 241
Citizen Kane 150
class 19, 45; *see also* working class
classical Hollywood cinema x–xi,
13, 18, 46, 62–3, 98
Close, Glenn 86, 111
close-ups 43, 215
closure 10, 210, 247
codes and conventions 22, 63, 64,
118, 125, 253; of actuality
filmmaking 228–9; generic 63,
83, 92; 'new brutalism' 225;
realist 100–1, 102–4, 107–8,
110, 115; use of mainstream
168
cognitive theory 123–30
coincidence 16, 18, 20
Collins, Jim 53, 92
colour 93, 108, 202, 215
comedy films 71–2
commonsense political discourse
148–9
composition 42–3, 102–3
compositional motivation 15, 63
computer simulation 76
concern alignment 135, 191, 234
conspiracy 151–2, 165
Constructivists 28–9, 31
contradiction, exposed by political
films 149–50, 151, 167
conventions *see* codes and
conventions
copycat violence 221, 247
Corner, John xiv–xv, 36, 189, 224,
226, 228–9
Costner, Kevin 163

Craven, Ian. 64, 66
Criminal Justice Act 221, 222
critical realism 3–4, 10–22, 149,
150
crtitcs: on *Cry Freedom* 160–1; on
*Henry, Portrait of a Serial
Killer* 236, 239; on *JFK* 164,
166–7; on *Man Bites Dog*
242–3; on *Saving Private Ryan*
118; on *Schindler's List* 172,
173–4, 175
'cross-over' films 52
Cry Freedom 153, 156, 158–61,
177, 178–9
cultural globalisation 187–8
Cumberbatch, Guy 222

Dallas 124
Dargis, Manhola 243
Dean, James 85
debate on realism 3–22
defamiliarisation 14, 15
detail 20, 43, 47, 80, 106–8, 115,
117, 200
Dial M for Murder 137–8
dialogue 51, 104
diasporic identity 196
Diawara, Manthia 52–3, 57
digital imaging 83
Dillon, Matt 86
Diorama 8, 9
discourse, hierarchy of 10, 11
distanciation 145, 147, 196
distribution of films 186–7
Do the Right Thing 104
documentary films 11, 31, 45; and
fiction 11–12, 35, 36, 226–30;
relationship to the 'real' 226–7
documentary realism 102, 196
documentary style 170, 176,
232–3, 236, 241; in fiction
films 35–7, 170; in social
realism 192, 208

domestic violence 204, 209, 215, 246
Double Indemnity 140
drama 7–8, 97, 98
drama documentary 35, 36, 227–8
dysfunctional family films 57–8, 209–16

editing 42, 103, 106, 165, 207, 234
effects research 222–3
Eisenstein, Sergei 27, 29–30, 31–2, 227
Eliot, George 5
emotional engagement 130–7
emotional realism 124
empathy 133, 145, 152, 191
English Patient, The 115–16
ensemble casts 84, 190, 192
entertainment, aggregate forms of 71
environment, effect on characters 184, 192–3, 208, 216–17
episodic structure 38, 43, 55, 60, 101, 104, 170, 171; in social realism 184, 192, 205, 206, 215; in spectacular realism 115, 117
establishing shots 47–8
ethical vacuum 225, 248
ethics 98, 99, 137; of good versus evil 76, 224, 225
events: alignment with 137–41; trivial 16, 20
everyday life 36, 39, 43, 189, 190
everyday reality 97–121
Executive Action 151
exoticism 74, 83, 115
experimental techniques 32, 69, 246, 247
exploitation films 230, 238
expositional realism 101, 104–10, 202, 225, 229

expression 18, 19, 84
eyewitness accounts 102, 116

facial expression 21
fact and fiction, mixture of 165, 166–7, 237, 239, 242–3, 246, 250, 251
fantasy films 82–4
fantasy of witnessing 175
Fascism 44, 148
feminism 146
fiction films 122, 124; documentary and 11–12, 35, 36, 227–9; realism and 24–5; see also fact and fiction
Fifth Element, The 83
film 11–13; as propaganda 35; separated from history 174
'Film-Eye' 29
film production 68–9, 79–80, 99, 188–9
'Film-Truth' 29, 30
Finney, Albert 47
Ferman, James 244
First Do No Harm 104
flexible specialisation 188
form xiv–xv, 14–17
formalism 14–17, 100, 101
Foster, Jodie 111
Free Cinema movement 45, 46
Freeland, Cynthia 248, 249
Full Monty, The 189

Gainsborough Pictures 36
Gan, Aleksei 29
gangster films 87, 88–95, 148, 157
Gasiorek, A. 10
generic categories 66–7
generic conventions 63
generic motivation xiv, 15
genre xiv, 65–96, 224
Gerhardie, W. 5
ghetto life 52, 56–60

Gledhill, Christine 18, 19, 70
globalisation 186–8; and the local
     188, 189, 195
Go Fish 105, 108–9
Godfather, The 69
Gorky, Maxim 7
Griffith Biograph films 20, 21
'gritty' dramas 106, 192, 233
Gunning, Tom 21

Haine, La 105, 106, 197, 205–8,
     209
Hanks, Tom 191
Hansen, Miriam 171, 172, 176
Heaven's Gate 69, 176
Henry, Portrait of a Serial Killer
     105, 110, 225, 229–30,
     233–40, 243–4, 249
heroic individuals, construction of
     112–13, 114
heroic realism 31
Hidden Agenda 151, 152, 156
high concept films 62, 64, 67,
     68–70, 92, 95, 100, 119;
     acting in 86
Higson, Andrew 35, 36, 38
Hill, Annette 251, 252
Hill, John 47, 48
Hindley, Myra 254n.25
history: challenging 161–7;
     depiction of 144–83; film
     separated from 174; as
     spectacle 119–20
histrionic code 21
Hitchcock, Alfred 80, 137–8
Hoggart, Richard 50
Hollywood see classical Hollywood
     cinema
Holocaust 167–9, 173–4, 175,
     176
home movies 102, 108, 110, 120,
     245
homosexuality, depictions of

characters 105, 108–9,
     111–12, 190–1
Horowitz, Sara 173
horror films 77–8, 83, 148, 248–9
humanistic values 17, 229, 253
hybridity of style 185, 192, 195–6,
     216
hypothesis formation 126

Ibsen, Henrik 7
Ice Cube 200–1
identification 130–7, 194; in 'new
     brutalism' films 244, 252;
     psychoanalysis and 130–1,
     244; in social realist films 194,
     200
identity 146, 163, 217; spaces of
     185–90
ideology 10–11, 29, 40, 129
illusionism 67
improvisation 84, 109
In a Lonely Place 140
In the Name of the Father 151, 154
Independence Day 77
independent production 99
infotainment 112, 232–3
intellectual alignment 134–5
interest alignment 135
interrogative narrative 152–3, 155,
     170
intertextual motivation 63
intertextuality 68, 70, 83, 118,
     119, 165–6; theme and
     87–95
Italian cinema, neorealism in
     40–5

James, Henry 5
Jancovich, Mark 77–9
Jaws 69
Jeanne Dielman 107–8
JFK 119, 120, 151, 156, 161–7,
     177, 179

Judge Dredd 78–9
Jurassic Park 83–4

Kassovitz, Mathieu 205
Keaton, Diane 86, 153
Kellner, Douglas 147, 151, 181n.8
Kennedy, J. F. 151, 162, 163
Kerekes, D. 231
Keystone films 71, 72
Killer of Sheep 54, 55, 56
Killing Fields, The 157
Kind of Loving, A 48, 49
King, Rodney 179, 180
Kinofot 29
Kinoks 32
'kitchen–sink' dramas 45, 46, 51,
    184, 190
Klute 12, 13
Knight, Deborah 210–11, 212–13
Kuleshov, Lev 26
Kundun 115

Lady Sings the Blues 150
Ladybird, Ladybird 104, 209,
    210–14, 234
Land and Freedom 152, 157
language 10–11; vernacular 46,
    102
Last Emperor, The 115
Lean, David 114
LEF 27, 31
legal drama 111, 112, 113
Leigh, Mike 109
Lejeune, Caroline 38
lens culture 3, 8
lesbians, depictions of 105, 108–9,
    111–12
liberalism 10–11
lighting 108
literary realism 4–5, 10–11
Lloyd, Howard 72
Loach, Ken 109; *Ladybird,*
    Ladybird 210, 213–14; *Land*

and Freedom 152, 157; *Riff*
    Raff 109
local, globalisation and 188, 189,
    195
local film cultures 51, 188–9,
    195–6
location shooting 16, 80–1, 104,
    170, 175; and neorealism 40,
    43–4; in New Wave 46, 47; in
    science fiction horror 78, 79
Look Back in Anger 46
Loshitzky, Y. 168–9, 170, 175
Love Story 69
Lovell, Terry 48–9
Lucas, Henry Lee 230, 233
Lukacs, Georg 5, 181n.6

MacCabe, Colin 11–12
MacIntyre, Steve 189
McKnight, George 214
McNaughton, John 230, 233
male gaze 139–40
Maltby, R. 64, 66, 76
Mama 55
Man Bites Dog 224, 225, 240–5,
    251
Man with a Movie Camera 32
Maori people 201–2, 205
marginalisation 190, 192–3
Margolis, Jon 164
Marxism 146
Marxist critique 50–1
masculinity 19, 163, 184–5, 189
Masilela, Ntongela 54, 55
Masood, Paula J. 57
Maupassant, Guy 5
Mayakovosky, Vladimir 31–2
Mayer, Louis B. 76
Mazursky, Paul 69
MCA 68
media violence 223–4; effects of
    221–3
Medved, Michael 220–1, 243

melodrama 6, 7, 8–9, 70, 88; realism and 18–22, 62
Menace II Society 56–7
Mercer, Kobena 53
Mermin, Elizabeth 53–4, 59
Messaris, Paul 142n.1
metalanguage 10, 11–12, 12–13
Method acting 84–6
Metz, Christian 122
Meyerhold, Vsevolod 29
MGM 76
Micheaux, Oscar 54
Millions Like Us 35–8
mimesis 4, 98
Ministry of Information Films Division 35, 39
minority groups 105, 191
Mirren, Helen 155
mise–en–scène 16, 63, 80–3, 84, 102, 217
Missing 151, 156, 181n.8
mondo 231–2
Mondo Cane 231–2
Money Train 221
montage 14,100, 163, 166; in British New Wave 49, 50; in Soviet cinema 26–7, 28–9; in British war-time films 37, 39; in high concept films 70
moral alignment 134, 135–6, 191, 211
moral panic 222, 230
morality 98, 137, 138
Motion Picture Patents Company 22
motivations 15, 77–87; character 111
Movement for Christian Democracy 222
MTV 246
Mulvey, Laura 139, 140–1
Murphy, Robert 50
music 70, 75; cultural specificity 195–6; in neorealist films 43; rap 200–1
musicals 72–3

Naked 105, 106, 108
narration 11–13: character-centred 104–5, 135, 162, 247; omniscient 113–14, 135, 213; voice-over 117
narrative 4–9, 55, 70, 75
narrative causality 13, 15, 63, 100, 247
narrative imperative 135
narrative integration 71–2
narrative logic 18, 20, 38
narrative motivation xiv, 63
narrative structures 16, 117; dual 190, 200; in 'new brutalism' 225; in political films 150–4, 164–5; in social realism 184, 192, 194, 210; see also episodic structure
Natural Born Killers 70, 225, 245–8, 250, 251
naturalism 5–6, 210–11, 212–13
neoformalism 14, 151–6
neorealism 40–5, 216
'new brutalism' 224–5, 251–2
New Moon 73, 74
'new sincerity' 92
'New Wave' films 33, 34, 45–51, 115
news footage 165, 16
Newson, Elizabeth 222
newsreels 37, 118, 119
Nil By Mouth 104, 189, 209, 214–16
Nixon 151
North by North West 80
novel 10, 11, 12
Novy Lef 27
Now Voyager 75, 76

objective realism 104
objectivity 5, 17, 106, 237
observation 5, 6, 21
October 31
Oldman, Gary 86, 214
On the Waterfront 107
Once Were Warriors 197, 201–5
Open City 42, 43
oppositional point of view xv, xvi,
    16, 17, 54–5
outsider characters 229; alignment
    with 156–7, 160

Pacino, Al 85, 91
parallel editing 113–14
parody of popular forms
    245–6
Pearson, Roberta E. 20–1, 22
perception 126–7
performance 104, 210; *see also*
    acting style
period referencing 119
personality 136
Philadelphia 104, 191
Philo, Greg 223
photographs, use of 165
photoplay 27, 28, 29
Pitt, Brad 86
place 48, 192–3; in expositional
    films 106, 107, 113
Platoon 162
plausibility 73, 74, 79, 124–5
point-of-view 55–6, 117, 139,
    155–7
political discourse 148–9
political film, as left-wing 149, 158,
    164
political issues 147–61
politics 146, 149; depiction of
    144–83
popular memory 167–76
pornography 230, 231
Postlethwaite, Peter 154

postmodernism 99, 146, 170–1,
    238
post-structuralism 10–12
Prince, Stephen 83
prior knowledge 127–8
product differentiation 62, 70, 80
Production Code 90
progressiveness 99, 146–7, 178,
    180, 229
propaganda, film as 35
psychoanalysis 130–1, 131–2, 244
psychological narrative 20–1
psychological realism 17, 18, 35,
    229
public opinion 123

radicalism 148
rap music 195, 200–1
rationalism 97, 98
'real-isations' 70, 73, 78, 83;
    spectacular 114–15; visual 8,9,
    64
realism x–xiii, xvi, 4–9, 253;
    discourse of 236, 237 *see also*
    expositional realism; rhetorical
    realism; spectacular realism
realist horror 248–50
reality effect 171
reality simulation 70–1
Reality TV 231, 232–3
Rebel Without a Cause 85
recognition 133
reconstruction 227–8, 229
Reds 152–3
referentiality 98, 99, 102, 119–20
reform movement 88, 98
religious thought 6–7
representation xii, 4–5, 15, 24,
    194, 204–5; of historical
    events 27, 31–3; of serial
    killers 234, 236, 240–1, 247
Reservoir Dogs 224, 252
rhetorical narrative 151, 152–3

rhetorical realism 101, 110–14
Rich, Matty 57
Richardson, Tony 49
Riff-Raff 109
Robins, Kevin 187, 188
Rock, Chrissie 211
romantic realist aesthetic 20
Room at the Top 46
Roth, Tim 86
Russian Left Front of the Arts 27
Ryan, Michael 147, 151,
    181n.8

Saltzman, Harry 51
Salvador 156, 162
Sandford, Jeremy 228
*Saturday Night and Sunday
    Morning* 48, 50
Saving Private Ryan 117–18,
    118–19
Scarface 89–90; remake 90–2
schema theory 129–30
schemata 126–7, 128
Schindler's List 119, 120, 151, 153,
    154, 167–76, 177–8
schizophrenic realism 246, 253
Schwarzenegger, Arnold 86
science fiction 64–5, 78–9, 82–4,
    148
scientific thought 7, 8
Scorsese, Martin 215
Screen theory xii, 145, 178, 238
Scruggs, Charles 60
Secrets and Lies 104
self-reflexivity 92, 250
sensationalism 89–90, 232, 233
'Sensations' exhibition 239
sequels 66, 67
serial killers: interest in 248;
    representations of 234, 236,
    240–1, 247
Serving in Silence 111, 112, 113,
    114

settings 80–1; in neorealist films
    43–4; in British New Wave 48
sexual relationships, depiction of
    46
Shackleton, Allan 231
Shaft 54
Shallow Grave 189
Shaw, George Bernard 7–8
Sheltering Sky, The 115
Shoah 170
shooting styles 47–8, 108–9; New
    Wave 46, 47–8; Soviet 28–9;
    see also camerawork
Shub, Esfir 29
Silence of the Lambs 234, 236, 237
Silkwood 112, 113, 114, 151
simulacrum 249–50
simulation 70–1
Singleton, John 52; *Boyz N the
    Hood* 197–201
situations 71, 137–41
slapstick 71, 72
Slater, D. 231
Sleepers 92–5, 100, 119
Smith, Murray 129, 131, 133–4,
    145
Snuff 231
snuff filmmaking 230–1
social and political issues 87–8, 95,
    98–9, 100, 101–2, 104, 228
social issue dramas 41, 47, 190–1
social justice 112, 113, 191
social problem genres 87–8, 95
social realism 46, 47, 50–1, 184–5,
    190–6, 210, 216–17, 233–4
socialist realism 32
Some Mother's Son 152, 155
Sorlin, Pierre 40, 41, 43, 44
Soviet cinema 25–33
space, in expositional films 106,
    107, 113
spaces of identity 185–90
Spanking the Monkey 107, 108

special effect of the real 174–5
special effects 76, 118–19
spectacle 30, 63, 69, 71–6, 77, 80;
    and realist horror 249
spectacular realism 101, 103, 104,
    114–20
Spielberg, Steven 118; *Schindler's
    List* 168, 169–70, 173–4, 176
Staiger, Janet 68, 167
star personae 63, 86
Stone, Oliver: *JFK* 161, 162–3,
    164, 165; *Natural Born Killers*
    246, 247, 248
Stone, Sharon 86
Straight Out of Brooklyn 54, 57–9,
    209
straight-to-camera soliloquies 240
Strasberg, Lee 85
Streep, Meryl 86, 111–12
Strike 29–30
Strindberg, August 7
studio production 79–80
subjectivity 122, 130, 139, 237
suspense 137–9

taboo subjects, depiction of 110
Tamahori, Lee 202, 205
Tarantino, Quentin 157, 225, 247
Target for Tonight 36–7
Taste of Honey, A 49–50
Taylor, Richard 32–3
technological innovation 46, 64,
    103
television xv, 100; and collapse of
    cinema audience 79; violence
    on 223–4
templates 128, 147
Thelma and Louise 141
theme, intertextuality and 87–95
This Sporting Life 49
Thompson, Kristin 15–17, 21, 41
time, in expositional films 106,
    107, 113

Titanic 66, 74–6, 117
Tomasulo, Frank 179–80
tourist gaze 195
Trainspotting 189
transparency 10, 12, 62, 63
true story films 116–17, 227, 233,
    234; rhetorical realism in
    110, 112; social realism and
    210
truth telling xiii, 34, 102
Tudor, Andrew 248
Twenty Four Seven 189
Twin Town 189
typage 31
typecasting 109

Underworld 88
United Kingdom: cultural
    devolution 188–9; debate on
    film violence 221–2; social
    realism in 190, 216; *see also*
    British cinema
urban life 192–3, 203

Vardac, Nicolas 9, 20
verisimilar code 20–1, 88
verisimilitude xii–xiii, 5, 18, 20, 88
Vertov, Dziga 27, 28–9, 30–1, 32,
    44
video diaries 102
videos 179; market for 186
Vietnam War 162
viewer engagement 107, 123;
    cognitive approach 123–9; in
    'new brutalism' films 238–9,
    240, 244, 248, 251–2; with
    political and historical films
    178–9; in social realism films
    214–16
violence: depictions of in 'new
    brutalism' 224–5, 252–3;
    effect of 220–1, 222–3;
    viewers and 39–40, 250–2

voyeurism 110, 238–9

Wall Street 162
Walton, Kendall 125, 251
war-time films 33, 34–40
Washington, Denzel 160, 191
Watt, Ian 10
Weaver, Sigourney 65, 67
Weber, Louise 87
Weissman, Gary 173–4, 175
Went the Day Well? 39
westerns 87
White, Hayden 166
Williams, Christopher 13, 51, 24, 27

Williams, Raymond 47, 97
Winston, Brian 4, 8–9, 226–7, 241
women: status in fictional representations 130, 142n; in urban dramas 203–4, 214
Woods, Donald 159
working class 49, 50–1, 189
World Apart, A 152
Wright, Basil 55
Wyatt, Justin 62, 69, 70, 86

Zelizer, B. 176
Zola, Emile 5